PLOUGHSHARES

Fall 1996 · Vol. 22, Nos. 2 & 3

GUEST EDITOR
Richard Ford

EDITOR
Don Lee

POETRY EDITOR
David Daniel

ASSISTANT EDITOR
Jodee Stanley

FOUNDING EDITOR
DeWitt Henry

FOUNDING PUBLISHER
Peter O'Malley

PLOUGHSHARES, a journal of new writing, is guest-edited serially by prominent writers who explore different and personal visions, aesthetics, and literary circles. PLOUGHSHARES is published in April, August, and December at Emerson College, 100 Beacon Street, Boston, MA 02116-1596. Telephone: (617) 824-8753. Web address: http://www.emerson.edu/ploughshares/.

EDITORIAL ASSISTANTS: Heidi Pitlor, Maryanne O'Hara, and Nathaniel Bellows. INTERNS: Paul Reilly and Monique Hamzé. FICTION READERS: Billie Lydia Porter, Emily Doherty, Anne Kriel, Karen Wise, John Rubins, Craig Salters, Loretta Chen, Barbara Lewis, Michael Rainho, Todd Cooper, Holly LeCraw Howe, David Rowell, Kevin Supples, and Tammy Zambo. POETRY READERS: Michael Henry, Jessica Purdy, Brijit Brown, Lori Novick, Ellen Scharfenberg, Tom Laughlin, Rich Morris, Lisa Sewell, Bethany Daniel, and Renee Rooks.

SUBSCRIPTIONS (ISSN 0048-4474): $19 for one year (3 issues), $36 for two years (6 issues); $22 a year for institutions. Add $5 a year for international.

UPCOMING: Winter 1996–97, a fiction and poetry issue edited by Robert Boswell & Ellen Bryant Voigt, will appear in December 1996. Spring 1997, a mixed issue edited by Yusef Komunyakaa, will appear in April 1997. Fall 1997, a fiction issue edited by Mary Gordon, will appear in August 1997.

SUBMISSIONS: Reading period is from August 1 to March 31 postmark dates. Please see page 252 for detailed submission policies.

Classroom-adoption, back-issue, and bulk orders may be placed directly through PLOUGHSHARES. Microfilms of back issues may be obtained from University Microfilms. PLOUGHSHARES is also available as CD-ROM and full-text products from EBSCO, H.W. Wilson, Information Access, and UMI. Indexed in M.L.A. Bibliography, American Humanities Index, Index of American Periodical Verse, Book Review Index. Self-index through Volume 6 available from the publisher; annual supplements appear in the fourth number of each subsequent volume. The views and opinions expressed in this journal are solely those of the authors. All rights for individual works revert to the authors upon publication.

PLOUGHSHARES receives additional support from the Lannan Foundation and the Massachusetts Cultural Council. Marketing initiatives are funded by the Lila Wallace–Reader's Digest Literary Publishers Marketing Development Program, administered by the Council of Literary Magazines and Presses.

Distributed by Bernhard DeBoer (Nutley, NJ), Fine Print Distributors (Austin, TX), Ingram Periodicals (La Vergne, TN), International Periodical Distributors (Solana Beach, CA), and L-S Distributors (S. San Francisco, CA).

Printed in the U.S.A. on recycled paper by Edwards Brothers.

CONTENTS

Fall 1996

Cover painting: *About Face* by Jane Kent
Printing ink on printed ground, 5″ x 4″, 1995

Ploughshares Patrons

This publication would not be possible without the support of
our readers and the generosity of the following individuals
and organizations. As a nonprofit enterprise,
we welcome donations of any amount.

COUNCIL
Denise and Mel Cohen
Eugenia Gladstone Vogel

PATRONS
Willard Cook
John K. Dineen
Scott and Annette Turow
Marillyn Zacharis

FRIENDS
Martin Geer
Richard and Maureen Yelovich

ORGANIZATIONS
Emerson College
Lila Wallace–Reader's Digest Fund
Council of Literary Magazines and Presses
Lannan Foundation
Massachusetts Cultural Council

COUNCIL: $3,000 for two lifetime subscriptions, acknowledgement
in the journal for three years, and votes on the Cohen and Zacharis
Awards. PATRON: $1,000 for a lifetime subscription and acknow-
ledgement in the journal for two years. FRIEND: $500 for a life-
time subscription and acknowledgement in the journal
for one year. All donations are tax-deductible.
Please make your check payable to *Ploughshares,*
Emerson College, 100 Beacon St., Boston, MA 02116.

RICHARD FORD

Introduction

If you don't like these stories, you should've read the ones I *didn't* take.

Even though that's not accurate, it's probably the only thing I could say in this space to truly arrest the attention of the curious soul bent on simply reading a few good stories (which, in fact, he/she will find here). But, after spending months reading, and wrestling with one's "tastes," splitting one's own hairs, urgently writing friends to send their work or the good work of their students, mulling self-importantly over the state of the American short story, the American literary magazine, the combined fate and character of the young American writer-in-training, plus one's own dubious fate, enmeshed as it precisely is in all these just-mentioned occupations—after doing all that and actually coming up with quite a few good stories to show for it—*to then* face the "need" of an introduction, seems, well...slightly awkward. Perverse, even. Unnecessary. A bit like putting a wiseguy vanity plate on a rental car: HUMDINGERS!

But, what *should* one say? Should I yammer on about what's good about these stories "taken together"—concoct some obscure, *ad hoc* category they either fully satisfy or invent anew, flattering thereby myself, the closet critic, and possibly also tripping up the stories themselves by making them bend even more lowly to my will? Good stories want only to create their own special terms each by each, satisfy them richly, and be done with it. A category of one.

Or maybe I should plot out my own well-burnished definition of what a good story Platonically *is*. Though that immediately risks ruling out something unforeseen and wonderful: a fresh new Donald Barthelme, for instance. So that wouldn't be a good idea. (The critic's job *is* a hard job.)

It's squeamishly tempting, only for the "sake" of the anonymous young writer, of course, to offer a short treatise on why stories (such as the ones I didn't choose) failed. How they attained what I saw as their inadequacies (lack of authority, lack of clear narrative voice—whatever that is—on and on and on). But who cares? Plus, as soon as I got my famous treatise all laid out neat, the last story I rejected—the classic of all unsuccessful stories—would show up in *The New Yorker*, win an O. Henry Award, and I'd start getting smirky letters with Iowa City postmarks, "thanking" me. Once, when I was teaching at Williams, a poet colleague and I thought about offering a course in which we would anatomize bad novels for an entire semester—again, all for the benefit of our writing students. For some reason, this seemed likely to be instructive. Only, we couldn't make ourselves read through our own syllabus, which *was* instructive, and we quickly forgot about the whole idea, following the wisdom that only good work counts.

Another possibility might be to enter mincingly into my own autobiographical mantra of the young writer "out there"; to recall my meatless days in heatless garrets in Chicago (while my wife was, of course, pulling down a handsome living for us), of dashes down to the mailbox, of envelopes ripped open, form rejections hungrily scoured for encouraging nuances in phrasing, or the slapdash "Pls try us again" appended by some work-study math grad student with a heart of gold, who at two a.m. and deep into reefer, begins to "feel for me" far away in the Windy City doing God's work unheralded and alone—and how all that made me work harder and get better while staying humble and uncynical. It wouldn't even be true. Moreover, it would be cloying and insulting to anyone actually trying to do God's work. Sad life stories, even pathetically sad life stories played for jokes, never offer much comfort to the truly serious.

Still another introduction topic might be the simultaneously-thriving-yet-still-somehow-beleaguered university writing program industry. Perhaps now would be the time and here the place to give it a good flagellating, put on my jeweler's loupe and scope out its flaws and corruptions. The French, after all, think we're a bunch of sillies for trying to "teach" writing. They, of course, think the way they do everything is the best way, and that becoming a writer is a gnostic, quasi-Zen, for-mandarins-only process that mustn't be spoken of in public—whereas we Americans will talk about anything forever. But who cares what the French think?

They're not satisfied with their own writers, either. Though plenty of American pseudo-mandarins natter on about this subject, too—usually toward the point that altogether too much writing's going on, that there're scandalously more writers than readers, that the writing gene pool is somehow being diluted and the world flooded with mediocrity, that the real writers don't teach, that editors are going brain-dead, on and on and on and on *again.* But unless I'm wrong, Tennessee Williams and Flannery O'Connor both went to Iowa. Barry Hannah went to Arkansas. Ken Kesey and Robert Stone attended Stanford. And as a group, these satisfy my requirements for being wonderful writers, their books wonderful books. What difference does it make where you learned what you learned, if you learned it well? If every holder of an M.F.A. isn't quite as good as these people, what's the harm, really? It seems like a victimless crime. Maybe they'll all become better readers of other people's good books. Plus, everybody has to be doing something, don't they? Would we rather more people were out in California designing video games?

And I'm sure there are other topics worth introducing this volume with: the influence on the American short story of deconstruction and the critical works of Frank Lentricchia. Web sites and hypertext. The "market." Venal agents. The "death" of first one thing and then another. But those introductions will have to wait for another day.

In compiling these eleven specimens, I have observed very few rules, only ones which I've hoped would benefit the random, unknown reader. Most of what's here are actual short stories, though I've not excluded parts of longer works if the integrity of the writing overcame the absence of a more succinct and purposeful structure. Gender, race, ethnicity, sexual orientation, and other such non-literary concerns have not mattered to the extent that I'm at all aware of them. Seriousness has not been enough, though funny stories would've needed to seem funny to *me.* Experimentation has not been suppressed, nor has literary heritage ("my story was probably influenced by Proust") been a selling point. I have not minded about why stories got written—reasons of personal therapy, self-expression, confession, risk-taking, insomnia, time to kill, the influence of Kenneth

Patchen or David Foster Wallace—but I have demanded that the writing concedes in some detectable way that I—the reader— exist and am doing my best to get with the story's program. To me, good writing manages at a very primary level to acknowledge that a reader is using his brain cells up as he reads, and needs from the writing to be rewarded. On the other hand, writing that seems indifferent to me and my lost brain cells invites indifference in return.

Finally, though I may be growing soft and patient with age, I liked the reading I did during these months. I did all my *Ploughshares* reading in Paris, and maybe I imagined I actually *was* related to my "uncle" Ford Madox Ford—fifty-ish, feeling underappreciated, mouth agape, editing, in that former Ford's case, *The Transatlantic Review* back in 1923: a "halfway house," he called himself, "between non-publishable youth and real money." A repeated feeling I've earned from my few years of writing stories is that I do precious little for anybody else—this, though my intention is avowedly other. And yet as I believe that what good writing mostly needs is a willing audience, I have simply tried during the last half year to make myself useful by hopefully and enthusiastically offering myself.

ANN BEATTIE

Buried Treasure

For more than a year, I thought Roman had disappeared from my life. If not for our very adequate postal service, he might have, but the last week of August, I open the mailbox to find an envelope that has been stamped: *Moved No Forwarding Address,* with an arrow drawn to the return address, tiny and wispily written in the upper left corner: *Roman Kelber, c/o Janet Peacham, rr. 11, box 8, Frankfort, ME.* There is no zip code. The arrow, drawn freehand, has been traced over several times, so that it is as bold as the return address is faint. The letter is addressed to a woman I don't know, Deirdre Smythe, in Providence, Rhode Island. Why Roman was writing her, and why he should have written his return address in care of me, is a mystery, but somehow I hesitate to open the envelope. What do you ever find out, with Roman, even when you pursue something, except that everything is complicated and inconclusive? Also, it isn't my mail. It is his mail, which he has apparently, for reasons of his own, indicated should be returned to me.

Roman visited the Maine house several times the summer Danny and I moved in—the year of the hurricane. A disastrous time, with a storm of sorts going on inside the house as well, caused by Roman and his lady friend, which exacerbated and complicated the problems Danny and I were having. But I've done my best to put that period out of my mind, and my resolve has been pretty effective, until the day I get the letter.

I hold it up to the light and run my thumb along it in horizontal lines, but I am hoping the words will be indecipherable, and they are, so that's a relief.

I consider opening it, but reflexively stop, hearing my mother's voice saying, "You *never* open another person's mail."

I look all around me—this is embarrassing, but I do—experiencing the irrational feeling that Roman, like one of those drawings for children in which the artist hides various animals in

9

bushes and cleverly disguises trees as elongated, vertical wolves, might be watching me and taking in my reaction. That is so paranoid that I immediately get another thought.

Being: Call Howie and tell him about the letter. See what Howie thinks.

Howie is my best friend. According to my ex-lover, Danny, he was a big part of the problem. As was Roman, of course. All those odd people imposing on him, ruining the silence, making their overt and covert demands on my time. The way I saw it, they had been my family before I met Danny, and I wasn't going to boot them out because I had a live-in boyfriend. I thought we had arrived at some solutions: guests on the weekends, not during the week; objectionable music listened to through headphones; consult Danny before mowing the lawn or trimming the bushes. You'd think he would have been grateful, not having to tend to the yard, but the noise of the lawn mower distracted him, he said. And sometimes he was painting the bushes, including them in one of his landscapes, so what was he going to do when they were suddenly dwarfed, just inflate them again in his imagination? He called Roman and Howie "the swallows," from the old song about the swallows returning to Capistrano, because he insisted on seeing them as homing pigeons, returning always to my— our—home. These were the things Danny said to his friends on the telephone. He'd have his friends think Roman and Howie were the gaping mouth that swallowed the cars of screaming couples as they rode into the fun house. He felt that Howie and Roman expected him to sit with his hands in his lap, listening, being subjected to whatever their speculative fun ride of the day turned out to be: anti-Lacan; pro-abortion; anti-Castro; pro-puppy. It really made him nervous that there might be a dog. He knew it would be a big responsibility, and Danny avoided as many responsibilities as possible: no marriage; no babies; no family obligations unless the request was made in obvious desperation.

I wasn't the only one who found him frustrating and uncompromising. I often remember Danny at his parents' fiftieth wedding anniversary, dancing with their neighbor, Mrs. Hill. Danny's sister's eyes had been trained on them, narrowed, as if by adjusting the distance between her upper lid to her lower in a fierce squint, she could lock them in place, keep Danny dancing with Mrs. Hill. That party was only a few weeks before the hurricane. He was furious that when we got home that night, Roman was there with a woman, screwing her on the floor of the study, while Jay Leno stood there giving his monologue on the television.

"It makes it seem like I'm a disapproving parent, and I don't have the slightest interest in playing that role," Danny said sulkily, upstairs in our bedroom, taking off his suit and punishing it for its presence at the anniversary party by throwing the jacket and trousers on the floor.

"If you can't beat 'em, join 'em," I said, slipping out of my clothes and lying on top of his discarded suit.

"What is this?" he said. "Three-dimensional sex, like three-dimensional tick-tack-toe? Probably Howie is down in the basement going at it with whatever man or woman he's picked up also?"

But that particular night, he knew Howie wasn't there. Roman had come alone, because Howie was at a funeral. Howie wasn't having any fun, sexual or otherwise. He'd already left a message on the machine saying he was so bummed out he didn't even plan to drive from Newburyport for the weekend. And Roman and his girlfriend had already told me they'd be going to a party in Vinalhaven—in fact, we expected them to be gone when we returned, but that was Roman: no sense of time; a conviction that what you don't do today you can do tomorrow. At any rate, the weekend, I thought at that point, was going to be just the two of us, just the way Danny liked it. But then the weather changed. There was a day's lull, during which Roman and Kathleen still did not leave for the party, and during which time Howie changed his mind and hopped a bus—Roman had Howie's car—and we picked him up at the Greyhound stop in front of the drugstore. Danny picked him up, because I was cooking.

Danny was not all bad. He was a talented painter, a generous man when the spirit moved him, and funny: he could mimic anyone. That night, in the bedroom, he screwed up his face to look like poor old Mrs. Hill's, and imitated the dance as she'd done it, favoring her right leg, trying to smile through her pain. Every so often he would stop and pretend to pick up the imaginary person and toss her to the ceiling, or drop-kick her—a tacit admission not only of his frustration, but that he was not always nice. It had me weeping with laughter: Danny, in his boxer shorts, recreating his earlier attempt at a fox trot, his caricature of his partner's gimpiness so convincing that I really saw her in the room, though she was elsewhere, and no doubt long asleep.

"You want to know what to do with a letter sent by Roman to some woman that got returned to you," Howie says. I can hear him tapping his finger on his computer. He's been playing a video game. It sounds like large things are quickly devouring small things: a combination roar and shriek. Howie works at home, designing publications on his desktop publishing system. As he works, he often listens to music, plays games on his portable computer, and converses with whoever calls through the speaker-phone. Eating or drinking something would also not be out of the question. For people of our generation, this simultaneous taking in of stimuli isn't all that unusual. An outgrowth, obviously, of taking drugs and functioning through their effects. These days, Howie only has the occasional beer, but he's retained his taste for constant input. I can hear the Japanese rock 'n' roll in the background. When Howie's playing a computer game and listening to weird music, you can guess the rest: Diet Coke; underwear or pajama bottoms; blinds dropped and lights out, the computer screen and the Jesus nightlight glowing.

"You know," Howie says, "I was just talking to somebody about Roman. And she predicted he was going to get back in touch. Maybe tomorrow a letter will be returned to me."

"Who were you talking to who said that?"

"A psychic."

"You're kidding me."

"No," he says.

"Well, let's hear. You went to a psychic. Was the psychic any good?"

"She had Girl Scout cookies on the table by her chair. Seemed our sort."

"What did you consult a psychic about, Howie?"

"Whether I should take the job in Silicon Valley."

"And?"

"I should, and rearrange my priorities, or I should stay where I am and admit that my current priorities make it impossible for me to move to California."

"We're talking Alice VanVleet?"

"I thought you never wanted to hear her name again. You just spoke the offending name."

"I'm trying to find out about the psychic."

"She impressed me. Had the mint Girl Scouts, not those new-fangled ones. She knew Alice's name without being told. She said, 'Your significant other is named either Alice or Ann.'"

Alice VanVleet is a bored, middle-aged fag hag. She dumps all her problems on Howie and expects him to make her complicated meals, besides, to which she contributes things she buys at the store, like bottled, fat-free salad dressing and wine only she drinks. She doesn't even keep beer for him in the refrigerator. Once, I got roped into going with Howie to her condo for dinner, and she spent the whole evening eyeing me every time I poured from her bottle of chardonnay, talking about her ex-husband's unwillingness to—as she put it—parent the children, all three of whom were in their mid- to late twenties and still living with her. From what she said, they seemed to do nothing but "be associated with" the Church of Christian Science and indulge their passion for sports.

"Did she know Alice VanVleet can't hold a job?"

"And she said you were a cynical bitch, and I should stay away from you," he says.

It takes a second, but when he snorts, self-satisfied, I know he's kidding.

"Now," he says. "Now: you have a letter and you're calling me to see what to do about it. I would suggest, if you've got an hour, you ask this psychic about the letter, as well as anything else you want. My treat. What to give the girl who has everything."

Another snort. When Danny left, he took half of everything. Everything consisted of his aunt's Limoges, a large collection of unisex winter clothing, such as long johns and down parkas, Salvation Army re-covered chairs, a sisal rug which he had drawn on with Magic Marker to make it look like marble (he took the rug), woven throw rugs with pug dogs on them we'd picked up at curbside in Somerville, Massachusetts (he left those), antiques bought cheap at auction, and the mahogany sleigh bed, which left me the mattress and box spring on which I sit as I talk to Howie, pleasantly distracted by my dislike of Alice VanVleet.

Abracadabra, and I'm in Howie's Chevy convertible, and we're off to see the wizard. Well—it takes him almost an hour to get to my house, but when he does pull in, I'm happy to see him, delighted the day is nice enough that the top can be down, resolved to either not mention Alice VanVleet or to say something nice about her, since Howie is so counter-suggestible. He fell in with Alice, come to think of it, just at the time he and Roman had the big fight. I'm not even sure who was to blame: apparently Howie backed out of going halves on a house in Umbria when he heard that Roman's girlfriend would be along, and Roman accused him of general cheapness and of having secretly made his own plans to invite what he sneeringly called The Cambridge Ladies, so it was hypocritical to pretend Roman had been the one to ruin the plans. It's always push-pull with Roman and Howie, though. They've had many of these fights, in which they haven't spoken for months, or even for a year or more. "He's such a prima donna," Howie has often complained to me. "He's so self-absorbed, he always wants to be in the spotlight, everybody applauding. He stands around the kitchen watching me cook like he's fucking standing at the end of the runway crowned as Miss America. Have you noticed the way he stands around, as if he's soaking in approval, as if everybody is just so fucking thrilled to see him preening while onions are being sliced?"

The psychic wears a beautiful intaglio ring and has delicate, long fingers with enviably manicured nails. She's younger than I expected—probably late thirties. She's painted the walls an odd lavender that seems to glow pink within. There is a ring of chairs in the center of the room, and nothing else except a small table next to the chair she sits in and, against the far wall, another table on which sits an answering machine, blinking. The overhead light is on a dimmer switch, and the room is neither bright nor dark. I briefly imagine Howie squirming in one of the chairs, talking to the psychic as if she were a giant daisy he could pluck, to find out whether he—Roman—loves him or loves him not. And then, all the petals gone, he would know, and she would be as she is now, her thin body in a longish green dress resembling a flower stem, her neat bubble of dark hair all that would remain: the black, black center of the daisy. What I at first take as a Cindy Craw-fordesque mole is actually a crumb, I see, as she licks it away. Today the cookies aren't on the table, though. Instead, she's reading a Jane Austen novel. Psychic myself, I realize the Chapstick must indicate she has dry lips.

"Yes," she says, "I can tell you what's in the envelope."

It sits where I placed it when I first came in, on top of *Pride and Prejudice*. She looks at it. I look at it.

"It's a map," she says.

"But what does the letter say?" I ask. Outside, I can faintly hear the music Howie is playing as he sits curbside.

"There is no letter," she says. "It's just a map."

"A map to what?"

"Buried treasure," she says.

I laugh. Instantly, before I can check my reaction. *Buried treasure?*

The perfectly painted fingernails play church and steeple. "The person has drawn a box. A pirate's chest. With a skull and crossbones on the lid. Pearls inside, it seems to me."

"You can't tell?"

She closes her eyes. Her fingers rest not on the envelope, but on one knee.

"It's a stereo," she says. "That's what's inside the chest. There's an amp. Receiver. Wireless speakers. CDs and tapes are dumped in the chest, too."

"You're serious?" I say. "Can you tell what the music is?"

"A pretty eclectic lot," she says. "Puccini. Marianne Faithfull. Astor Piazzola."

They're all musicians Roman loves. In fact, when I picked up a *People* magazine in the dentist's office recently, I wondered if

Roman had heard that Marianne Faithfull was coming out with a new album. I had been thinking about him, shortly before the envelope arrived.

"Are you interested in anything besides the envelope?" she says.

"Your intaglio—" I begin.

"Zeus," she says. "The stone is an old carnelian."

"Beautiful," I say. I lean forward in my chair. "The setting is rose gold, isn't it? It's so beautiful, but so simple."

"Rose gold," she echoes. "Simple, yes. The setting is simple; he wasn't."

"I beg your pardon?"

She says, sounding slightly world-weary, "A complicated man, Zeus. Like so many others."

"My friend Howie—" I say, in an impulsive burst. I know what I want to ask, but still I hesitate, because I don't want to hear the answer. I want to know about his health, exactly how long I can plan on our being able to knock around together. Most of all, I want to know, and do not want to know, the day and time of his death. And: what exact thing will that death also kill off in me? My sense that the world can be a pleasant place? My love of gardening, because every flower might forever after look like what I'd seen in a spray of flowers at a funeral? Morbid. Morbid. The thoughts I always quickly push out of my mind, though after a while they assert themselves as a headache.

"See the pyramids...," Patsy Cline sings from Howie's tape deck. My question unfinished, the psychic waits politely. Does this mean she can't read my mind? Or that she isn't obliged to, if I can't at least do the work of finishing a sentence? She adjusts the ring, twirling it slightly with her right hand. It makes me wonder whether it might be possible that she's finding the answers in Zeus's head, not her own.

"Your friend," she says, tired of waiting for me to speak. "I think your friend will soon transcend his personal problems."

It's not until I'm in the car that I realize what she said could be interpreted two ways, and that the second of those ways might be transcendence through death. I turn to him, and he is as real, as solid, as the car itself. He looks bright-eyed, healthy. Happy, even.

"See Janet Peacham's life passing before her eyes," I say. "What remains constant? That Howie and Janet go on excellent adventures, consulting psychics about how everything will be." I look at him. "Do you realize you just spent a hundred bucks to receive news of buried treasure? *Buried Treasure!* And do you know what it turns out to be? Not jewels and gold coins, but stereo equipment. He must be telling her he's bought her a stereo in lieu of a dozen red roses." Here, though, I bog down, considering this. "Do you think he drew her a map to tell her where to find her present?" I say finally.

"Open it," he says. "Let's see where it's buried."

"Then what? We go excavating? We find it, and what do we do? Take it over to the woman's house and tell her, 'Hey, here, this is from Roman'?" I slide lower in the seat. "I'm sure he's given it to her by now."

"But if he hasn't," Howie says, "if for any reason he hasn't, it falls to us. Correct me if I'm wrong here, but this Smythe woman doesn't live where he thinks she lives, the letter comes bouncing back to you, all but hollering, Open Me! Open Me! What do you say, we go there, dig up the lady's treasure, keep it in the garage, if you want, until he shows up, and then tell him that the joke's on him. We both know he's showing up, right? Did the psychic tell you he was going to get back in touch with you, too?"

It breaks my heart. Under any conditions, he wants us back together again. Not just him and Roman, Howie and Roman and Janet—and we've all become such different people. Is there any chance that if we met now, for the first time, we'd still be drawn to each other? Of course, I'm more fond of Howie than anyone else I can think of, but that's because he revealed himself to me so long ago, because our friendship evolved, because we've lost our families, and friends have become surrogate families. I wouldn't know how to break down Howie's barriers if I met him today. And Roman: did either of us, ever, really get close to Roman, or is he still orbiting around us, teasing, no greater possibility he'll plunge to earth than your average meteor?

"He follows through on everything," Howie says, thinking out loud. He's completely caught up in this; he's experiencing it as virtual reality. "And if she doesn't write him a thank-you note, or whatever it is he expects, he'll get in touch with you and make some half-assed explanation about it all, and, bottom line, he'll want to know if his goods are okay."

"Let sleeping dogs lie," I say.

"Yeah, but buried Bang and Olufsen?"

"What does it matter? Why involve ourselves in some peculiar courtship ritual of Roman's? I can pretend not to know anything about it, particularly when I return the sealed envelope."

"So you know he's coming," Howie says.

"Yeah," I say, surprised, myself, at the tone of defeat in my voice. "I know he'll show up eventually." I look out the window. No pyramids, though Patsy Cline is trying to conjure them up for me; just the shopping center.

"He's in love again," Howie says.

Years ago—many years ago—Roman was in love with Howie. When Roman became infatuated with me, it became a triangle. Then Danny came along and struck the side, and took me away. Danny has always been militantly heterosexual, but it intrigued him that I was bisexual. He'd missed the sixties sitting around graduate school, studying law, as his parents insisted he do, until he finally took a stand, dropped out of school, and worked at a dull job in an accounting firm, and then, when he'd saved enough money, went to art school. He'd had several successful shows by the time I met him. We lived in London, where a gallery was representing him at the time. Later, the gallery owner jumped out the window, and the gallery folded. Then we went to Seattle. Then we went to Washington, when Danny got a job with the State Department, before he quit trying to work at pointless jobs just for the money and decided to devote all his time to painting. When he did resign, we were lonely because for some reason his friends from work all seemed to gradually drop him, and there we were, back in the States without our friends from Europe, or our friends from the Pacific Northwest. So we moved to a summer home in Maine and invited my old friend Howie to visit us, and who did Howie bring but Roman? They'd just gotten back in touch, after a month-long snit, and Howie thought it would be perfect if their reunion included me. To my surprise, nothing was there: no *frisson*, no deep feeling at all, except that Roman's being there seemed vaguely dangerous. For some reason, though I'd often talked about Howie, I'd never really discussed Roman with Danny.

Soon Roman began to drop by the house alone. He wasn't flirting with me, I quickly decided; he was a little put out I hadn't kept in touch, and he was jealous of my happiness, but for a while I actually thought he wished me well. He was never charitable toward Howie, so why would I have thought he'd feel kindly toward me? What happened next was that he asked if he could introduce us to his younger sister, who had seen one of Danny's paintings in New York and greatly admired his work. You can guess the rest: Danny fell in love with Roman's sister. She was a senior at Yale, a Fine Arts major, a painter herself. A winsome little thing, physically small, at five foot one, with her Janis Joplin tumbleweed hair and sparkly vests she wore over T-shirts to cover her flat little breasts. The first time we met her, she was wearing too-short cutoffs and make-a-joke-on-housewives mules, her pink polished toes protruding from the little vee in front, her pumiced pink heels naked in back. So Howie and I grew closer, as we'd been back in undergraduate school, taken aback by Roman's outlandish offering of his sister, Marielle, who so gladly modeled for Danny in exchange for critiques of her paintings.

Meanwhile, Roman began to show up on the weekends with an assortment of girlfriends. There had been other periods when he saw women exclusively, but this time his interest was lasting longer than usual. Danny and I never found the women much fun, though, and they tended to baffle Howie. Their conventionality bothered me, and the sheer quantity of them offended Howie, who was used to the occasional foray into heterosexuality, but still: young women in Ann Taylor business suits whom Roman, it turned out, had picked up on the train? One of them was there the afternoon the hurricane blew up, a paralegal named Angie, who ended up camping out with him for days in the trailer that had belonged to the former caretaker when we bought the house. In retrospect, I think she might have been too shy, or embarrassed, to spend much time with us. Roman was fifteen years older than she, and he took every occasion to let her know he had greater wisdom. Did she really care for him? When she returned to me the jeans and tops, the underwear and nightgown,

I'd lent her—she expected to be there only for dinner—something about the way she handed back the soiled, neatly folded clothes made me think she valued them, and I had seen her express none of that care, none of that respectful carefulness, toward Roman. She had spoken little in his presence. There seemed no joy there. All of which reminded me of Roman's trial by fire of me and of Howie, years before. We had stood our ground and prevailed. We had won, in a way—though look what that winning got both of us: more years of testing our loyalty, tempestuous fights, pronouncements like flash floods, waves of information about the way things should be (his way).

The trailer kept its power when the main house went black. From our various rooms, and for our various reasons, we'd look at that beacon in the night, glowing oddly, the nucleus stained to shine under the microscope. It was obvious that Danny had begun to desire Marielle; I had begun to desire—not to physically desire, but to depend upon with a kind of fierce desperation that my trust be returned—Howie, the one person who could best understand my own surprise and confusion at the way events were shifting. Wind blew. Wine was uncorked to toast its wildness. Candles burned to stubs. The power lines were down, and it was dark, dark, dark—except for the constant glow of what Howie came to dub "the love boat," the trailer sinking into the muddy field. Roman took long walks around the wet, wind-lashed land, no doubt malevolently whistling as he walked. Because his strategy to undermine my relationship with Danny was working as forcefully as if he had been able, himself, to whip up a storm and permanently alter the ground we stood on.

Roman, returning? Howie has to be right, but what is this strange approach? And if—as he'd written to Howie in a letter after the hurricane—he has nothing to feel guilty about, but only feels sorry that he has to be honest in telling Howie that the menopausal Cambridge Ladies are too pointless and depressing to be part of his planned idyll in *Italia*...if, as he maintains, it is his curse to have become the messenger who has to reveal Danny's lack of love for me...if he is only poor Rosencrantz, or poor Guildenstern, and if he's been functioning blindly and blamelessly, why disappear for so long? He left his job, put the brownstone in the South End on the market, moved out before it was sold (we heard this from Roman's mother, who was searching for him, as confused as anyone), wrote a self-justifying letter, which he mailed from St. Thomas to his mother in New York and to his father in Palm Beach, with a "cc" at the bottom to Mr. Daniel Obersham (*Mr.?!*) and to a psychiatrist he'd seen many years before, as well as leaving a copy tacked to the door of his office (the histrionic flourish has never been lost on Roman), claiming that the negative energy released during the hurricane, combined with the toxic effects he now doubted he would ever overcome, following his years of chemical dependency, had left him with unmanageable emotions that often took on a life of their own, causing him to provoke those he loved. Only on Howie's letter was there an asterisk—at least, there was no foot- note to the letter Roman's mother forwarded to Howie, and the psychiatrist told Howie on the phone that there was no physical mark, including a signature, on the letter he received. The asterisk was not typed, but hand-drawn, and it looked a little the way a gnat does when it flies too close to your face. At the bottom of Howie's letter, underneath a larger, darker cluster of splayed strokes, was written: *You I have hurt most, not even Janet, yet you know I love you, Howie.*

Well, indeed. Indeed Howie did know it, but for most of the time he'd known Roman, that love had been a confusing thing, announced at odd times, something Roman used to manipulate Howie, a standard, almost, to which Howie could either measure up or, more often, and just as pleasing to Roman, fall short of.

For more than a year after the hurricane, everyone felt they had had more than enough of everyone else, and even Howie and I hardly talked. I received one drunken phone call late at night from Danny and listened for only a few seconds before I hung up. If it hadn't been for the excruciatingly bad news that Howie tested HIV-positive—if he hadn't called me from a phone booth just after getting the news, barely able to talk because of his chattering teeth—I might have continued to stay separate from all of them. The voice control button had been activated on my answering machine, and when I heard that it was Howie, and what Howie was saying, I slowly slid the volume down to off for one second in which to compose myself before I picked up the receiver. The one second stretched to two, three—enough time for many emotions to sift through my understanding: the shock; the acceptance of the unthinkable; a hundred plans for reversing the news; vivid memories of my friendship with Howie, from meeting at age eighteen until that moment, which seemed like many long, painful moments until the time when I would rush toward him, find him leaning up against the side of the plastic hooded phone he'd called from, looking blankly into a gutter as if he were watching water's effluence, while leaning against the rail of a ship.

We were sailing nowhere. We were moving slowly. Hardly at all. Back to his apartment, because where else was there to go while Howie said over and over again, like a mantra, "I haven't slept with you for years, I haven't slept with you for so many years, there couldn't possibly be a problem. I haven't slept with you..." Of course, people overheard him, and looked after us as we wove down the street, Howie shaking, me trying to steer him and shush him at the same time, Howie saying through chattering teeth: "I haven't slept with you..."

An observation: people's personal pain is just another box that will tumble from the back of the truck, spilling your possessions all over the street; people's contentment, even their happiness, is the orchid that once bloomed with such waxy perfection they forget it can become blighted; special moments are the kite carried high by the breeze, when the same day, a plane caught in a downdraft of wind plunges to the ground. You're lucky if no one you love is traitorous; you're blessed if your friends, however peculiar, remain loyal; you're admirable if the rug is pulled from underneath you, and you improvise a gawky dance.

That's what I am thinking this morning, just a few weeks after our convertible ride, trying to keep my thoughts as abstract as possible, walking from the parking garage to the hospital, feeling sorry for Howie, because his white blood cell count has begun to sink alarmingly, sorry for myself because I am so little up for this; and also sorry for the passengers of the USAir plane that crashed, for the orchid Howie sent me for my birthday that I threw out prematurely at the first signs of yellowing, for the moving men who gathered up what they could from a big box containing Howie's pans and spine-bent books and broken crockery. He decided that if he was getting sicker, he didn't want to be a sick person in the city. And what was his solution but to rent a house close to mine, in Maine. In the winter he'd think about where he would relocate to get out of the cold. Alice VanVleet, either stupid or intent upon not confronting the specifics of Howie's situation, was lobbying hard for Virgin Gorda. Even Howie found this amusing. "Doesn't the woman know there's no going back?" he asked me.

Suddenly, there is a short, fat nurse running into the hospital ahead of me, pushing the up button of the elevator, doing an impatient little sidestep routine as she watches the control panel, then runs onto the elevator and rises to her floor as I stand next to her. Whatever floor she gets off at will inevitably be permeated by the cardboard and sugar smell of hospital kitchen–prepared tomato sauce. She gets off at 3, and I continue on in the elevator, alone, to the fifth floor.

I'm not expecting anything good when I exit the elevator, and naturally I also am not expecting to see Roman. He is there in the corridor, though. And he's at least had the sense not to drag some woman Howie wouldn't know to his bedside. As I come off the elevator, I know it is Roman, even though his back is turned to me and his hair has grown quite long, pulled back in a spout of a ponytail. He is wearing corduroy pants and a jade-green shirt.

"He's using the portable toilet," Roman says, nodding toward the room's closed door.

"Hello to you, too," I say.

"Don't be mean to me," he says. "I just found out, from my mother."

"Your mother? In New York? How did she know?"

"She called him because he can always tell her what she's missed on the Sunday crossword puzzle. The paramedics were there."

"I sent them," I say, as if I feel the need to explain my place in all this. "He was so out of breath when we talked on the phone, he couldn't finish a sentence."

"They've given him a transfusion," Roman says.

We both look at the closed door.

"Were you planning to be in the area, anyway? A letter you sent got returned to me the other day. A letter to some woman."

He looks confused. As always, when he is confused by something, he looks much younger.

"Roman," I say, "you put your name, in care of me, as the return address."

"I don't know what you're talking about," he says.

"Roman, what is the point of this?"

"A letter from me to someone else was returned to you? How is that possible?"

It is on the tip of my tongue to say *buried treasure,* but I don't. A woman and a teenage girl, looking grim, walk by, arm-in-arm. The elevator doors open again, and three more people get off. One woman walks quickly, holding her black patent leather purse in front of her, like a shield. A man with a limp walks behind her. Another woman, obviously dizzy with nervousness, walks crookedly to the window of the nurse's station.

"Who is this letter to?" he asks. At least this time there is a slight hint of doubt in his voice. He shifts his weight from one foot to the other, standing in the familiar way with his left hip thrown out and his right foot turned outward, an almost balletic position.

"Some woman. Some woman you probably picked up on the train, or wherever. Remember when the phone would ring, and you'd say *'Just some woman'* if anyone expressed any curiosity?"

"What is this?" he says. "Your feminist sensibilities being offended?"

"I just asked a straightforward question. Howie's been going downhill for months now. Neither of us had any idea where you were, since you've always conveniently appeared and disappeared according to your own schedule. Excuse me for being curious about whether you were in the area to begin with."

"I drove from Derry, New Hampshire," he says. "That's where I live now."

I look at the dizzy woman hurrying by, mouthing something silently to herself. Howie's move to be close to me I understand, but what does Roman have in mind? He has never liked the cold, and what can there be for him in Derry, New Hampshire?

"Other than this disastrous news about Howie, how was your summer?" he says. "You know, 'Other than that, Mrs. Lincoln—' "

"Roman, forgive me, but after all that's happened, I really can't stand here and be asked questions about whether I had a pleasant summer."

"I always change things," he says. "I'm cursed with being a catalyst. I don't expect you to be sympathetic, obviously—"

"That's good."

"I don't think I expect enough," he says, suddenly, quite seriously. "The way I see it, I'm going with the flow, but it's a mystery to me: other people see me as the one who's in control. They look to me for answers. They try to make me into some sort of authority figure that I'm not. You and Howie have always acted in collusion, like everything that happened between us so long ago was all my idea, something I coerced you into. Why was it all my doing? Think about it." He frowns at me. "She asked me if she was correct in assuming that he was attracted to her."

"What are you talking about?" I say.

"My sister. Marielle, who stole your boyfriend."

It surprises me, when he mentions it so blatantly. Somehow, I had been wondering about the envelope—the envelope which he addressed just as I said he did—but while I was thinking about that mystery, he was thinking about the past.

"They've cut me off, you know," he says.

"I didn't know, because I haven't been in touch with anybody except Howie."

"You're living in Maine year-round now, aren't you?" he says.

"What does it matter?"

"Just a question," he says. "You know, like your asking whether I intended to be here, anyway."

An orderly wheeling a patient on a gurney passes us, wearing a gray jumpsuit and moon-landing boots. A nurse comes up quickly behind him, then opens the door to the room next to Howie's so he can push the patient in.

"Good," Roman says, more to himself than to me. "Howie's still got the room to himself."

It is the first moment I remember that Roman can be kind, considerate. The person Howie and—amazingly—I once cared so much about.

"Why did they cut you off?" I hear myself ask.

"Ooooh," he says, drawing it out, seeming to really be thinking. "My guess? My bisexuality. He's a pretty straight arrow for an artist, Danny. And of course she's always been Little Miss Goody Two Shoes. If things don't hit her in the face, she doesn't care to see them."

"Your sister didn't know anything about your life?"

"Didn't, apparently, until I hit her in the face, in a manner of speaking. Took a guy with me when we went . . . this is going to kill you: the four of us went on a reggae cruise one night. Sailed out of Portsmouth."

The orderly passes by, says, "How you doin'?"

"Good, thanks," Roman says.

I offer a false smile, although he's already passed by. I stare at the backs of his boots. They are enormous; they seem to have been inflated with an air hose. But this is certainly not the moon. Very few people, except for visitors leaving, are taking one giant step here. Everyone moves slowly, bent under the weight of their worry or grief. A woman holding on to an IV pole wheels it along, a needle centered in the side of her wrist, smiling apologetically as she passes.

"God, this is awful," I say.

He drops his arm around my shoulder. I feel myself stiffen, then slump tiredly. Why had Roman been the one in charge? Because he was better-looking than either of us. Because, embarrassing as it is to admit as a grown-up, the most beautiful person got to be the one in charge. It didn't hurt that he was the most charismatic, either, or that he had his own apartment. Because Howie and I had both been weak, in a way, smitten with beauty, and we'd both wanted to be captivated, wanted to be instructed, wanted to take some of what Roman had, just through osmosis. As if on cue, the minute I figure all that out, the red light above Howie's door comes on. He is finished; he is calling the nurse to help him back to bed. There is no nurse anywhere in sight.

"You go," I whisper, drawing back. It seems clear that Roman should be the one to help him off the toilet. I feel sure that would embarrass Howie less.

At the door, only three steps away, Roman stops. He turns. He says, "A couple of times I've driven by your house. I was trying to get up the nerve to come in and apologize. I had a rehearsed speech—a pretty good one. And then one time I decided to rely on that old dependable charm, I felt like luck was with me that particular night. That our stars were aligned, or something. I got there, and there was a Jeep in your driveway."

"How you doin'?" the orderly says, passing by, as if he hasn't greeted us before.

"So that stopped you," I say, finishing his thought for him.

"Right. It stopped me."

"I do have friends," I say.

With that he nods, then turns and opens the door, starting the difficult but still no doubt familiar process of going toward his old friend Howie, turning his back on his old friend Janet. It is symbolic, I think, feeling sorry for myself. It isn't just a turned back, it is the back he's turned before, more times than he should have. And that is when the unexpected image comes to mind: the three of us, in bed, twenty years before, a not-yet-sex-sated Roman turning toward Howie, his ass jutting into my groin as I push forward to curl against him, his vertebrae pronounced because of his thinness. Drugs were food, and sex was love. I remember that moment in great detail: the way I used the tip of my nose like a finger, running it lightly up his spine, breathing in the smell of Right Guard and sweaty skin, which had been synonymous, at that time in my life, with actually inhaling freedom.

Later, after a slowly eaten dinner, we go to my house. The Jeep is parked in the driveway; the neighbors' daughter's prized vehicle, which there is no place for in their two-car driveway. I don't explain it. I pull a bottle of wine out of the old oak mailbox that functions as a wine rack. There are two bottles, and I take the better of them out, uncork it wordlessly, pour two glasses half full, push one glass closer to Roman.

"You're careful, aren't you?" I ask.

"About drinking?" he says.

"No. About sex."

He looks at me, genuinely surprised. "Yes," he says, after a minute. "Of course I am." He is suddenly not only looking at me, but staring. Can he possibly, madly, mean his steady gaze to be a come-on?

"Of course I'm careful, and of course it's no fun," he says.

I lower my eyes, sure now that it's not my imagination; he *has* been holding open some possibility. Sex isn't *fun*? He and I could have *fun*? In my house, half-emptied of furniture, with absurd rugs thrown here and there with pug dogs woven into them, in this place that I meant to live in so happily with my lover, visiting with my dear friend and soul mate Howie when he was well, physically well, no nightmare disease hanging over anyone . . . in this context, today, now, Roman and I could fall into each other's arms? Uneasily, as I've done before, I look around me because I sense some presence. Is it guilt creeping in, because for half a second I was happy he was offering something? Or do I still think the younger Roman is hovering somewhere, hidden like the wolf in the tree, the Roman whose ghost hangs over us both: a ghost that Roman can't exorcise any more than I can—that dynamic, seemingly fearless person that Roman used to be.

I get the letter. Along with letters to be answered and bills to be paid, it's been in one of the cubbyholes of the mailbox. I hand it to him, and, again, he looks surprised. "Well, look at it carefully," he says, finally. "It's my handwriting on the address, but it's Marielle who . . . why would she have done this? She obviously filled in the return to be in care of you. Why would she do that?"

"I thought they'd cut you off," I say.

"They have. I haven't seen them for months, since the boat ride." He puts the letter on the table. He says, "I had it in my jacket pocket that night, I think. I remember now. She wore my jacket because it was cold once we got out on the water. That's right; she did. She even wore it home in the car. She must have thought she was doing me a favor by mailing the letter the next day, but she didn't know my address, because I'd just moved to Derry. So she asked Danny what your address was, and he told her."

"Sherlock Holmes," I say, raising my wineglass in a toast.

"But why didn't she put her own address on it?"

"You tell me," I say.

"Maybe because she thinks about you a lot. She's guilty, and it makes her preoccupied with you."

"She thinks about me? What does she think?"

"I don't know. She used to bring you into conversation all the time. Like she could banish his memory of you by talking about you. What do I know?"

"Well," I say, handing him the letter, "I hope you weren't expecting a quick reply."

"Actually, she saved me from making a fool of myself. It was a pretty intemperate letter. I was angry because a woman I'd been seeing—"

"*Some woman*," I say jokingly, mocking myself as much as him.

"Yep. *Some woman*, indeed. Issued me an ultimatum—could have told her that wouldn't work, right?—insisting I set a wedding date, or the relationship was over. I'd never misled her about anything, and it set me off. I wrote her and told her I'd been straight with her from the first—what was she doing, suddenly demanding things like that?"

For a moment, I'm too surprised to react. He was serious enough about the woman in Rhode Island that she thought he'd marry her? Because she was hoping against hope, or because he might truly have indicated that was a possibility?

"What did she say?" I finally ask.

"You're holding my letter," he says. "She never got it. Maybe she's so dumb she thinks I'm still mulling it over."

My thoughts are flooding: *The buried treasure; the buried treasure... the skull and crossbones. The stereo equipment. Tapes by Astor Piazzola.* But I can't mention those things. There's no way I can contradict him without having to explain. Why is he making up such a detailed story? Why tell me about the messy situation at all, if all he's going to do is lie?

"Open it," I say. "It would be like old times. I could see what you sound like these days when somebody pushes your buttons."

"It's better forgotten," he says.

"You won't open it? You won't even read me the first few sentences?"

He frowns, then shrugs. He hands me the envelope. "Read them yourself, if you really want to, Janet."

This is even more perplexing. The envelope is suddenly in my hand. When he hands it to me, though—when he gives me permission to open it—I realize instantly that whatever the psychic said had to have been mere invention. She was a charlatan, just as I'd suspected. It is not a map; it is an irate letter, telling a woman in Rhode Island that what she wants will never come about. The fortune-teller was another person, another thing, Howie put his trust in inadvisably.

I rip open the envelope. Then I get my next surprise.

Where I expected a letter, there is, instead, a map. On one corner, someone has drawn a tornado or, more likely, experienced some frustration getting ink to flow out of the pen. Just as the psychic said, there is a fairly detailed map, with a pirate's chest in the lower corner, with the top braced open, spilling from it not jewels and coins, but revealing stereo components and many tapes. In another drawing, a maze of streets leads to the chest. The streets are named, and arrows point the way.

Coming up beside me, Roman says, "What the hell is that?"

"Buried treasure," I say, at last.

"What the—" He grabs the piece of paper from my hand. "My God, she's completely crazy. She really is completely crazy. What did Marielle do, steam it open?"

If he weren't so earnest, I wouldn't even half believe him, but I do half believe him. I decide that there is at least a fifty-fifty chance that he thought it really was the letter he just described to me.

"Unbelievable!" he says, pronouncing every syllable, staring at the piece of paper. "I knew Marielle didn't like her, but I mean, this is nothing a sane person would do with a letter that..."

"What is it?" I say, helpless now in my confusion.

"It's what you said it was. It's *buried treasure*," he says. "It's even got...look at the road names. She's written the street names right on the page. She's lost her fucking mind!"

I sit on a kitchen stool, frowning.

"Somebody broke into Deirdre's apartment one weekend when we were away. They—Jesus!—there's no *they* about it. My insane sister did it. She took her stereo and hid it in the woods, obviously, and then, on top of that, later she steals my letter and sends Deirdre a map showing her where the stuff is, and naturally, since it's in *my* handwriting, what would Deirdre think but that I was responsible. That I put somebody up to the break-in. My God! What if this hadn't come back to you?"

I take it all in. It does seem bizarrely malicious. Also, he does seem incredibly lucky. But more than that, I see that for the millionth, billionth time, I'm involved in his life again, helpless and awed by the madness, fascinated but repelled. Roman becomes Pac Man, eating up time. That's what he's like; he's like Howie's game of Pac Man, a little figure racing around the screen, voracious, wildly energized, everything magnetized by his megalomania. It's just another moment in Roman's life, in which so many colleagues are jealous of his brilliance there's always a movement afoot to get him fired, but this time—this time it's his own sister who's tried to do him in. Earlier, in the hospital, Roman was onto something. He sensed something similar to what I'm thinking now; he was on the track of himself, when he made the remark about being a catalyst. I take a deep breath, wanting to organize my thoughts, wanting to explain that it's because of the way he lives that he invites these things. Yeah, sure, he finds people who are complicit, but since I've been one of those people, I've developed a lot of sympathy. You stand at the shore, wading in gradually, and suddenly there's a tidal wave, an undertow, Roman arranges it so there's no lifeguard but him, and when you finally escape—grateful to him; always grateful to the savior—your metabolism is set a little higher, those endorphins have been set loose, the next day, you need the next high. The beach was just a mirage, though. You look everywhere for where you were, but it isn't there, or never was. But Roman is there. So you attach yourself to Roman, to the great magnet who pulls you slowly in.

So how did I lose my charge? I wonder now. How did I ever escape to the extent that I did, and what is it that made him let me go? Because I sorted out my sexual allegiances? Because of all the time I spent with Danny, before Roman found a way to intervene? Or because I'd opted for true friendship years before—because it quickly became obvious that I liked Howie better: reliable, unglamorous Howie. That conclusion must have hurt Roman, but the more I drifted, the weaker his pull became, so that all he could do was stay in close proximity. Let me see what being a loser in love was like. Let me experience loneliness. Wait until illness threatened to take my best friend away. See if that didn't make me go running back to his side. And he is now to be found in New Hampshire, a state conveniently adjacent to Maine.

"I'm afraid of her," he says. "I'll be honest with you. I'm too freaked out to go home tonight. I'm afraid I'd call my sister and say some very, very regrettable things to her. You've got to protect me from what I might do. I've got to stay calm. She's stark raving mad—you see that, Janet, don't you? I've got to figure out the best way to deal with this."

The guest room, the one painted blue, has always been referred to—because he always chose to sleep there, those rare occasions he was without a girlfriend he wanted to screw all night in the quiet of the trailer—as "Roman's Room." He is telling me now that he must spend the night there—the first time he'll have been in the house overnight since Danny left.

"You know what, Roman?" I say. "All the time you've been talking, I've been thinking the most terrible things about you."

"When have you not?" he says, taking my hand. "When, ever, have you not?"

Sitting in the red Jeep in my driveway, late that night, I relive it: the time Roman arrived with Howie, bringing the hurricane on their heels. No, of course Roman couldn't determine the weather, but how fortuitous—how fortuitous the facts of Roman's life have so often been: the sky flashing bright with lightning, trees dropping like pick-up-sticks in the gusting wind, candles lit as the power went out, the panes of glass shaking in the old windows in need of reglazing. That unremitting, wild weather that always leads people to band together to resist nature with all their strength.

I meant to stay safe inside. While Howie and Roman and Danny took silly chances, chasing after ambulances and fire trucks on foot, going to inspect huge fallen oaks with power lines tangled like deadly IV tubes through them, Danny—so I'm told—

stripped and jumped in the river, laughing and bobbing crazily as spiky waves lashed him. So much physicality must have come as a relief. In spite of his cynicism about life in general, Howie always retained his schoolboy crush on Roman. He must have suffered when he faded into and out of Roman's affections, even as a friend, and taken it personally not only that Roman chose women over men, but that those women were most often such small, pale, compliant creatures. The parade of women was like a parody of the two of us; they'd inevitably have little energy, little to say, they'd seem, perhaps, only to have one hidden agenda, and that would be their desire to marry Roman. Then, if any got close enough, he'd tell them our history, and if that didn't work, he'd repel them by going to a bar and dancing, or flirting, with men.

Sometimes I fixate on the night of the hurricane, and this is turning out to be one of those times. The neighbors' daughter didn't have a red Jeep then, she had a different car that I let her keep parked in my driveway, a banged-up Buick that was painted a nondescript brown. She'd given it the nickname "The Mudmobile." Although I was alone the day after the hurricane hit, I'd gone outside to clear my thoughts. It saddened me that so many large, substantial trees had been uprooted; the snarled power cables were dangerous snakes of electric current coiling through the maples and elms; more wind than I expected blew up around me, forcing tears from my eyes, so that after a few minutes of standing and staring, I took shelter in the driver's seat of the Buick. While I was sitting there—a silly sight; a driver going nowhere, I reflected even at the time—mulling over the first dramatic arrival of Roman in Maine, accompanied by his amazing singing tiger, Howie (truly, he had introduced Howie to Danny this way, casting himself as the person who cracked the whip, and at the same time making fun of the tiger-striped scarf Howie wore around his neck)—well: it was Howie who was my friend, and, however unadvisedly, he had brought Roman, but the way Roman presented it, he was running the show, Howie was just one of the acts. I wasn't even on the billing anymore. I had been sitting in the car, thinking about that, thinking about Roman's unkindness toward Howie, envisioning a circus—a real circus, Barnum and Bailey—remembering how excited I had been as a small child to be seated with my mother at ringside, when suddenly, or maybe not so suddenly, because my eyes had been closed, and I had been in another world, there was a tap on the car, and I jumped with alarm. Frightened myself, I had also frightened the person who'd done the tapping: Roman's girlfriend of the moment, Angie. I rolled down the window.

"The men are all off inspecting the damage, aren't they?" she said.

"Yes," I said, "Right." Flustered. Embarrassed to have been so lost in thought that I'd been easily frightened.

"I know you're his best friend," Angie said. "I hope it doesn't put you on the spot if I ask you a question."

"Whose best friend?" I said.

Naturally, she looked at me a little strangely. Then—I should have thought to offer—she walked around to the passenger's side and opened the car and got in. "Roman's," she said, pulling the door shut with a click so delicate I wasn't sure the door was closed. She was a sweet, gentle girl. She found it difficult to make eye contact. "I know you've known each other since you were eighteen. He says you're the only person he totally trusts."

"I didn't see Roman for quite a long time," I said. "For quite a while after I got together with Danny, I found I really did not have any desire to see Roman."

"Ms. Peacham," she said. "What are you doing in the car?"

"Is that the question?"

"No," she said. "But what are you?"

"I wanted to get out of the house, but it was a little too wild out here for me. So I thought I'd sit in the car for a minute."

"The trailer's sunk in the mud," she said. "Roman says it's going to have to be pulled out with a tractor."

We both looked at it, through the car's streaked windows, lopsided and glowing. I remember thinking that we inherited such odd things. I was looking at a trailer, on a triangle of land across from my house in Maine. Inside were plants. Gesnariads. The caretaker who'd lived there—or more likely his wife—had grown them under grow-lights clipped to pole lamps and window ledges. They were almost all dead when we bought the house, and I started trying to nurse them back to health. I had the sudden thought that Angie might think the plants were mine. That I had no better idea of how to care for plants. It seemed important to tell her that certain things had just befallen me. I was about to describe our move to the house, when she did, finally, meet my eyes as she turned toward me in the seat. She was in her early twenties, but she could have passed for a teenager, her face bare of makeup, her eyes startlingly large and quite lovely without it. She looked a little the way I'd looked when I was her age, but she had real natural beauty.

"I don't think he loves me, do you?" she said.

After quite a long pause, I said: "No. I don't think he does."

She swallowed. "Is it because he loves you?"

"No," I said. I said it instantly, reflexively, though I'd been taken aback by her question. "You know when a person loves you. Roman has never loved me."

"Did you ever feel the way I do?" she said. "I mean, did you ever want him to?"

I decided to give her slightly more than she'd asked for. "Roman is our friend, but I think Howie and I both were worn down into friendship. He's very demanding, as I'm sure you've noticed. There's a real bond, but it's not friendship, exactly, and it's not love, either. To the extent that he cares about anybody, he cares about me and Howie, but he doesn't love either of us, and he never did."

The information registered, I saw.

"Does he always set women up? Want to fight with them, I mean." She was biting her bottom lip, her eyes averted, her flaxen hair falling forward, nearly obscuring her face.

"Women, in particular? I've never thought about it. I think he just likes to be provocative. He prefers to be the center of attention."

"Is this what your life is like?" she said. Her voice was almost a whisper. She was wearing my white T-shirt—the clean one I'd told Roman to give her that morning, along with a pile of other clean clothes, as he was returning to the trailer after having his breakfast and coffee.

It was an excellent question: Was it? A person sitting in her driveway, world torn up around her, power out, food in the refrigerator spoiled, an odd hostess hostessing an odd party, taking time out from the talk and the games and the "remember when's" that would continue for many more nights, amid burning candles, in the aftermath of a storm.

"You could leave," she said. "Couldn't you leave?"

Not so long after that, it was Danny who left. Intermittently, Roman and Howie arrived, and then departed. Now Howie may either be in residence full-time, or, if he's unlucky, he may never be in the house again. And Roman. Right now, Roman sleeps in Roman's Room.

The girl, though, is long gone—someone who meant to be kind, whose sincere curiosity I managed, in the moment, to pass off as a rhetorical question. For our own reasons, that day, because of Roman, and also because so much of what she and I wanted to believe in had been uprooted, toppled like big trees in the storm, our levels of unhappiness had risen to the same level at the same time. When she slipped her hand in mine, it was as if we were momentarily powerful, contiguous. It was as if we were one great river, not separate bodies holding their own courses.

IRA SADOFF

The Tragic Stiletto of Trabzon

We were sipping grappa, watching *The Tragic Stiletto of Trab-zon* on an old Zenith TV in a suburban public square outside of Patras. Though it was dusk, and the images were murky, the film looked familiar, like a dim photo resolving in its pan. My wife and I were trying to read the lips of the dubbed and now dead third-rate British movie stars from the forties. An exotic theft held our interest—an amulet pared directly off the heroine's neck—while soldiers lined the rim of the square to defend the town against any drunk who might raise his fists in a distant recollection of Democratic Greece. It was 1972, a few years before I'd start my life over again, but I'm getting ahead of myself, because it was the words, not even the movie, *tragic stiletto,* that brought back a hazy memory, a critic over my shoulder, chastising me for something shamefully asinine I'd once said or done. I couldn't remember for sure who'd said it, and I'm not certain to this day whether I even wanted to remember or to forget.

My wife's handbag, including her passport and traveler's checks, was lifted off the back of her chair, that's how distracted we were while locals made faces at us behind our backs: our American dollars were desirable, whereas in the flesh we were banal and expendable, or, as I remembered reading in the paper a few days earlier about a couple in a rented Renault, explodable. We had reason to be distracted. Earlier, we'd missed the ferry to Brindisi. At least we thought we'd missed it. Some clerk told us the last boat had departed an hour before. "This time of year we're very busy," he said, meaning in the heat of August, "and we sell out tickets fast." So we bought our non-refundable tickets for the next morning, parked our car at the pier so we'd be first in line, and sat, until an hour later we saw another ferry leave the harbor. When I went back to shout at the swindler, he said, "Oh, I thought you meant our boat. The other has holes. Completely unsafe." After that, everything else had to be our fault: if there is a country of Omens and Signs, it has to be Greece.

In the movie an anonymous dark-skinned swine took a dagger out of some elaborate draping that served as his belt, and, after taking the amulet, stabbed our blond heroine three times, presumably to further the plot so her lover could scour the city and avenge her loss. My wife, I was reasonably certain, had recently slept with someone else, and I kept the hurt close to me, like a cold medallion on my chest, all through Europe. So we sat silently before the screen, until eventually she decided it was stupid to sit in the open air listening to dialogue that sounded like ugly murmurs (that's what she thought of Greek) while the smutty traffic drove back and forth through town: that is, dark-haired young men looking to lure pretty women in what they saw as their luxurious rusted-out '57 Fords.

I saw the movie twice. Once as a boy and once as a man. Once while my mother peeled carrots into a pot, cursing at the screen and crying, and once with my wife at my side shaking her head and rolling her eyes. "Did he say Boris or boring?"

"What else would you like to do?" I asked.

"Go to bed," she said, "so we can get an early start for Brindisi. I can't wait to get out of this fucking country."

It was still hot, probably still over ninety degrees after six. I was wearing a white oxford shirt and khaki shorts, and they were both saturated with sweat. We had spent the morning on the beach, so our thighs and our shoulders in particular were almost crimson. My wife wore a brown sundress that seemed to have faded after a week in Greece, and you could see the pale edges of her unexposed skin; her long brown hair, parted in the middle, was stringy wet. Being in the square, with its cloudy scent of smoked meat wafting out of every window, intensified the feeling of being skewered. My wife's handbag had been one of those colorful hemp-knit shoulder purses they used to call Greek bags. But now this whole scene is growing too literal, reduced to discussion, so the light around it grows dim. The point is, I tore into her for what she wore around *her* neck. It looked like a birthmark, but the purple perforated oval had been made by lips and teeth, someone else's, so I couldn't bear to look at her. Besides, everyone else was looking. I was therefore extraneous.

My mother came from Russia, was stern in spite of herself (and hardest on herself), and never lost the *k-k-k* sound to her consonants, and never lost the sea tide lilt to her sentences, so every family in our suburban block was slightly frightened of her, and during the height of the Cold War, I'd heard rumors that she was supposed to have been a spy. A spy who had difficulty getting out of her nightgown until late afternoon. Which must be why the Ruskies lost the Cold War and now run around with cheap imitations of Levi's, while they mope, jobless, on their street corners. At least that's what we saw when we went to visit my mother's homeland without her the week before we took the plane to Greece. "Take pictures of my old house," she'd said. Her old house, which was now in another country. Or had been taken down from there so all that remained were tire tracks from a Russian tank.

Every Zimmer and Motel we went to refused us a bed for the night, including a place called Zorba's, which had been recommended in our guidebook as particularly friendly to Americans. So what did we do? After we left the movie, we walked to the closest "department store" we could find, paid too much for a double sleeping bag, a small pup tent (my wife thought it practical since in Italy we could camp along the coast), along with pots and pans and utensils. I even bought a Swiss Army knife, the knife all my friends had owned when I was a boy but my mother had prohibited because she thought it too dangerous. It had a scissors and a corkscrew and a fingernail clipper and a screwdriver. Even at twenty-eight, I thought it astonishing. We walked around for a while with the tent on my backpack, until we found a restaurant whose sign said "Kamping." Some of the locals were eating dinner there, and those who bothered to look up to sneer at us made us feel as if we had not been sufficiently humiliated at the movie. "Maybe we're too old for camping," she said.

"After what we just spent?" I shrugged. "Look, it's eight-thirty. You want to sleep in the car?"

"Forget it," she said.

The owner was jovial, he called us Mr. and Mrs. America, he still loved Americans, he knew the difference between a country and a government, and then he lowered his voice to say again, *"I* know the difference between a government and a country, even if I can't say so in a normal human voice. So you come here," he said, and took us to a square gravel of field about fifty yards behind the restaurant. "It's off-season," he said, "so you might have the place to yourself. If you need to use the bathroom, it's right behind my place." He pointed to what looked like a large outhouse behind the restaurant. "Cold showers, too."

"Off-season, my ass," my wife said as he left, and I'm sure he heard us. "Camping in a fucking parking lot."

As we set up the tent in the dark, the foggy images of the piers of Trabzon came back to me, because the hero of the film, for most of it, couldn't see three feet in front of his face. And neither could I. I couldn't see the other end of the tent in the dark, so I didn't even know if the poles were straight or if my wife was standing by me.

You see, earlier in the evening I'd refused her offering. Just before we sat down to dinner, she'd taken out of her handbag—so I know she had it then—a small box wrapped in elaborate paper laced with gold thread. "Not now," I said. I didn't know what it was. "Please," I said, waving my hands in front of my face. "Not now. I just feel too raw."

I'd been cruel in the only way I'd known how, by being distant and indifferent during our whole vacation. We'd saved up for the past five years to travel, and now I wanted to be sure I made her suffer for hurting me. So you don't get to really know her, you don't get to see her close-up, which is not to say she ever admitted she'd made a mistake, that she had any regrets, that she even knew what she was doing, though I forgot to say she was French, the brightest person in her graduating class at the Sorbonne, she spoke without a trace of an accent, and consequently got taken for an American. I don't want to tell you how once she loved me deeply, she couldn't be happy unless she called me at work once a day, she made me presents out of construction paper and made collages of my favorite movie scenes on video. I held her through nightmares, one of us worked while the other went to school, we wept together when it was impossible to bear a child. You know why I won't let you? Because this isn't a story about love lost. And I refuse to give you metaphors about what it felt like to be so alone in a foreign country among enemies who should be friends. Don't even make me think of what it felt like to slice my finger to the bone with a bread knife the next morning: the shock of it— how long did it last?—was like an out-of-body experience. And you don't get to meet any of the people who were nice to us in Greece either.

During the movie, I remember now, my mother had cursed the Turks because her own father died in 1916 at their hands in the Dardanelles, but during commercials, my mother offered a long, familiar riff on my father, which she issued with bitterness and rage, though in a soft voice, and with parenthetical apologies, saying she knew that my relationship with him differed from hers, but it was stupid for me to defend him, that I couldn't possibly know how he treated her once the bedroom doors were closed, and then she opened her nightgown, exposing one of her breasts, and showed me a thin pink seam on the breastplate. Whether it was a burn or a slash, I didn't know, and at eleven, I didn't want to ask. "But your father is kind to you," she said. And when he came home from work, she always wrapped her arms around him tightly, as if she had amnesia, as if she knew, being a mother of the fifties, that she'd be on the street if she left. "He's proud of you, as he should be. For that I give him credit. I don't want to be unfair." The Russian way she said credit, with the *c* sound about to deliver phlegm from her throat, I won't forget it. So when I think of my mother, I think of spit.

The hero—his name, I think, was Frank (the names were as straightforward as the movies and the age)—was lost without his love. When he saw couples kissing on the waterfront, he covered his eyes with his hands. There were gypsy-looking women—I know it was Turkey, but in those days, every foreign country looked alike—who seemingly wanted to seduce him. There was no one left to trust. And when he saw someone from behind who looked like the thief of Trabzon, his face welled up with that manufactured rage you only find in old third-rate movies, as if the medium had not yet made the successful adjustment from theater, where feelings had to be so visible you could not mistake them: that's actually what I wanted, as I revisit my mother peeling those carrots (saying something innocently ugly to me, cursing at the hero)—why do I feel numb every time her name is mentioned?—and thinking then about how I'd let my wife die from me, and how now I had to lie beside her in a tent in a foreign country where we were both, rightly—since we'd given their dictators guns and dollars to prop them up—despised.

Just before I thought of the words *The Tragic Stiletto* (earlier and later I mistakenly called it *The Magic Stiletto*), about three quarters of the way through the film, after it was completely dark, three junta soldiers armed with American AK-47's picked up a young man around nineteen or twenty by the shoulders and took him away. It was all done silently, with dignity, and everyone who wasn't sitting at that particular table, meaning his mother and girlfriend, acted completely absorbed by the melodrama on the television screen. The young woman tried to follow them, but her way was blocked by another soldier, while the older woman sat at the table holding her head in her hands. My wife—I'll tell you her name, Justine—actually said, "Should we contact our embassy?"

I looked at her and shook my head. "They're probably behind it." So you see what dialogue does, how it takes away more than it supplies, because you can't know what it felt like for her to hear that from me, whether she felt stung or relieved or saddened by my cynicism, or whether she was even listening. And I certainly can't remember the inflection in my voice.

It took us at least an hour to set up the tent. Justine focused the flashlight on the instructions, and I spread the materials out. The instructions were in French, probably written by Bulgarians. We were missing a pole. I found a stick in the olive orchard that tore a hole in the canvas material. We sighed and cursed. Even with our clothes on the ground as a buffer, the sleeping bags could not soften the hard and bumpy gravel, and I couldn't help but think of Hindus sleeping on beds of nails, thinking they were welcome to them. I wished they were Greek.

We had some grappa we'd bought at the department store, and once the tent was up, we sat briefly inside it (it was too small to stand in), cross-legged, and passed the bottle as if it were a peace pipe. "So this is our vacation," I said, looking around the tent.

"No, this is our life," Justine said. "It's just a mirror image."

"What can we do about it?" She didn't say, so I continued talking. "You know, I've been thinking about that guy."

"At the movie?"

I nodded, though I wasn't sure she could see my face. "But not him, really. The woman at the table with him, how she wanted to get up to help him, but couldn't."

"They just would have thrown her in jail."

"Yeah. But he probably thinks she doesn't give a damn. For all he knows, he's going to rot in jail till the firing squad shoots him."

"That's melodramatic. Now you're just projecting."

"Please, Justine, I hate that kind of talk. I'm just telling you how I felt."

"No you're not, you're guessing at what *he* felt."

"Right." I felt the sting of her judgment simultaneously with the rightness of it. "I'm sorry I jumped on you." Then we were silent for a very long time before I said, "I want to forgive you, but I can't."

"Because I'm unforgivable?"

"Of course not. No one's unforgivable."

"The junta's unforgivable."

"Yeah," I said laughing, "but you're not the junta."

"Yeah, but that's what it feels like?" I nodded. "I'm sorry," she said. "I wish I could say it won't happen again."

I wish I could say I asked her why. I wish I could have told her I felt ripped open, not about her sleeping with someone but about everything, not just what was happening to us. But it wasn't talk we needed. So I closed my eyes and reached over to feel her hand, which was still burning feverishly from the hot afternoon sun. And then I heard vaguely in the background as I drifted off some accordion music and the clapping of hands, but I was too tired to try to figure out if it came from a dream or not.

You can probably guess what I dreamed of. In the movies I might have gotten a telegram that my mother had died, but in fact I was just hovering over her while she cried, asking her again and again, "What's wrong, why don't you do something?" The dream had actually occurred several times in what we call real life, and I'd often leave our house thinking, *She doesn't have to be alone if she doesn't want to. She's torturing me.* But in the dream, I'm like an angel, the angel I want to be, as well as the boy sitting beside her watching the movie, telling her I understand, I want to make her feel better, what can I do? She doesn't have to do anything, just let me help. And when she reaches for my hand, she has a ring, or a coin, for me.

When I woke up, when I was awakened, it was by a man's voice murmuring in Greek to a woman, and she was saying something like *No, no,* but in a tender voice, and it was clear after a while that he was trying to cajole her it was all right, nobody would know, it would feel good, whatever Greek man say in seducing a Greek woman, and behind them I heard loud music coming from the restaurant, but I knew I wasn't dreaming. Justine elbowed me and whispered, "How could you sleep through this?" Then she asked if I'd get out of the tent and ask them to go away.

"What, in Greek? At least you speak good French. They'll go away." And they did, after he apparently pushed her to the ground and gave it to her hard, and after she stopped protesting and later called his name passionately, Yannis. Justine and I were so ashamed. But as we lay down in our sleeping bags, the rocks pressing against our spines, I'm thinking I can't wait till morning; but then I hear a number of voices, I don't know how many, and then I hear one of them laughing and unzipping his pants. I know it's his pants because a moment later he's saying, *Amerikani,* and he's pissing on the tent, so I have to get up, I have to unzip the tent and stand before them in my underwear, but before I do, I slip into my jeans and feel my Swiss Army knife in my pocket, and I'm suddenly furious, at Justine and the Greeks and the stupid movie and anybody who's in my way. *Amerikani,* I hear, they're calling to us, laughing, they're calling me out, and I unzip the tent with my knife flashing, saying, "Bastards, you bastards. Rapists, murderers, thieves."

They back away, but their fists are up, so I move toward them, stabbing the air, I move them toward the restaurant, knowing full well Justine has no passport as I walk away from her, and I lead them toward the bar, which is raucous and crowded, which smells of the tarry scent of Greek liquor and lamb and cigarettes—it all unfolds unbearably slowly like the movie—and I'm scanning the room to see who it is—what—I have to *kill,* before I see the owner holding up a shot glass, and spying me doubling over in laughter, wrapping his arms around himself, and then he's shouting in English, "My hero, my hero," so there's nothing else I can do but put the blade between my teeth and act like a pirate or an ape, swinging my arms loosely back and forth, jumping on a table and gesturing wildly until we're all laughing, until I sit and drink with them and their girlfriends, each of us happily babbling in our foreign tongues.

At the Edge of the New World

How do you begin to judge your father? The Coast Guard and the insurance company investigators would list my father as blameless in the boating death of Lamar Locklear, our next-door neighbor and my father's business partner. The boat—a sportsfisher—was christened the *Nell,* a name my divorced parents had chosen for me had I been born a girl. My father and Lamar considered the *Nell* firm evidence that, when I finished college and married Lamar's daughter, Holly, and joined their electrical wiring company, we would all be well underway towards something better than our backlashed lives along the Haw River in North Carolina. We couldn't afford to berth the sportsfisher, so the *Nell* rode out snowstorms and summer cloudbursts on a trailer which straddled a drainage ditch dug as a property line. Then, when hurricane season lowered the coastal rental rates, we hauled the sportsfisher to Hatteras Island, where each year we vacationed at a sound-side cottage, complete with a widow's walk my mother had waved from in happier times, before my parents' divorce. A breezeway which reeked of creosote connected our cottage to an identical one that our fathers rented for prospective clients.

My father and Lamar were happiest these two weeks of each year, especially at dusk, when the cottage smelled of bacon-wrapped mackerel steaks and Old Bay–seasoned water set to boil, clattering with crabs from our trap. Each evening, when the lighted mainland across Roanoke Sound seemed a piece of the night and stars poured down, my father and Lamar made a ceremony of lighting their boat.

"No more arguments or complaints," my father always said. "The Italian has passed over." It was one of his favorite expressions—the code words to the Allies that the A-bomb had exploded. Lamar then plugged in a drop cord strung from the cottage to the rickety dock where the *Nell* was moored, illuminating its outline with Christmas lights. My father and Lamar each threw an arm around the other's shoulders and hefted their Seven and Sevens: they had escorted us across the sound to a land of latticed cottages built on stilts, to a world where executives and senators summered and where the first English attempt to found a colony in the New World had failed. My father and Lamar were determined their beachhead would not give or falter.

The night the Lucases were due to arrive, we gathered in the kitchen after the ceremonial lighting, and my father toasted, "Here's to the Lucas deal." Frank Lucas was a purchasing agent from Southern Bell. He and his wife had been invited to the island for a fishing trip, and they would be staying in the adjacent cottage. Lamar had bid on the wiring for a new Southern Bell plant which would house satellite construction. Up to that point, most of our company's jobs had involved houses or restaurants, and were very earthbound.

"Here's to the big executives," Lamar's wife, Wanda, said. "Ha." She sank into a wicker chair in her housecoat with her knees at angles against the armrests. "You call renting this cottage during hurricane season a damned vacation? Holly, you take note of this. Richard," she said to me, "you, too. I could have married anyone, but who did I pick?" Around the kitchen were cans Wanda had opened and left sitting. Wanda Locklear opened cans when she got drunk and angry.

"Our ship will come in," promised Lamar.

"It already has." Wanda pointed to the sportsfisher strung with lights like a celebration no one had bothered to attend. She was a nurse, an LPN, hooked on gin and codeine, who got cranky when we limited her supply. Holly helped her mother to the bedroom to ready themselves for the Lucases. I slipped in after them while Holly combed her mother's hair. After Wanda promised not to manufacture a disturbance that night, Holly fed her a pill from the supply she governed.

On the mainland, once or twice each year, Wanda wouldn't come home from work, turning up usually at an interstate motel or, once, drunk and naked in the back of her sedan at an all-night carp fishing pond. When the police brought Wanda home on these occasions, Lamar would meet the squad car at the edge of our shared driveway, wearing Wanda's housecoat over his underwear and seeming much older than his forty-five years.

"You're a bastard," Wanda would scream at Lamar and the sleeping neighborhood. "I want everyone to know you've made me into what I am." Money would be passed so her name wouldn't appear in the newspaper. Soon she would sob she had done nothing wrong—she had just gone out for a little fun, and now everyone thought the worst of her. Once, after the police left, Lamar struck her so hard she lost an incisor. Wife beating and noisy front-yard battles were part of our world. Lamar took Wanda inside and put her to sleep. Then he ambled back outside and unchained his German shepherd, Lucky, who slept beneath the raised bow of the *Nell*. As he dragged the dog to a drum filled with used motor oil, its splayed paws cut sharp lines in the dirt. The dog had a perpetual spot of mange on its flanks, and old motor oil was thought to be a home remedy for the disease. Lamar always lifted the mutt by grabbing handfuls of flesh along the withers and rump, so that its muzzle was stretched into a grin. Again and again he dunked the German shepherd as it howled. Upon release, the dog shook and rolled in the drainage ditch. As if in need of regaining its master's good graces, Lucky brought a stick to Lamar, and they played fetch at first light, while down by the Haw River you could hear the mill generator's high-pitched whine as it struggled to convert water into a substance as ethereal as electricity. I watched them from my bedroom window, convinced that their sorrow would never be my own. I was twenty, and I actually believed I could escape where I came from.

The Lucases were a mismatched couple who warred openly. They brought their clothes to the cottage in steamer trunks like refugees. Frank Lucas kept asking why we hadn't invited a swatch of local residents and a senator or two to celebrate his arrival. My father, embarrassed that as renters we knew no one here, blamed the lack of revelers on the stormy Coast Guard forecast. During cocktails, Frank Lucas launched into his life story. Two tall drinks later, his North Carolina rags-to-riches account had exhausted itself. On the third drink, he wanted to arm-wrestle "Mister College." He beat me twice, though I tried until my molars ached to slam his arm to the table.

"You've been pushing too many pencils and not enough iron," he said. He was very proud he had risen to purchasing agent without a college education. "Look at what all I got." He flexed his bicep and pointed to the balcony, where the woman he alternately called "Cheri" and "wife number two" shook her hair back and laughed at something Wanda or Holly had said. Cheri was closer to Holly's age than her husband's, and a foot taller, and she wore her boredom as beautifully as any negligee. She and Wanda had struck up the quick, intense, suspicious type of friendship of people who have excesses in common. They discussed which pills to mix with others, and exact proportions. As the women wandered onto the patio, Frank Lucas claimed he golfed weekly with the governor—a man he knew dirt on.

"Now *that's* power," he said.

"You're doing fine," my father said. "You're living the sweet life."

"Damned right." Frank Lucas thumbed his barrel chest and crunched on a pretzel as he splashed out the last of the drink he was waving. "I can make you or break you."

"You up for king mackerel fishing tomorrow?" Any hint of a business deal collapsing made my father skittish. "I bet you've caught trophy kingfish before."

"I've hauled in tarpon and marlin." Frank Lucas imitated a man setting a hook. "Now *there's* two game fish for you."

"You'll like king mackerel," my father assured him. "They fight like hell."

"*I* fight like hell." Then Frank Lucas went to the bathroom.

"This guy's a jerk," said Lamar. "What does he mean, make us or break us?"

"He's just an obnoxious drunk," said my father. "I bet he throws up all day tomorrow while we fish."

"Hey, bub, where's my drink?" Frank Lucas yelled from the bathroom.

"Take him a damned drink," my father said to me.

"Let him get it." I was not taking him a drink while he pissed.

"Let him stick it up his ass," whispered Lamar as the women meandered inside.

"I've got Frankie-boy his drink," said Cheri Lucas. "He likes to bellow a little and blow up after he's had whiskey." She winked at Wanda. "But he's really harmless." She smiled openly at Lamar. "You're part Indian, right?"

"One-quarter Lumbee," said Lamar. "Don't know how the other three quarters got here."

"That's priceless. I've heard Indians are big savages."

"I don't like what's going on here," said Frank Lucas, coming back into the room.

"You don't have to like it." Cheri let her eyes linger on Lamar where they wanted.

"Hey, bub. You flirting with my wife?" Frank Lucas got between Lamar and Cheri. "No one flirts with my wife unless I let them."

"No one is flirting with anyone," said my father. "Hey, we're all friends here. We're all having a few drinks and a nice time."

"That's right, Frank," Cheri said. "No one is flirting here because you don't want them to, and besides, we're all friends." Then she walked over and threw her arm around Wanda, who smiled at everyone from the safe place the pills had carried her. "We were talking origins, Frank. I was remarking about the Indian in Lamar."

"I'm part Lumbee," said Lamar again. "The Indians who took in the Lost Colonists." According to legend, the ill-fated first colonists had searched for gold and bickered instead of planting crops and securing their precarious position at Manteo. When winter arrived without Sir Walter Raleigh's supply ships, they were either killed in a surprise Indian attack or forced to wander inland and lose themselves amidst whatever grace a wilderness had to offer.

"I've got conquistador blood in me," Frank Lucas said. "I got a coat of arms to prove it."

Cheri Lucas rolled her eyes. "Frank sunk a reasonable fortune into a trace-your-family-tree deal. They give you lists of famous people—Louis IV, George Washington, you know. Frank chose Hernando Cortex."

"Cortés, damn it."

"Cortex, Cortés, whatever. Frank's choices were limited because he's a strict *Catholic*." She relished the word's hard *c*'s. "Catholics never divorce themselves from their past."

Frank Lucas gave her a look that warned this was not the time for this.

"You," she said to my father. "How did you get here?"

"By Buick LeSabre," he said.

"That's *rich*," Cheri said. My father rarely got a joke, so to hide this fact he laughed hardest. This moment of goodwill uncoiled when Cheri suggested they all get raving drunk and have a toga party aboard the *Nell*. Frank Lucas was quick to produce a camera after they had all changed into bedsheets and Wanda had remarked that a crazy moment like this needed saving. He adjusted the fancy Instamatic on a tripod and fine-tuned the lens and set the timer. Then he grouped us family-style in front of a wide net with cork buoys and dried starfish decorating a wall. As the bulb flashed, I remembered being a kid thumbing through our photo album thick with people left behind from all the new beginnings my parents had launched their hopes upon. Then the feeling passed, and I took my place with the others as we waited for the picture of our new lives to develop.

That night while everyone else toured the sound, Holly and I made love in our room, which adjoined the widow's walk. Discarded furniture salvaged from a yard sale or the attic of the owner's inland home gave the room the temporary feel of a place you visit but never fully inhabit. A salty breeze curved the curtain of the storm door. I stripped and lay naked and proud on top of the covers, smoking a joint to the distant collapse of waves as Holly drew her bath water. While the tub filled, she smoked a little with me and giggled when she coughed. Standing up, she stretched and slowly undressed, allowing me to explore the parts of herself untouched by the sun. Next she sat before the mirror, combing and twisting her hair into a bun. She clenched the hairpins with her mouth and set into place the coil I would pull down. Finished, she appraised herself in the mirror and checked her teeth. *There will be no hurrying this,* I thought as she touched up the nail polish on her toes and swung around and blew them dry at me. Holly was most beautiful, women are most beautiful, when caught in the purposeful act of readying the gift of themselves for you. They sense in their preparations the enormousness of simple things—the hair held with the exact number of pins needed to fall when pulled free, or the nails painted bordello-red because she appreciates the fact that you like them that way. As she bathed I thought of her before the mirror, and we seemed in no way connected to our parents out squabbling over spilled drinks and lewd passes and which star to mark a course by. First love is that much of a happy conspiracy.

"Don't smoke so much of that stuff that you go sullen on me." Holly toweled herself in the doorway. Too much pot carried me to a place from which only sufficient sleep could retrieve me. Holly led me onto the widow's walk. She kneaded my shoulders and soothed me with easy questions: Were summer school classes hard? (Yes, I answered, but I had passed them.) Did I think the Lucases were a sad couple? (No sadder than our parents.) How soon after graduation would we marry? (We would decide that my senior year.) Did I feel our engagement was constraining us?

"What do you mean?" I asked.

"Do you miss seeing other women?"

"No," I lied. Certain weekends when Holly didn't drive up to Chapel Hill, I slept with a sorority girl named Lisa McQueen, whom everyone called Queenie.

"I wouldn't like to share you with anyone," Holly said.

"Do *you* feel constrained? Is Ron Ramsey still lit up with love for you?" Ron Ramsey was an apprentice electrician with a stutter and a crush on Holly. She worked as a receptionist-secretary for our fathers' business, and once, to demonstrate his love for her, he had unscrewed a sixty-watt bulb, stuck his finger in the socket, and smiled at the bulb's flickering while his body conducted the current.

"He's nothing for you to worry about." When she turned me around, we helped ourselves to each other. A previous vacationer had abandoned a lawn chair, and we tested all the positions its unfolding would allow. The weavings made adhesive noises as we shifted love's positions. By the time we had both finished, we had moved back inside to watch our joining in front of the mirror. We stood like that until we re-inhabited ourselves and became embarrassed. Then we stretched on the bed to spoon.

"You *do* understand we don't have to know everything about

each other, don't you?" Holly had pushed my head into the secure place between her breasts, and instantly I feared she suspected my whole affair with Lisa McQueen. Then I remembered that, before smoking pot, I had told her the story of a college pal and his girl-friend. My pal's girlfriend had walked into his dorm room one morning with a travel bag full of dresses. She asked him which one he liked. After the shade went down, she tried them all on for him. She danced around in a front-buttoning dress like country girls wear, a miniskirt which barely hid the sweet cleft of her but-tocks, an evening gown with slits up the sides, and a shift so loose he crawled under it like a kid. Between each modeling, they made a regular feast of their love. She had even brought over the ingre-dients for mimosas. "I want to dress for *you* today," this woman had said. "Choose." My friend told her the miniskirt made him want to bay like a dog. He even howled a few times—hell, he had been drinking champagne and making morning love. Spring break was the next day, and they were traveling to different places, so they stocked up on the way that skirt made them feel. When school resumed, she confessed she had worn his choice to the abortion clinic. Though my friend didn't want the baby—he was pre-med and his life was on a certain schedule—he broke up with the girl. When he got drunk, he'd repeat the anecdote, as if it meant something whose message he had yet to divine. This was the story I had told Holly earlier. Now, I pulled my head from her breasts and aligned my eyes with hers.

"Are you pregnant?" I asked. "Did you stop taking the pill?"

"Nope." She thumped my head. "I was thinking about how that girl should never have told him about the abortion. It was some-thing he didn't need to know."

"They should have discussed it together," I said. "They should have talked things out."

Holly started laughing.

"What's so funny?"

"When she came over with those dresses, she had already decided to go through with the abortion."

"But wasn't she dishonest?"

"Oh, Richard. That woman *wanted* him to leave her. By telling him what she had done, she was showing him the way out. Come here," and Holly smiled as she guided my dick back inside her. Downstairs the revelers had returned; ice was cracked for drinks, and glasses were filled, but we didn't stop, even when I heard someone climb the steps. I could feel them out in the hall, watching. Then whoever it was seemed to understand what was going on in the room, and they shut the door gently, as if we were feverish but sleeping children whose dreams they were hesitant to disturb.

The next morning, when the sun shaped the offshore clouds into brooding continents, I readied the *Nell* while Holly rowed Wanda and Cheri a few hundred yards into the sound and anchored our old skiff for flounder. I oiled the big Penn reels and changed steel leaders on the Russel lures. Anything that might heave or toss got battened down. I packed the long coolers with block ice my father had bought before rousting me. Then I chipped two blocks for mixed drinks and iced down the beer. We had gathered two bushel baskets of out-of-season oysters the day before, and I shucked them after enjoying the first few's salty freshness. In the distance a workman hammered at the first of several weekend attempts to winterize his cottage, while out in the sound the women laughed about something.

Much of my adolescence was spent rebuilding that skiff or larger boats, for when anything went wrong in our lives, my father bought and renovated a boat. We replaced keels, fiberglassed hulls, covered seats with Naugahyde, and stitched canvas covers to shield us from the elements. Watching Holly and Wanda and Cheri fish, I was reminded of earlier vacations with the Locklears in rented cinder-block bungalows we could barely afford. Somehow, we seemed happy with the cold tile floors and two-burner gas stoves. These places smelled of homemade oil-and-vinegar suntan lotion and leaking air conditioners and the peculiar odor of previous tenants' lives. A tube of discarded lipstick rounded by some woman's lips and hidden in the back of the medicine cabinet confirmed my simple-minded suspicions that others had passed through these rooms, too. Nights, Holly and I peeked from the room with bunk beds we shared. Like cousins, we were pajama-ed and giggling. Our parents danced slowly in the kitchen. Their inland, quarreling existences had been left behind. We slept to their laughter as they played rook or poker or some all-night board game of chance.

Some people reel backwards through time when they smell woodsmoke while children build snowmen, others go giddy over a field of summer fireflies, but I am reduced to a blob of sentiment by *Paralichthys dentatus*—the common summer flounder. They still seem strange, flat fish left over from fossilized times. We hooked them at the edge of sandbars with a piece of the first-caught flounder's belly cut into finger-sized strips to imitate a minnow.

When my parents were still married, my mother fished alongside Holly and Wanda. I was nine or ten the first time I saw her fish. Kerchiefed, she sat like a man with her feet apart on the gunnel. How had she learned to unhook a flounder so quickly or so easily? Because of her nervous lapses into hospitals and other men's many-bedroomed houses, she had always seemed the ghost of my childhood—moody, seasonal, a creature of shut doors and unexplained absences—but when she fished for flounder, I understood my father's love for her. Each time she hooked one, the rod curved into a smile and the line sang. She cursed if the fish bit the leader, then giggled with Wanda like schoolgirls at naughtiness. Wanda would be braiding Holly's hair, and my mother would mix gin-and-tonics while my father and Lamar yelled to row in, the carburetor was fixed and the *Nell* was seaworthy. *What do they see in that damned boat?* Wanda or my mother would remark. I would pull hard at the oars and practice my oarsmanship. On the way in, the talk would shift to how deliciously bohemian it was to play cards all night and dance at dawn and then drink tonics at nine in the morning.

"It's times like this that I wish your mother hadn't jumped ship on us," my father said, boarding the *Nell*. He handed me the shrimp he'd boiled in the cottage. I tossed them in the cardboard box as he poured on the seasonings. We would eat oysters and shrimp all the way to the fishing grounds. He looked at his watch—wishing we were offshore by now—then tuned the shortwave radio. A song on a distant channel mixed with the Coast Guard warnings of moderate to high seas. As my father listened, his face wore the same look as when he talked to my mother with the special telephone extension he had wired from his bedroom window to the fighting chair aboard the trailered *Nell*. She still owned a share of the business, and he consulted her like an oracle whose luck he felt compelled to court. He gave her counsel on her boyfriends and listened patiently to her confessions. The fact that he couldn't have her made her maddeningly desirable. Both my parents loved the Titanic quality of their love. My mother had called just before this vacation to say she was flying to England with some chiropractor. "Don't let your father screw up this business deal," she had said to me. "You don't know the trouble I went through to set this thing up."

My father pitched me a clean bandanna, which I tied on my head pirate-style as he had taught me. "Piece of advice, Richard," he said out of the blue. "Be careful what you wish for—it might come true." Absently, he picked through the shrimp and ate some small ones, shell and all. Out in the sound, Holly yelled and held up a doormat-sized flounder she had caught. My father laughed and bellowed to quit scaring the fish and get busy catching more. He watched them for a long time, then he turned to me. He had been trying to get his bandanna just right, but the little flap of triangle kept missing the knot. I fixed it for him. I could tell my fingers on the back of his head gave him barbershop memories of when my mother kept our hair cut. He had even bought her a barber's chair at an auction in a clumsy attempt to jump-start their marriage. His gift was exactly the wrong thing; even the garbage men refused to lug it away.

The predicted storm system stalled, and the wind lay. Aside from the bilge pump, the *Nell* performed like a shipwright's fantasy on a maiden voyage. The rough seas would not arrive until late that night, and the ocean was like a sheet of plastic connected to the sky by a seamless horizon. I mixed drinks for Frank Lucas and Lamar, and we ate with our hands from the pail of shucked oysters. When my father yelled from the bridge to send him up a few, I carried him a coffee cupful, along with a beer. We were men on water, passing around lemon wedges and Tabasco sauce as we estimated what luck the day would bring. As first mate, my job entailed keeping Frank Lucas liquored up and happy. I shoved the box of shrimp his way and told him to weigh in. There is a pecking order aboard boats, and he was *last*. When Frank Lucas sucked the heads, too, I almost began to like him. We ate until the last mile buoy, when my father gave the sportsfisher full throttle, and we made what felt like Godspeed with the old Chrysler engine humming on all eight cylinders. We planed at twenty, got a smooth bow spray going, and outdistanced our problems as we sped towards where you must reckon by charts and compasses. When I realized we had long since passed our usual fishing grounds, I gave my father a what's-up look. *Blue water,* he mouthed. *Gulf Stream.* We had never taken the *Nell* this far from shore.

Out where the land fell from sight, I got an inkling of why the old-timers called what they saw the New World. It had something to do with inland feelings and left-behind places. You can't look at a continent from that distance without imagining a life in its interior. Before, the closest I had come to understanding this were certain autumn afternoons, during high school, when Holly and I drove my motorcycle into the Haw River countryside. We sped by old clapboard, two-story houses set back handsomely from the road. The yards were big enough to be mowed by tractors, and entire families raked and burned leaves. Kids jumped over flames when their parents' backs were turned, and brothers dumped on bedsheets full of damp leaves, which sent up smoke signals before igniting. Fathers leaned on rakes and watched another end of summer burning. Holly ran her hand beneath my shirt and fingered my navel as she pressed her breasts into my back. On the straight stretches, the Harley topped eighty as we rocketed into the illusion of the road suddenly ending. I imagined I lived in one of those houses with Holly, that *I* had stopped raking to watch two lovers zoom by. Would I wave at how young I had once been? would I remark that their speed tempted Providence? would I wonder at how far inland I had wandered from such recklessness? That day aboard the *Nell*, I was a young man getting his first glimpse of an old feeling called the New World.

"This is the goddamned life," yelled my father. He motioned me up to the flying bridge. He claimed I should learn a thing or two about navigating; after all, the *Nell* would be mine and

Holly's whenever we wanted. I had driven countless times before, even weaving safely through the shoals of Cape Hatteras when he and Lamar were incapacitated. But my father made a production that day of handing over the wheel. He fetched two cold beers and called out headings as I marked the course. We took the *Nell* to blue Gulf Stream water, where big mackerel ran so deep we used downriggers. Whole acres of the ocean's surface boiled with menhaden, and I trolled through them to catch the kingfish feeding on the school's bottom. Whenever the *Nell* felt sluggish, my father snuck below to hand-pump the water the bilge would not siphon.

We filled the boat with big kingfish that Frank Lucas fought. Lamar and my father clubbed and gaffed them, and even when there were two fish on, Frank Lucas got angry if he were not allowed to fight both fish to the boat. We played the part of genial fishing guides, even taking pictures as he proudly displayed the largest. Frank Lucas couldn't get enough of catching mackerel, and a greedy part of himself wouldn't allow us to release any. This was before there were ceilings on the number of fish you could keep, and a part of myself was ashamed that we kept fish beyond what my father called "a gentleman's limit." Our haul was illegal by modern standards.

On the ride back from fishing, my father sipped whiskey beside me on the bridge and fiddled with the shortwave radio while I held the *Nell* on course. I hoped that he didn't see me at the helm as something other than it was. I expected and dreaded a father-son chat: When would I be ready to learn the subtleties of bidding? Would Holly and I buy a house near his? Would we give him one grandchild or seven? When this conversation never happened, I was relieved. *Don't go into business with your father,* my mother had warned. *Strike out on your own.* This was my last conversation with her, and she had promised to have a drink for us as she crossed the Atlantic. I had thought it a crude remark, but sitting there beside my father, I understood she meant it as a salute, as people at a wake toast a life that has passed. When I caught my father looking up at the sky and whistling, I remembered today was the day she was flying to England with her chiropractor.

"We'll make the dock right at nightfall," my father said. Behind us, Frank Lucas was tipsy and singing "What Do You Do with a Drunken Sailor." Lamar led him like a choir director. We habitually sang that when homeward bound, and my father and I joined in, too. Then Lamar remembered that on *real* fishing cruises, you strung up the fish like those little triangular flags at used car lots. By the time we reached the first mile buoy, the *Nell* was fringed with mackerel. Lamar even ran up a small one like a Jolly Roger on the outrigger. The Christmas lights got hooked to the generator, and a loose connection made them blink. Fisherman on other boats heading back to port pointed at us and waved the thumbs-up sign. A few displayed their meager catches. When another sportsfisher tried to run up a mackerel and it fell off, there seemed nothing funnier. The gossip on the radio informed us that the other boats had heeded the warnings and not risked blue water.

"Landlubbers." My father clapped me on the back. "Bunch of goddamned featherweights." Then he broke into all the channels and began broadcasting our adventure. The liquor had gotten to him, and he kept explaining that luck must be pushed and tested. My father believed that the day's catch was an omen that his own luck was not ruined.

When you push circumstances beyond normal limits, you risk discovering things you don't want to know. Back at the dock, we called the women down to applaud our catch. Mackerel five deep lined the pier like cord wood. Frank Lucas seemed disappointed when my father explained that no one mounted mackerel. We were shirtless and red from the sun and liquor, and we needed a shave and a bath, but we exuded a *good* sort of frontier feeling. The women sensed and admired this. Holly worked lotion into my shoulders and giggled when the imprint of a quick kiss to my neck disappeared.

"Let's have one hell of a party tonight, mates." Frank Lucas had begun calling us that offshore. "Sex and drugs and rock 'n' roll— isn't that how the song goes?" He called marijuana "hooter" and asked my father and Lamar if they partook.

"I'll try anything once," said my father.

"Righto, mate." Frank Lucas claimed he had pills, too—speed and Quaaludes. "I'm a walking goddamned pharmacy." When he produced a fifty and asked would I take care of the fish, my father said that wasn't necessary.

"Don't insult me," said Frank Lucas. "If I want to give him fifty, I will. Where I come from, it's customary to show your gratitude like this." I felt like a valet as I tucked the bill in my pocket. Frank Lucas strung his arms around my father and Lamar and said it was time to get down to some righteous partying and serious business. They walked up to the cottage with Cheri and Wanda following while the ice in their drinks jingled.

"Cheri's not a bad person, but she's not his wife," said Holly. She explained her mother and Cheri had been drinking all day and confessing. Frank Lucas couldn't get a divorce from his first wife because he and she were strict Catholics. When Holly asked if I could imagine what it must be like to know the person you loved would never marry you, I said I couldn't.

"Just put in an appearance, mix them some drinks, and come upstairs to me," Holly said. "I'll be naked."

I set about cleaning our slaughter. The dock had a fish cleaning station with a spigot and a humming streetlight high on a pole. I worked in the cone of light. The wind had increased, and the sound was whitecapping. The clouds hid the stars and moon and lidded in the darkness. There were so many fish that I scored them vertically and pushed out nuggets of mackerel tenderloin instead of steaking them. This was as wasteful as shooting buffalo for their tongues, but I didn't care. The best part—the cheek meat—I left on the fish. I slung the carcasses out into the dark sound for the crabs. By the time I finished, I had bagged and iced over a hundred pounds of mackerel nuggets.

When I walked into the cottage, I saw that Frank Lucas had made good on his promise. Wanda snored with an open mouth on the couch, while Cheri twirled like a dancer around the living room. She spun my way and kissed me wetly on the cheek. Then she started spinning again like an out-of-kilter gyroscope.

"Whoa, now," said my father. "Which way do these things go?" He held a joint in each hand and seemed genuinely confused. He saw me and announced that I was his son—as if that were an astounding and philosophical statement. "Here." He handed me a joint. "We've never done this together before." When I took a big lungful, its quality widened my eyes. This was Thai stick—good pot laced with opium. Lamar wobbled from the kitchen with a tray of drinks, looked at Wanda, and gave me hers. Three or four more tokes on the joint made me forget my promise to Holly. I reasoned the wait would make going to her more pleasurable.

"Frank," Cheri said. "You're a bastard, and I'm passing out." She lay down like a tired child on the hard floor and closed her eyes. Frank Lucas gave my father and Lamar a what-can-you-do-with-them look and launched into business. He stroked his chin whiskers and calculated. He seemed neither drunk nor high. How long had he waited for this first scent of the end of a deal? He assured us he had done his homework; without his contract, our company would go under.

"Point number one." He looked at my father. "Your ex-wife owns one quarter of the business. She handles her personal life so sloppily she *could* be persuaded to force you to buy her shares. You can't afford to." He looked at Lamar. "Point number two. My friends on your local police force tell me you've offered bribes on several occasions—not that they ever accepted them." Then he looked at me. "There are all types of fellowships available for an enterprising young man, especially if the governor made a few calls."

"You know dirt on him," I said brashly.

"You're such a bright boy." He looked at Cheri and seemed to falter. "She *is* beautiful, isn't she? It's a shame she's lying there like that. Is there a more comfortable place she could sleep it off? Could you help me carry her? All of you."

Wanda's bedroom was the closest. I followed with the high heels Cheri had kicked off. Without any ceremony, Frank Lucas stripped her. I was so high that it seemed like a dream.

"That's not even his wife," I said to my father and Lamar.

"Bingo, Mister College," said Frank Lucas. "What I need is a little help here. You see, after I'm dead, there's a good chance she'll claim common-law wife rights, and I don't want that. I want everything to go to my real wife and kids. If we could just get some pictures of a little *fake* love here, I'd be grateful. I'm talking snapshots of one of you penetrating her, or, say, in her mouth. Hell, she's so Quaaluded she'd never know the difference. I'd put the pictures in a safety deposit box and will my executor the key. No matter what claims Cheri made, the pictures would invalidate them. My lawyer suggested this." I felt a trickle of pity for his indiscreet scheme until I realized we were all desperate.

"What say, mates?" Frank Lucas produced a doubloon from his pocket, which he claimed his grandfather had given him for luck. He suggested a coin toss to pick the leading man. He left and came back with the Instamatic, and he promised he wouldn't get any face except Cheri's in the picture. I realized we were all shirt-less and half-naked as we fumbled with his proposition. Then I felt someone at the door. It was Wanda, stoned. She focused for a moment and comprehended. I understood she had been in rooms like this before—terra incognita—and that she didn't like them any more than we did.

"You all are no better than I am," said Wanda. Cheri moaned and moved in her sleep, and from where Wanda stood, it must have seemed the naked woman was a willing participant. "Oh, Lamar," she said. "What will we do now that I think the worst of you, too?" When she shut the door, I realized she had seen Holly and me the previous night, and I was ashamed at this room's dif-ference.

"She won't even remember this happened," promised Frank Lucas. I didn't know if he was talking about Wanda or Cheri. We stood there, three men fighting the invitation to violate her sleep-ing beauty. If I had been asked, I do not know if I would have participated in the coin toss. I only stayed long enough to know that Lamar would be in the pictures. He ungirded himself and set about the sordid business at hand. My father looked hard at me—as if about to apologize that our search for the good life had landed us here—and our eyes met for the first time as regretful men. Whole ages passed between us in that sad moment. Frank Lucas readied the Instamatic, and I remembered that, as a kid, I had believed the way the image developed before my eyes was sheer magic.

"Richard, get the hell out of here," my father said—the last command he gave me that I would ever follow—and as I shut the door, I knew that I would never picture any of us the same way again.

Up in our room, I confessed everything to Holly, except Lisa McQueen. I began with my nervousness concerning our proposed marriage and ended with our fathers below us sealing a deal. My heart wanted out of my chest, and I couldn't sit down, nor stop talking. I chain-smoked cigarettes by the widow's walk and said I would *not* join the business. Then I cried the tears of a person who wanted sympathy.

Holly allowed me to cry, then said, "Grow up."

"What do you mean?"

"Everything comes with a price. Do you think I *like* playing secretary to save expenses so you can go to college? Don't you think that *I* worry about our marriage? Whatever my father did, he did for all of us. You're so naïve it's almost endearing. You wouldn't..." But she stopped when my father and Lamar staggered outside and began yelling at each other. The widow's walk afforded a box view of their argument. Lamar wanted my father to ride with him to the first mile buoy to air their heads. My father explained the *Nell* was not seaworthy in such rough seas. He screamed, had Lamar drunk so much that he didn't understand the bilge pump was malfunctioning?

"All I'm asking for, mate, is a little pretend love," said Lamar. They laughed as if it were the best joke they had ever heard and clapped each other on the back. Lamar claimed they would take a little spin like old times, when they were teenagers who had dropped off their dates and spent whole nights debating love's mysteries. My father unmoored the *Nell,* but before he could hop aboard, Lamar gunned the sportsfisher from the dock. My father jumped up and down and shouted curses, but Lamar kept going. *I am washing my hands of this foolishness,* he yelled. He motioned the-hell-with-you with both palms and zigzagged back to the cottage.

"He'll just putter around the sound and probably anchor off a sandbar and drink until he feels better," I told Holly. "It's like when he dunks Lucky."

"I hope so," she said. Holly and I watched Lamar ease around the buoy which marked the channel to Cape Hatteras. The Christmas lights made the *Nell* resemble an all-night party cruiser out for an aimless celebration. He sang a drunken sailor's ditty whose words were lost over the grumbling of the engine. Was he simply drunk, or was he running from the part of himself he and my father had traded to close a deal? My father would have no stomach for electrical wiring after that night. He would sell the company at a profit, thanks to the bid Frank Lucas would award. What no one had counted on were the four sizable life insurance policies Lamar had taken out on himself. Each different policy listed one of us as sole beneficiary. The *Nell* would flounder so close to the shore off Hatteras that the lights of senators' cottages must have winked at Lamar as he drowned.

But I didn't know any of this that night I stood with Holly on the widow's walk. We simply watched him leave, and I found myself wondering what got rabble like us to this place billed as an earthly paradise. A people like mine were not pleasure-fearing Pilgrims, nor the landed aristocracy of the Virginians who would write the Constitution. We would have never crossed the ocean in an organized migration. What got *my* ancestors here was any situation in which you decided a change in geography might cure your luck. As the anchor dropped, all we would own was queasy stomachs. Once inland, we became whatever the new landscape required: reluctant but rum-fortified revolutionary soldiers; willing purveyors of smallpox-infested blankets; traders of horses and human flesh; sharecroppers and tent revivalists and, later, owners of used cars and second mortgages and damaged dreams. I *do* know that whatever feeling Lamar was full of as he drove off—drunkenness or loathing or devil-may-care—fueled the journey from the old world to the new one where Holly and I were standing.

"We will not be like that," she said, and I understood we already were. She looked hard at me, the way a woman does when she is deciding something important. I'm not sure what words could have saved us then. I remembered my father's advice—*Be careful what you wish for*—but it seemed an old man's useless warning.

"Ron Ramsey and I are more than just friends." She let this information sink in. She was giving me a way out. I started to give her tit for tat, but she put her hand over my mouth, as if she had guessed about my dealings with girls like Lisa McQueen and had already forgiven me. We stood like that until she decided whatever it was she was thinking and it felt safe to take her hand away.

Is that what happens when two people find themselves marooned at a new place in each other, wrestling not with angels nor each other but with the sadness of passages? Once the insurance money came through, we would all move to different neighborhoods and separate lives. I marveled at the newly discovered place in myself which could make love on a widow's walk to someone I loved but would leave because a greedy part of myself wanted more. I was still young enough to risk my future without her, but old enough to know that the youngness didn't matter. Suddenly, I was as ashamed of myself as I have ever been, yet oddly, I was elated.

For the first time in my life, I made love as an adult, without innocent explorations and with a desperate, hungry roughness. We cursed and clawed and bit. The knowledge that Holly would allow me to be the one to leave made me want to plunder something as mysteriously familiar as her body. I felt full of something I can only describe as the sorrow of conquest—a feeling my ancestors must have dismissed as second thoughts when the sight of the New World took their breaths, while at their backs tugged home and those parts of themselves travelers must leave behind. There would be no end to the new beginnings this fresh-found part of myself would exact. Now, I ask you, what can you do but hope—like your forefathers—that a course can be charted for a lifetime of moments like that?

Two Altercations

The calm, early-summer afternoon that "in the flash of a moment would be shattered by gunfire"—the newspaper writer expressed it this way—had been unremarkable for the Blakelys: like the other "returning commuters" (the newspaper writer again), they were sitting in traffic, in the heat, with jazz playing on the radio, saying little to each other, staring out. Exactly as it usually was on the ride home from work. Neither of them felt any particular pressure to speak. The music played, and they did not quite hear it. Both were tired, both had been through an arduous day's work—Michael was an office clerk in the university's admissions office, and Ivy was a receptionist in the office of the Dean of Arts and Sciences.

"Is this all right?" she said to him, meaning what was on the radio.

"Excuse me?" he said.

"This music. I could look for something else."

"Oh," he said. "I don't mind it."

She sat back and gazed out her window at a car full of young children. All of them seemed to be singing, but she couldn't hear their voices. The car in which they were riding moved on ahead a few lengths, and was replaced by the tall side of a truck. *Jake Plumbly & Son, Contractors.*

"I guess I'm in the wrong lane again," he said.

"No. They're stopped, too, now."

He sighed.

"Everybody's stopped again," she said.

They sat there.

She brought a magazine out of her purse and paged through it, then set it down on her lap. She looked at her husband, then out at the road. Michael sat with his head back on the seat top, his hands on the bottom curve of the wheel. The music changed—some piano piece which seemed tuneless, for all the notes running up and down the scale, and the whisper of a drum and brushes.

She looked at the magazine. Staring at a bright picture of little girls in a grass field, she remembered something unpleasant, and turned the page with an impatient suddenness that made him look over at her.

"What?" he said.

She said, "Hmm?"

He shrugged, and stared ahead.

No ongoing conflict or source of unrest existed between them.

But something was troubling her. It had happened that on a recent occasion a new acquaintance had expressed surprise upon finding out that they had been married only seven months. This person's embarrassed reaction to the discovery had made Ivy feel weirdly susceptible. She had lain awake that night, hearing her new husband's helpless snoring, and wondering about things which it was not normally in her temperament to consider. In that unpleasant zone of disturbed silence, she couldn't get rid of the sense that her life had been decided for her in some quarter far away from her own small clutch of desires and wishes—this little shaking self which lay here in the dark, thinking—though she had done no more and no less than exactly what she wanted to do for many years now. She was thirty-three. She had lived apart from her family for a dozen years, and if Michael were a mistake, she was the responsible party: she had decided everything.

Through the long hours of that night, she arrived at this fact over and over, like a kind of resolution, only to have it dissolve into forms of unease that kept her from drifting off to sleep. It seemed to her that he had been less interested in her of late, or could she have imagined this? It was true enough that she sometimes caught herself wondering if he were not already taking her for granted, or if there were someone else he might be interested in. There was an element of his personality that remained somehow distant, that he actively kept away from her, and from everyone, it seemed. At times, in fact, he was almost detached. She was not, on the whole, unhappy. They got along fine as a couple. Yet on occasion, she had to admit, she caught herself wondering if she made any impression at all on him. When she looked over at him in the insular stillness of his sleep, the thought blew through her that anything might happen. What if he were to leave her? This made her heart race, and she turned in the bed, trying to put her mind to other things.

How utterly strange, to have been thinking about him in that daydreaming way, going over the processes by which she had decided upon him as though this were what she must remember in order to believe the marriage safe, only to discover the fear—it actually went through her like fear—that he might decide to leave her, that she would lose him, that perhaps something in her own behavior would drive him away.

In the light of the morning, with the demands of getting herself ready for work, the disturbances of her sleepless hours receded quickly enough into the background. Or so she wished to believe. She had been raised to be active, and not to waste time indulging in unhealthy thoughts, and she was not the sort of person whose basic confidence could be undermined by a single bad night, bad as that night was.

She had told herself this, and she had gone on with things, and yet the memory of it kept coming to her in surprising ways, like a recurring ache.

She had not wanted to think of it here, in the stopped car, with Michael looking stricken, his head lying back, showing the little white place on his neck where a dog had bitten him when he was nine years old. Just now, she needed him to be wrapped in his dignity, posed at an angle that was pleasing to her.

She reached over and touched his arm.

"What?"

"Nothing. Just patting you."

He lay his head back again. In the next moment she might tell him to sit up straight, button the collar of his shirt (it would cover the little scar). She could feel the impulse traveling along her nerves.

She looked out the window and reflected that something had tipped over inside her, and she felt almost dizzy. She closed her eyes and opened them again. Abruptly, her mind presented her with an image of herself many years older, the kind of wife who was always hectoring her husband about his clothes, his posture, his speech, his habits, his faltering, real and imagined, always identifying deficiencies. It seemed to her now that wives like that were only trying to draw their husbands out of a reserve that had left them, the wives, marooned.

"What're you thinking?" she said.

He said, "I'm not thinking."

She sought for something funny or light-hearted to say, but nothing suggested itself. She opened the magazine again. Here were people bathing in a blue pool, under a blue sky.

"Wish we were there," she said, holding it open for him to see.

He glanced over at the picture, then fixed his attention on the road ahead. He was far away, she knew.

"Is something wrong?" she said.

"Not a thing," he told her.

Perhaps he was interested in someone else. She rejected the thought as hysterical, and paged through the magazine—all those pictures of handsome, happy, complacently self-secure people.

Someone nearby honked his horn. Someone else followed suit; then there were several. This tumult went on for a few seconds, then subsided. The cars in front inched ahead, and Michael eased up on the brake to let the car idle an increment forward, closing the distance almost immediately.

He said, "I read somewhere that they expect it to be worse this week, because the high schools are all letting out for summer."

They stared ahead at the lines of waiting cars, three choked lanes going off to the blinding west, and the river. He had spoken—her mind had again wandered away from where she was. And she had been thinking about him. This seemed almost spooky to her. She started to ask what he had said, but then decided against it, not wanting really to spend the energy it would take to listen, and experiencing a wave of frustration at the attention she was having to pay to every motion of her own mind.

"How could it be worse?" he said.

She made a murmur of agreement, remarking to herself that soon he was going to have to turn the car's air conditioning off, or the engine might overheat. She looked surreptitiously at the needle on the temperature gauge; it was already climbing toward the red zone. Perhaps she should say something.

But then there was the sudden commotion in the street, perhaps four cars up—some people had gotten out of two of the cars, and were scurrying and fighting, it looked like. It was hard to tell with the blaze of sunlight beyond.

"What is that?" she said, almost glad of the change.

He hadn't seen it yet. He had put his head back on the rest, eyes closed against the brightness. He sat forward, and peered through the blazing space out the window. It was hard to see anything at all. "What?" he said.

She leaned into the curve of the window as if to look under the reflected glare. "Something—"

"People are—leaving their cars," he said. It was as though he had asked a question.

"No, look. A fight—"

Scuffling shapes moved across the blaze of sunlight, partly obscured by the cars in front. Something flashed, and there was a cracking sound.

"Michael?"

"Hey," he said, holding the wheel.

The scuffle came in a rush at them, at the front of the car—a man bleeding badly across the front of a white shirt. He seemed to glance off to the right.

"What the—"

Now he staggered toward them, and his shirt front came against the window on her side; it seemed to agitate there for a few terrible seconds, and then it smeared downward, blotting everything out in bright red. She was screaming. She held her hands, with the magazine in them, to her face, and someone was hitting the windshield. There were more cracking sounds. Gunshots. She realized with a spasm of terror that they were gunshots. The door opened on his side, and she thought it was being opened from without. She was lying over on the seat now, in the roar and shout of the trouble, her arms over her head, and it took a moment for her to understand that she was alone. She was alone, and the trouble, whatever it was, had moved off. There were screams and more gunshots, the sound of many people running, horns and sirens. It was all in a distance, now.

"Michael," she said, then screamed. "Michael!"

The frenetic, busy notes of jazz were still coming from the radio, undisturbed and bright, under the sound of her cries. Someone was lifting her, someone's hands were on her shoulders. She was surprised to find that she still clutched the magazine. She let it drop to the floor of the car, and looked up into a leathery, tanned, middle-aged face, small green eyes.

"Are you hit?" the face said.

"I don't know. What is it, what happened? Where's my husband?"

"Can you sit up? Can you get out of the car?"

"Yes," she said. "I think so."

He helped her. There were many people standing on the curb, and in the open doors of stopped cars. She heard sirens. Somehow she had barked the skin of her knee. She stood out of the car, and the man supported her on his arm, explaining that he was a policeman. "We've had some trouble here," he said. "It's all over."

"Where's my husband?" She looked into the man's face, and the face was blank. A second later, Michael stepped out of the glare beyond him and stood there, wringing his hands. She looked into his ashen face, and he seemed to want to look away. "Oh, Michael," she said, reaching for him.

The policeman let her go. She put her arms around him and closed her eyes, feeling the solidness of his back, crying. "Michael. Oh. Michael, what happened?"

"It's okay," he told her, loud over the sirens. "It's over."

She turned her head on his shoulder, and saw the knot of people working on the other side of the car. Her window was covered with blood. "Oh, God," she said. "Oh, my God."

"We'll need statements from you both," the policeman said to them.

"My God," Ivy said. "What happened here?"

He had been thinking about flowers, and adultery.

One of the older men in the admissions office, Saul Dornby, had sent a dozen roses to his wife, and the wife had called, crying, to say that they had arrived. Michael took the call, because Dornby was out of the office, having lunch with one of the secretaries. Dornby was a man who had a long and complicated history with women, and people had generally assumed that he was having an affair with the secretary. He was always having affairs, and in the past few weeks he had put Michael in the position of fielding his wife's phone calls. "I know it's unpleasant for you, and I really do appreciate it. I'll find some way to make it up to you. It would break Jenny's heart to think I was having lunch with anyone but her—any *female* but her. You know how they are. It's perfectly innocent this time, really. But it's just better to keep it under wraps, you know, the past being what it is. After all, I met Jenny by playing around on someone else. You get my meaning? I haven't been married four times for nothing. I mean, I have learned one or two things." He paused and thought. "Man, I'll tell you, Jenny was something in those first days I was with her. You know what I mean?" Michael indicated that he knew. "Well, sure, son. You're fresh married. Of course you know. Maybe that's my trouble—I just need it to be fresh like that all the time. You think?"

Dornby was also the sort of man who liked to parade his sense of superior experience before the young men around him. He behaved as though it were apparent that he was the envy of others. He was especially that way with Michael Blakely, who had made the mistake of being initially in awe of him. But though Michael now resented the other man and was mostly bored by his talk, he had found that there was something alluring about the wife, had come to look forward to talking with her, hearing her soft, sad, melodious voice over the telephone. Something about possession of this intimate knowledge of her marriage made her all the more lovely to contemplate, and over the past few weeks he had been thinking about her in the nights.

Sitting behind the wheel with the sun in his eyes and his wife at his side paging through the magazine, he had slipped toward sleep, thinking about all this, thinking drowsily about the attraction he felt for Dornby's wife, when something in the static calm around him began to change. Had his wife spoken to him?

And then everything went terrifyingly awry.

He couldn't say exactly when he had opened the door and dropped out of the car. The urge to leave it had been overwhelming from the moment he realized what was smearing down the window on his wife's side. He had simply found himself out on the pavement, had felt the rough surface on his knees and the palms of his hands, and he had scrabbled between stopped cars and running people to the sidewalk. It had been just flight, trying to keep out of the line of fire, all reflex, and he had found himself clinging to a light pole, on his knees, while the shouts continued, and the crowd surged beyond him and on. He saw a man sitting in the doorway of a cafeteria, his face in his folded arms. There were men running in the opposite direction of the rushing crowd, and then he saw a man being subdued by several others, perhaps fifty feet away on the corner. He held on to the light pole, and realized he was crying, like a little boy. Several women were watching him from the entrance of another store, and he straightened, got to his feet, stepped uncertainly away from the pole, struggling to keep his balance. It was mostly quiet now. Though there were sirens coming from the distance, growing nearer. The gunshots had stopped; and the screams. People had gathered near his car, and Ivy stepped out of the confusion there, saying his name.

He experienced a sudden rush of aversion.

There was something almost cartoonish about the pallor of her face, and he couldn't bring himself to settle his eyes on her. As she walked into his arms, he took a breath and tried to keep from screaming, and then he heard himself telling her it was all right, it was over.

But of course it wasn't over.

The police wanted statements from everyone, and the names and addresses. This was something that was going to go on, Michael knew. They were going to look at it from every angle, this traffic altercation that had ended in violence, and caused one man to be wounded in the abdomen and another to be shot in the hip. The policemen were calling the wounds out to each other. "This one's in the hip," one of them said, and another answered, "Abdomen here." It was difficult to tell who was involved and who was bystander. The traffic had backed up for blocks, and people were coming out of the buildings lining the street.

There was a slow interval of a kind of deep concentration, a stillness, while the police and the paramedics worked. The ambulances took the wounded men away, and a little while later the police cars began to pull out, too. The Blakelys sat in the back of one of the squad cars, while a polite officer asked them questions. The officer had questioned ten or eleven others, he told them—as though they had not been standing around waiting during this procedure—and now he explained in his quiet, considerate baritone voice that he needed everybody's best recollection of the events. He hoped they understood.

"I don't really know what was said, or what happened," Michael told him. "I don't have the slightest idea, okay? Like I said, we didn't know anything was happening until we heard the gunshots."

"We saw the scuffling," Ivy said. "Remember?"

"I just need to get the sequence of events down," the officer said.

"We saw the scuffle," said Ivy. "Or I saw it. I was reading this magazine—"

"Look, it was a fight," Michael broke in. "Haven't you got enough from all these other people? We didn't know what was happening."

"Well, sir—after you realized there was gunfire, what did you do?"

Michael held back, glanced at his wife, and waited.

She seemed surprised for a second. "Oh. I—I got down on the front seat of the car. I had a magazine I was reading, and I put it up to my face, like—like this." She pantomimed putting the magazine to her face. "I think that's what I did."

"And you?" the policeman said to Michael.

"I don't even remember."

"You got out of the car," said his wife, in the tone of someone who had made a discovery. "You—you left me there."

"I thought you were with me," he said.

The policeman, a young man with deep-socketed eyes and a toothy white smile, closed his clipboard and said, "Well, you never know where anybody is at such a time, everything gets so confused."

Ivy stared at her husband. "No, but you left me there. Where were you going, anyway?"

"I thought you were with me," he said.

"You didn't look back to see if I was?"

He couldn't answer her.

The policeman was staring at first one, and then the other, and seemed about to break out laughing. But when he spoke, his voice was soft and very considerate. "It's a hard thing to know where everybody was when there's trouble like this, or what anybody had in mind."

Neither Michael nor his wife answered him.

"Well," he went on. "I guess I've got all I need."

"Will anyone die?" Ivy asked him.

He smiled. "I think they got things under control."

"Then no one's going to die."

"I don't think so. They got some help pretty quick, you know— Mr. Vance, over there, is a doctor, and he stepped right in and started working on them. Small caliber pistols in both cases, thank God—looks like everybody's gonna make it fine."

Michael felt abruptly nauseous and dizzy. The officer was looking at him.

"Can you have someone wash the blood off our car?" Ivy asked.

"Oh, Jesus," Michael said.

The officer seemed concerned. "You look a little green around the gills, sir. You could be in a little shock. Wait here." He got out of the car, closed the door, and walked over to where a group of officers and a couple of paramedics were standing, on the other side of the street. In the foreground, another officer was directing traffic. Michael stared out at this man, and felt as though there wasn't any breathable air. He searched for a way to open his window. His wife sat very still at his side, staring at her hands.

"Stop sighing like that," she said suddenly. "You're safe."

"You heard the officer," he told her. "I could be in shock. I can't breathe."

"You're panting."

In the silence which followed, a kind of whimper escaped from the bottom of his throat.

"Oh, my God," she said. "Will you please cut that out."

She saw the officer coming back, and she noted the perfect crease of his uniform slacks. Her husband was a shade to her left, breathing.

"Ivy?" he said.

The officer opened the door and leaned in. "Doctor'll give you a look," he said, across her, to Michael.

"I'm okay," Michael said.

"Well," said the officer. "Can't hurt."

They got out, and he made sure of their address. He said he had someone washing the blood from their car. Michael seemed to lean into him, and Ivy walked away from them, out into the street. The policeman there told her to wait. People were still crowding along the sidewalk on that side, and a woman sat on the curb, crying, being tended to by two others. The sun was still bright; it shone in the dark hair of the crying woman. Ivy made her way to the sidewalk, and when she turned she saw that the polite officer was helping Michael across. The two men moved to the knot of paramedics, and the doctor who had been the man of the hour took Michael by the arms and looked into his face. The doctor was rugged-looking, with thick, wiry brown hair, heavy, square features, and big, rough-looking hands—a man who did outdoor things, and was calm, in charge, perhaps five years older than Michael, though he seemed almost parental with him. He got Michael to sit down, then lie down, and he elevated his legs. Michael lay in the middle of the sidewalk, with a crate of oranges under his legs, which someone had brought from the deli, a few feet away. Ivy walked over there and waited with the others, hearing the muttered questions bystanders asked—was this one of the victims?

The doctor knelt down and asked Michael how he felt.

"Silly," Michael said.

"Well. You got excited. It's nothing to be ashamed of."

"Can I get up now?"

"Think you can?"

"Yes, sir."

The doctor helped him stand. A little smattering of approving sounds went through the crowd. Michael turned in a small circle, and located his wife. He looked directly at her, and then looked away. She saw this, and waited where she was. He was talking to the doctor, nodding. Then he came toward her, head down, like a little boy, she thought, a little boy ashamed of himself.

"Let's go," he said.

They walked down the street, to where the car had been moved. Someone had washed the blood from it, though she could still see traces of it in the aluminum trim along the door. She got in, and waited for him to make his way around to the driver's side. When he got in, she arranged herself, smoothing her dress down, not looking at him. He started the engine, pulled out, carefully, into traffic. It was still slow going, three lanes moving fitfully toward the bridge. They were several blocks down the street before he spoke.

"Doctor said I had mild shock."

"I saw."

They reached the bridge, and then they were stopped there, with a view of the water, and the rest of the city ranged along the river's edge—a massive, uneven shape of buildings with flame in every window, beyond the sparkle of the water. The sun seemed to be pouring into the car.

He reached over and turned the air conditioning off. "We'll overheat," he said.

"Can you leave it on a minute?" she asked.

He rolled his window down. "We'll overheat."

She reached over and put it on, then leaned into it. The air was cool, blowing on her face, and she closed her eyes. She had chosen too easily, when she chose him. She could feel the rightness of the thought as it arrived; she gave in to it, accepted it, with a small bitter rush of elation and anger. The flow of cool air on her face stopped. He had turned it off.

"I just thought I'd run it for a minute," she said.

He turned it on again. She leaned forward, took a breath, then turned it off. "That's good." She imagined herself going on with her life, making other choices; she was relieved to be alive, and she felt exhilarated. The very air seemed sweeter. She saw herself alone, or with someone else, some friend to whom she might tell the funny story of her young husband running off and leaving her to her fate in the middle of a gun battle.

But in the next instant, the horror of it reached through her, and made her shudder, deep. "God," she murmured.

He said nothing. The traffic moved a few feet, then seemed to start thinning out. He idled forward, then accelerated slowly.

"Mind the radio?" she said.

He thought she seemed slightly different with him now, almost superior. He remembered how it felt to be lying in the middle of the sidewalk with the orange crate under his legs. When he spoke, he tried to seem neutral. "Pardon me?"

"I asked if you mind the radio."

"Up to you," he said.

"Well, what do you want?"

"Radio's fine."

She turned it on. She couldn't help the feeling that this was toying with him, a kind of needling. Yet it was a pleasant feeling. The news was on; they listened for a time.

"It's too early, I guess," she said.

"Too early for what?"

"I thought it might be on the news." She waited a moment. The traffic was moving; they were moving. She put the air conditioning on again, and sat there with the air fanning her face, eyes closed. She felt him watching her, and she had begun to feel guilty—even cruel. They had, after all, both been frightened out of their wits. He was her husband, whom she loved. "Let me know if you think I ought to turn it off again."

"I said we'd overheat," he said.

She only glanced at him. "We're moving now. It's okay if we're moving, right?" Then she closed her eyes and faced into the cool rush of air.

He looked at her, sitting there with her eyes closed, basking in the coolness as if nothing at all had happened. He wanted to tell her about Saul Dornby's wife. He tried to frame the words into a sentence that might make her wonder what his part in all that might be—but the thing sounded foolish to him: *Saul, at work, makes me answer his wife's phone calls. He's sleeping around on her.*

I've been going to sleep at night dreaming about what it might be like if I got to know her a little better.

"If it's going to cause us to overheat, I'll turn it off," she said.

He said nothing.

Well, he could pout if he wanted to. He was the one who had run away and left her to whatever might happen. She thought again how it was that someone might have shot into the car while she cringed there, alone. "Do you want me to turn it off?" she said.

"Leave it be," he told her.

They were quiet, then, all the way home. She gazed out the front, at the white lines coming at them and at them. He drove slowly, and tried to think of something to say to her, something to explain everything in some plausible way.

She noticed that there was still some blood at the base of her window. Some of it had seeped down between the door and the glass. When he pulled into the drive in front of the house, she waited for him to get out, then slid across the seat and got out behind him.

"They didn't get all the blood," she said.

"Jesus." He went up the walk toward the front door.

"I'm not going to clean it," she said.

"I'll take it to the car wash."

He had some trouble with the key to the door. He cursed under his breath, and finally got it to work. They walked through the living room to their bedroom, where she got out of her clothes, and was startled to find that some blood had gotten on the arm of her blouse.

"Look at this," she said. She held it out for him to see.

"I see."

The expression on her face, that cocky little smile, made him want to strike her. He suppressed the urge, and went about changing his own clothes. He was appalled at the depth of his anger.

"Can you believe it?" she said.

"Please," he said. "I'd like to forget the whole thing."

"I know, but look."

"I see it. What do you want me to do with it?"

"Okay," she said. "I just thought it was something—that it got inside the window somehow. It got on my arm."

"Get it out of here," he said. "Put it away."

She went into the bathroom and threw the blouse into the trash. Then she washed her face and hands, and got out of her skirt, her stockings. "I'm going to take a shower," she called to him. He didn't answer, so she went to the entrance of the living room, where she found him watching the news.

"Is it on?" she asked.

"Is what on?"

"Okay. I'm going to take a shower."

"Ivy," he said.

She waited. She kept her face as impassive as possible.

"I'm really sorry. I did think you were with me, that we were running together, you know."

It occurred to her that if she allowed him to, he would turn this into the way he remembered things, and he would come to believe it was so. She could give this to him, simply by accepting his explanation of it all. In the same instant something hot rose up in her heart, and she said, "But you didn't look back to see where I was." She said this evenly, almost cheerfully.

"Because I thought you were there. Right behind me. Don't you see?"

The pain in his voice was oddly far from making her feel sorry. She said, "I could've been killed, though. And you wouldn't have known it."

He said nothing. He had the thought that this would be something she might hold over him, and for an instant he felt the anger again, wanted to make some motion toward her, something to shake her, as he had been shaken. "Look," he said.

She smiled. "What?"

"Everything happened so fast."

"You looked so funny, lying on the sidewalk with that crate of oranges under your legs. You know what it said on the side? 'Fresh from Sunny Florida.' Think of it. I mean nobody got killed, so it's funny. Right?"

"Jesus Christ," he said.

"Michael. It's over. We're safe. We'll laugh about it eventually, you'll see."

And there was nothing he could say. He sat down and stared at the television, the man there talking in reasonable tones about a killer tornado in Lawrence, Kansas. She walked over and kissed him on the top of his head.

"Silly," she said.

He turned to watch her go back down the hall, and a moment later he could hear the shower running. He turned the television off, and made his way back to the entrance of the bathroom. The door was ajar. Peering in, he saw the vague shape of her through the light curtain. He stood there, one hand gripping the door, the rage working in him. He watched the shape move.

She was thinking that it was not she who had run away; that there was no reason for him to be angry with her, or disappointed in her. Clearly, if he was unhappy, he was unhappy with himself. She could not be blamed for that. And how fascinating it was that when she thought of her earlier doubts, they seemed faraway and small, like the evanescent worries of some distant other self, a childhood self. Standing in the hot stream, she looked along her slender arms, and admired the smooth contours of the bone and sinew there. It was so good to be alive. The heat was wonderful on the small muscles of her back. She was reasonably certain that she had dealt with her own disappointment and upset, had simply insisted on the truth. And he could do whatever he wanted, finally, because she was already putting the whole unpleasant business behind her.

ALAN CHEUSE

Midnight Ride

Where did I get the idea for this picture? It was the year of El Niño—the current, I mean, and not anything else that I knew about at the time—and the meteorologists were telling us to expect strange events in the atmosphere.

They didn't say anything about events at home, where it hadn't been good between me and my housemate, Gary, for nearly a month now, ever since one of our late-night script sessions turned into a mistaken encounter in my bedroom. Still, except for the color of the sky—low clouds, smog, the kind of weather we don't usually advertise, especially when it comes in the middle of summer—it was kind of lovely outside that afternoon, warm, with an inviting breeze blowing up over the bluffs from the ocean. It was that same wind that pushed all the crappy air back up against the mountains east of the city, and when you drove up to the top of the road and looked down in our direction, you could see it hanging there like some slightly soiled yellow scrim that someone had tacked up over the hills. From that hilltop, I wound my way down into the adjoining neighborhood and threaded the car along through four or five more all the way to the mall. I didn't like driving the freeways much, because I always thought of Joan Whatshername's heroine Maria, played by Tuesday Weld, and the way she drove and drove. That's how you get out here—probably all over America, since I don't feel much different about it than I did when I was living in Illinois—seeing life in terms of movies. Or a better, more truthful way to put it, seeing life *as* a movie. What else was I supposed to believe when I pulled into a parking space at the mall and who should drive up along-side me but my favorite actress friend Bunny?

"Yo, Bee," she said, rolling her window all the way down. She was wearing shades and had bound up her long hair in a snood—a sort of *Sunset Boulevard* look. From her lips dangled the usual cigarette. I hadn't seen her since Gary and I had gone to one of those chamber music evenings over at Milt Markowitz's. I think she had been going out with the viola player. I remember saying to Gary, That girl looks like my little sister, Harriet—except Bunny could never live in the Chicago suburb where Harriet and her banker husband have settled, with two kids, a dog (though no cat), and a little behind-the-house pond with a rowboat—but Gary was too busy flirting with the viola player himself to pay much attention.

"So, you ready for it?" Bunny said, puffing out some smoke from between her teeth in that schoolgirl way—what a school-girl!—that Gary had said, correctly, was so right for the part of Harmon Root, the runaway rich girl in the carnival story we were pitching.

I beeped shut my car and slouched over to Bunny's window, leaning over the way you see the CHPs do on the freeway when some poor jerk screws up. Her perfume—it was Calandre by Paco Rabanne—twisted my nose into a knot.

"Ready for what?"

"Our big dinner tonight," Bunny said. I looked blank. "You don't remember? Roger and Balu Maginnes?"

"Shit, how could I have forgotten that? But I did!" What? Was I crazy, or just depressed? Roger and Balu weren't a pair whose invitations you took lightly—the big bald producer with the drop-dead beautiful actress wife was how I first noticed them at the evening at Milt's house, and I remember that my heart started to flutter when I got introduced to them.

"I'm amazed Gary didn't say anything," Bunny said as I pulled back from her window and looked around at the gray-orange sky.

"He was lost in his new cowboy script," I said. "*Showdown at the Gay Corral.* I'm the one who should have remembered. Our big chance to pitch the carnival story again! We thought it was dead!"

"So go inside and buy yourself something to cheer you up, and we'll charm them tonight. A nice shirt, maybe. That's my thing when I'm down. A shirt. Or maybe a scarf? I don't know you that well, Bee. Are you a scarf chick?"

"No," I said. "I'm a cat person. When things get tough, I go and buy something for my Meow."

"I'm glad you like animals."

"You are? Why?"

She gave me a mysterious smile and said she'd see me tonight, and with a little wave drove off.

I walked slowly across the lot, a vast metal beach of gleaming sports cars and sedans, and wandered along the walkways of the mall, strolling from shop window to shop window—the leather dresses, velvet coats, platinum-rimmed eyeglasses, gloves made from the skin of antelope, emeralds and rubies in the most bizarre settings, ropes of pearls, and telescopes and video phones—you name it. I found a juice bar, drank a papaya smoothie for lunch. There was a pet store, of course, so I went in and bought a little bag of catnip on a string. Then I found another shop, where the brightly lighted window was filled with stuffed lambs, rabbits, and bears. Like a sleepwalker, I made a purchase.

Then I drove back the way I'd come, the blue blaze of ocean on my horizon, the urine-colored curtain of smog behind me, and this sort of gave me hope, though for what exactly I couldn't figure.

I wanted to share my good feeling with Gary when I got back, except that he had gone out, saying in a note left on the front table that my mother had called.

I took out the little gift for Meow, and tossed her the bag on the stick. It didn't take but a few seconds for her to begin tearing around with it on the rug, crazed with the scent of the catnip. So having made at least one creature happy, I dialed my mother's number.

"I called you earlier," she said after picking up on the first ring.

"I got the message, Mom."

"It shouldn't always be my call that makes you call me."

"I'm just a wayward daughter," I said.

"Don't talk that way, Bee. If you say something, you could make it happen."

"That's sort of a primitive way of thinking, Mom."

"I don't know what you're talking about. Tell me, have you been getting around?"

"Getting around?"

"Have you been meeting any nice young men?"

I held the receiver at arm's length. Outside the window, a stray gull swept from the beach on a lifting wind. It swooped past our orange tree and disappeared at an angle into an otherwise empty sky.

"I don't get out much, Mom," I said, "because I stay home and work. With Gary. We—"

"Friends are friends, Bee," she cut in, "but I don't have to tell you that you're not getting any—"

"Younger?"

"If you've heard me say this often enough to know it by heart, then you ought to know enough to believe it by now. I don't mean to nag, darling, but just woman to woman, I have to tell you that when you get to my age, you won't be able to look back on your work and get much comfort from it."

I took a deep breath. "You're right. I should have some children that I can call on the phone and make miserable because I'll be alone and pissed off at—"

"Please don't speak to me that way, Bee."

Another breath. "I'm sorry. You don't bring out the best in me when you raise this particular subject."

"Well, tell me, then, have you seen any movie stars lately? You're always telling me about seeing people like that at lunch."

"You just shut off one thing and pick up another?"

"I thought you wanted me to stop talking about the other thing."

"I just want to have a talk with you, Mom. In a pleasant way. You know, like, 'How are you?' and 'How was your day?'"

"Family isn't always pleasant in that way, Bee."

"So why do you want so much for me to start one?"

I could hear my voice sail into the highest register.

I was still close to tears when Gary came in the door. He was wearing his usual jeans and thin T-shirt with his cigarettes rolled up in the right sleeve. But despite that tough-guy stuff and his wispy mustache, he had that little-lost-dog look.

"Have a nice shopping trip?"

On cue, Meow came tearing through the room with her catnip ball, did a roll, a leap, and another roll, tossing the ball of herbs and then catching it again before it came to a stop.

"My big purchase," I said.

Gary looked puzzled. "Did you call your mother?"

"That's why my eyes look red."

He came and peered into my face. "Ah, so..."

I rubbed my nose with my fist and turned away.

"At the mall?" I said when I looked back at him.

"Uh-huh?"

"I saw Bunny."

His tongue slipped out from between his teeth, the way it does when he's working on a line of dialogue and you know even before it comes out that it's going to be a snapper.

"Oh, my God, that's so dumb! I just remembered! But I can't go. I've got a date."

We were standing there looking at each other when the telephone rang.

It was Bunny. "Better wear pants," she said.

When I hung up, I turned to Gary.

"Did you know?"

"Know? Oh, about the ride?"

I nodded.

"Yeah," he said. "I mean, I knew, but then I forgot about it. Look, Bee, if you want me to go with you, I'll break my engagement."

I shook my head. "I can do it myself. I just need to rest," I said. "Before I go."

And so I left him standing there—not a very nice thing, but it was what I thought I had to do. I went into the bedroom and lay down, feeling a little dizzy at the thought of what was to come. There's one thing Prozac does, though. No dreams. At least not for me. I touched my cheek to the pillow and went out.

The next thing I knew, Meow was purring furiously in my ear. I sat up to see the sky outside turned to lavender and fading crimson. "Hi, little puss," I said, a croak in my throat as I ran my fingers along her long back. It was late, I was sweating, but it wasn't the middle of the night, so I couldn't just turn over and go back to sleep. So I hauled my butt out of bed and dragged myself into the shower. In just thirty minutes, I was driving down the Ventura Freeway, heading south. The traffic began to slow, and I thought to myself, Oh, girl, here it comes, this is why I hate these roads, and then I saw the orangey flickering on the horizon and figured that someone else had bigger troubles than mine. After the next curve, I could see the dance of fire on the other side of the road, lower than the palm trees, higher, much higher than the retaining wall.

Two cars were burning like slabs of meat on a grill, and the small auxiliary fire truck that had pulled up alongside them wasn't doing much to put out the flames. Inching along on my side of the freeway, those of us moving away from the accident could see the rolling lights and hear the wavering whine of more engines approaching. God help the passengers if they were still inside! I rolled down my window and tried to look back, but our lane was moving too fast now to do more than get a good whiff of the fire. It stayed with me all the way to the restaurant, Cactus Cantina, in Burbank, surrounded on either side by stables, dark animals milling about in the corrals, steeping the air around the place with odors different from the rest of the city.

Two rows of faces greeted me inside the restaurant. There was Bunny, sitting alongside Roger and his beautiful blond wife. A half-dozen other couples I didn't know and Milt Markowitz filled out the table.

"Your friend Gary called to say you were going to be late. So I had the idea we could play the old switcheroo," Milt spoke in that appealing Long Island nasal voice of his. "I'm not into punishment, and I don't know if I can make it back."

Seeing my puzzled expression, Bunny piped up, "Milt rode with us, but he'll drive your car home for you and take a taxi from there if you ride his mount back over the mountains."

"I love what she said. My mount! My mount! I love that word!" Milt looked up at the papier-mâché piñatas dangling from the ceiling.

"When you didn't show at the stables," Bunny said, "I gave up on you. I'm glad you remembered the restaurant."

"Me, too," I said, noticing that Roger Maginnes was smiling up at me while his wife dabbled with her spoon at some dessert.

"My mount! My mount!" Milt kept on. "I love that word. My *mount!*" He paused and took a breath. "Except I had a saddle with teeth and it chewed up my *tuchas.*"

"The white Rabbit," I said to him enigmatically as Maginnes's wife looked over at me and I turned away to dig in my bag for the keys.

"The bronze-colored mount," Milt said and lifted the keys from my hand.

Next thing I know, people are pushing back from the table, tossing their napkins onto their used dessert plates, and Roger Maginnes is saying at the top of his voice, like a character in a picture he's much too subtle to make, "Troop, mount up!" I'd missed dinner.

In the corral behind the restaurant, I met my mount, a chestnut mare named Madonna. As the groom held her reins, I stared at her in the light of the spots above the stable doors, feeling her edgy vitality under my fingers as I stroked her flank, though I went a little weak in the knees from the pungent power of her smell. The young Mexican groom motioned for me to mount, and as I hoisted myself into the stirrup, I felt his hand pushing up on my ass, and then I was sitting high in the dark, the big animal twitching menacingly beneath me. Roger Maginnes pulled up alongside me sitting atop a huge black gelding.

"You've done this before, right?"

"At Honey Cartwright's house every summer when I was a girl," I said, watching as his horse shimmied sidewise and then jerked away forward, but not before I caught a glimpse of the round white globes of the gelding's eyes.

Honey! I hadn't thought of her in years, her big house north on the lakeshore, what we used to do after dark with the black grooms from the deep-city neighborhoods. Grooms! It never occurred to me until now what richness lay in *that* word!

The other horses, jittery, snorting, stamping in the dust, moved with a clatter out of the corral.

"Troop! Foh-ward!"

"Roger," I called after him into the dark beyond the gate, "you should make a western!"

Now, if you have ever wondered—and I myself certainly hadn't before this evening—just how a posse of folks on horseback would take a ride across Los Angeles, here is how you do it. The first thing is you cross the freeway, and you do this by means of a long dusty trail that curves away from the stables and declines gently toward the racing lights and roaring vehicles on the road and then ducks beneath the road into a long tunnel swirling with dust and clanging with the rebounding sounds of hoofbeats. This was our first ten minutes, and my mouth clogged with the thick choking clouds we kicked up as we moved along with only the faint glow of arc lamps at the far end.

Coming out of the tunnel was like coming up for air after a long dive! I took deep gulps of fresh wind, snorting along with the horses and giving myself over to the batting rhythm of Madonna as she chugged along, bouncing me mercilessly in the saddle. I looked ahead for Roger, but all I saw was the huge rump of his mount as he and a couple of other riders took advantage of the flat stretch between the road and the hills to make their horses race.

"Hey-yo!" Voices drifted back to me over the clatter of the hooves. And then we began climbing.

"It's beautiful," I called out near the crest of the trail, catching up with Bunny, who bounced along smartly atop a broad bay mare.

"You having fun?" she said.

"I'm having a ball."

Roger just then turned his horse back toward us, and in the faint glow of the quarter moon, I could see a strange smile pass across his face.

"There's that, and there's that," he said, nudging his beast into another graceful turn and coming up alongside me. He pointed up at the sliver of moon and then at the trail that opened into a field of odd machines and smoking pipes poking out of the ground.

"What is that?" I said, staring at this weird landscape.

"Methane farm," he said. "These hills were built up out of garbage. As it decays, it gives off methane gas."

"We're riding across mountains of garbage?" I watched now with fascination at the little puffs of smoke that burst from the ends of the buried pipes.

"You got to look at it another way. It's all a metaphor," he said. I'd never heard anyone in the business, except for Milt, talk about anything like it was poetry. "They pile it on here, and it makes a mountain, and then we ride over it and catch the view. I mean, look at that down there, Bee." Roger pointed to where the dark hill fell away into the vast ocean of illumination below us. Whatever he meant by what he said, I couldn't take my eyes off that luminescent plain fluttering with bursts of bright lights here and there—in which somewhere that fire I saw on the way over or another fire in another part of the city or a fire that would burn before I knew it was adding to the glow. Our horses held fairly still, only their occasional snorts and heaving breaths clotting the air, while faintly in the distance at the bottom of the great decline, the tiniest whines of sirens and rumbling of the freeway drifted up to us.

"Bunny," Roger said, "would you ride up ahead and see how they're doing?"

"Sure, pardner," Bunny said, throwing me a strange look—the moonlight, however faint, clearly showed her arched eyebrows and puckered mouth—and then peeling away up the trail.

"Bee?" Roger urged his horse closer to mine so that he could reach over and take my mare's bridle.

I was surprised at this.

"Did I do something wrong?"

"You're so cool, Bee," he said. "Loosen up a little."

"What are you talking about?"

He got—somehow—his horse to edge even closer, so that when he leaned across his neck, it was almost as though we were sitting together on some stiff, old-fashioned upright divan and his head was nearly resting on my shoulder.

"Don't misunderstand me," he said.

"What?"

"In my position, I could get misunderstood. There's always girls, you know." He nodded toward the dark, and I thought that he might have meant something about Bunny. "That's not what this is about."

"What is it about, Roger?"

Madonna jittered in place, nervous to walk, I figured. Uncomfortable wouldn't describe what I was feeling then.

"Troop's got to get moving," he said.

"Yeah, we should."

"So?"

He tried to reach for me, but my horse backed away, spooked a little by his sudden move.

"Easy, girl," he said.

"Who are you talking to, Roger?" I said.

"Very funny," he said, turning in his saddle and looking up the trail into the darkness where all the other riders had long disappeared. "But we should talk."

"I think we should."

Madonna calmed down again, and I felt so good sitting so high up on her, as still as the stillest part of the big mass of her body.

"I think we could talk," Roger said. "Bunny tells me that you have a treatment."

"That's right, pardner," I said.

"Then we can talk." Roger's gelding shied just then at some invisible menace in the dark, stamping back a few paces and then letting out a blubbery snort.

I remained still, and in that moment Madonna took it upon herself to gush out a long hot stream of particularly pungent flow, the sound of which rushed through the space between Roger and me.

"We'll talk," he said, and gave his horse a kick that sent them moving up the trail at a rapid rate of speed.

"Wait for me," I called after him, digging my heels into Madonna. I might as well have been urging a statue to move. "Come on, girl!" I shouted, kicking harder as Roger dissolved into the blackness ahead.

And then the dark kicked back, because at that instant these terrible cramps nearly folded me over double in the saddle, and I sat there in agony, unable to get the horse to budge. Tears rolled down my cheeks, the stink of the animal jammed all the way up my nose like slivers of bamboo under the fingernails of some victim in a thirties movie about the Orient.

"Jesus!" I called out into the dark, alone up here, and hurting. For a moment the only sound after my voice faded away was the

gentle hissing of the methane tubes and the faint tumult of the
city below, a whirring, shushing sound that branches make when
stirred by a forceful wind. My insides twisted around knotted up.
Oh, Mama! I started to cry. Somebody please come and help me!

I looked up to see mist passing before the moon and the chill of
it all settling over me like the gauzy curtain before a big empty
screen.

And then it came to me, right then and there, just what a scene
it would make! The girl, stranded out here on horseback, her guts
churning—but why? not just like me because she had cramps,
though I was thankful that they arrived at last, but something else,
what? like maybe she was pregnant and going into premature
labor? but then why would she even think about going for a ride
like this? wait, because she wanted to lose the child? because... she
was carrying one man's child—say, someone like Roger? and
wanted to marry the other, say, Gary? but how would it go? how
would it go? and who is she, anyway? rich girl on her own horse?
or working girl on a rented mount? a career girl from the Midwest,
say? who came out to work in... what? not the movies, not that,
but then what? a girl my age, pretty, but not sure of herself, attrac-
tive to men but not really liking herself all that much, and she
drifts into one hurtful affair after another, and she's got some talent, sure, but there's something inside of her, some need she has
that she doesn't want to admit to herself, the opposite of the wild
side, of the desperate hope and chance that brought her out here,
because... because even though it's a cliché, she's had to admit it,
she feels the biological clock ticking away in her, and she's not sure
of either man, maybe, but she goes along with it, because it's the
business, she gives her whole life to the business, and even though
things are going well, say, her mother calls and it all comes to her
in the middle of the conversation just how sad she feels, you can
see it on her face as she talks on the telephone, she tells herself it's
okay, it's going to be all right, and maybe she can have both things,
the work and a family when the right guy comes along, and she
thought she had found him in this young—what?—screenwriter?
okay, okay, but I thought she wasn't going to be involved in the
movies?—but say that he is a screenwriter, or a lawyer? or what?
say he runs a restaurant? no! or maybe a stable, yes, a riding stable

just at the foot of the Santa Monicas, a surprising thing like that, something most people not living out here would ever imagine, a stable in the middle of this huge city, and horses that travel in tunnels under the freeways, kicking up clouds of dust that rise into the air and fade into the smog, and say that they go out for a midnight ride, this woman and her friend, the man she loves, the man she adores, and it turns out that she's pregnant and doesn't even know it, maybe she's just missed a period and she's had some irregular periods in the past when she was under a lot of stress, and he tells her—what? that he's met someone else? or that he's gay? maybe that? which leads to the problem of the child and whether or not the man is infected, and say that the baby's going to be HIV? and they're going through hell because of it? and he decides to say the hell with it all? and takes off on his mount? his mount! and she races after him in the dark up the trail into the hills of garbage, calling out to him that she doesn't care, that she loves him no matter what? and in the dark she's galloping along— think of the scene, this scene, the dark trail, the city like an ocean all around this island made of trash—and the horse stumbles and throws her and the baby dies?

"Bee?"

A woman on horseback came trotting back up the trail, calling my name as she rode.

"Hi," I said, giving the uncooperative Madonna another kick. But I still had trouble.

"You all right?" It was Balu Maginnes. "We thought you might have fallen."

"Where is everybody?" I said.

"Almost back at the stable by now, I'm sure," she said. "Roger sent me after you. I'm a better rider." She reached for my reins, but I pushed her hand aside.

"I'm okay," I said. "I've ridden before."

"So what were you doing up here?"

"Admiring the view," I said.

And then suddenly she turned her horse, and Madonna began to move and followed her mount along the trail past the rest of the methane pumps and then down along the sloping ridge and into the utter darkness of the steeply descending path. My cramps returned ten times worse than before. The trail went down and down, and I dared to turn in the saddle to try and ease my pain, and looked back up to where I had been lingering, dreaming all that time.

I could hardly breathe by the time we reached the stables. My nose and mouth and throat were so filled with dust, and my cramps had gotten even worse. Gary was standing there, his small hands planted on his slender hips, looking more miffed than worried. Bunny was waiting with him. So was Roger Maginnes. By the time I turned my horse over to the groom and got out of the bathroom in the stableman's office, Roger and Balu had already gone.

"They said they had an early call," Gary said. "But I couldn't abandon you."

"Your legs are really going to hurt in the morning," Bunny said as she walked with us to the parking lot.

"And yours won't?" I said.

"It's just like fucking," she said. "You have to keep in shape."

Gary was staring at me. "Are you all right?" he said once we were inside the car.

"Yes, I'm fine."

I tried to sleep on the drive home, but the horse smell lay too thick on me, and I sat there, eyes closed, going over and over the treatment I had imagined in the dark. Once we got to the house, I asked Gary to feed the cat while I stripped off my clothes, tossed them into the washer, and took a hot soak. Bunny was right. My thighs resonated in the stinging water.

After that, I lay in bed with Meow curled up into a purring ball near my head and the stuffed lamb I had bought at the mall tucked against my rumbling stomach. Next thing I knew, Gary was in the room, saying, "Telephone."

"Oh," I said, picking up the receiver.

"I woke you, didn't I?" Milt said in his nasal way.

"That's all right."

"I would have left a message on your machine, but I hate those things. I just wanted to say thanks in person. So, thanks."

"You're welcome," I said.

"I'm vell-come," he said.

"You are," I said. I looked up at Gary, who shrugged and left the room.

"Am I vell-come enough to maybe take you to dinner tomorrow night?" Milt said.

"You don't owe me anything for what I did," I said.

"I wasn't thinking about it like that," he said. "Nobody owes anybody anything. This would just be a dinner-dinner. So?"

"Milt, can I think about it?"

"Okay," he said, and I was sorry to hurt his feelings. But I was too tired to explain anything anymore that night. Though after I hung up, I lay there a while listening to Meow's insistent breathing and the distant hum of the spin cycle on the washer. I was still awake when the next call came.

"Hello?"

"I told you we could talk."

"Roger," I said, "it's so late."

"I do some of my best business this time of night," he said.

Coming and Going

The man at her door was bald and wore a blue windbreaker. She had asked him twice what he wanted, but he had only said, "Are you Emily Fletcher?" as if he knew she was, but needed confirmation.

It struck her from the man's salutary tone that she might have won something—an envelope was about to be handed over with a check inside for a million dollars. She was sixty-five years old. It was about time.

"Yes," she said, and heard her tone cascading downward, as if she were stepping onto an unsteady footbridge over a high mountain pass. The man looked harmless enough, there in the doorway. On closer observation he seemed less sure of himself, as if he couldn't quite fathom why he was there. So many things had seemed unfathomable since her husband's recent death that she'd begun to accept "unfathomable" as an ongoing state.

Emily suddenly remembered she'd left Hanson, her lawyer, waiting on the telephone. It had taken her three phone calls to get a return call from him, and now the dollars were ticking away while she stood there with this awkward stranger. She looked him over again and felt the moment seize her in which women hurriedly judge a man safe with the scantest evidence—that split second in which they lunge past fears into a hastily assumed and unreliable security.

"Please step inside," Emily said. "I won't be a minute." She moved back to allow the man into the entry, then shut the door behind him and automatically turned the deadbolt. She knew it was crazy, to lock people in after she'd locked them out, but at least no one else would come in. She'd been interrupted by the telephone as she'd been taking a quilt from its shipping package. She had draped the gift from her sister across the back of a hall chair. She left the man standing as if he'd come to a halt before the flag of some unknown nation.

Speaking again to Hanson, she experienced the odd sensation of being in two places at once. She heard her voice going out over the phone lines, but she was also uneasily aware that her side of the conversation was entering the acutely attentive but uncommunicative head of the stranger in her entryway.

"Nyal spent a month in Italy while the house was under construction, but it wasn't a vacation!" she said to Hanson. "Martin tells me this woman called him before his father died." She revealed this almost involuntarily. Martin was their son, and she had confided unnecessarily to the lawyer during their last discussion that she feared Martin was a womanizer. She hated how she found herself blurting the most personal things to the business people she dealt with now. "It was while Nyal was very ill, and the woman must have intended to put pressure on him by calling Martin." She paused here to calculate the echo factor of the stranger's overhearing this last piece of information. Though what did it really matter? The man had no context in which to place these fragments of her life. Hanson's incisive voice, heading for the crux of the matter, began impatiently sweeping aside what he seemed to consider mere female baggage.

"The legal issue is: did your husband modify, use, or appropriate another man's house design? And if so, is that man's widow entitled to recompense? The statute of limitations unfortunately has not run out on this. You're further involved because Nyal completed this job under the business partnership you both formed to reduce his tax liability. You signed off on this work and took payment with him in the partnership."

"I recall something about it," Emily said. "But Nyal took care of all that." She'd signed whatever Nyal had asked her to sign. At the time they'd formed the partnership, paper had flown by with blizzard force. But, as representative of her husband's estate and also in her tutelary capacity as his surviving business partner, she would now, Hanson had reminded her, be the defendant in any action. The other woman, also a widow, and representing her own deceased husband's estate in Rome, would be the plaintiff. On his behalf, she claimed part ownership in a house design. Nyal had only been asked to modify the design. The plans had resulted in a construction in Italy which Emily had never seen, but which her husband had supervised. Both men who'd contributed to its design were now dead—her husband from cancer and the architect named Riccardo from a stroke in Rome some ten months previous.

During the final months of her own husband's illness, Emily had been aware of murmurings from the widow in Rome, who believed Nyal owed her payment for Riccardo's original design. Ultimately a letter had arrived, full of allegations. And Nyal, on his sickbed, had reasserted it was nonsense. Riccardo himself had invited him to modify the plan. Riccardo's widow knew this all very well. It was unfortunate Riccardo wasn't alive to corroborate it. But the whole matter would subside on its own. No, they needn't hire a lawyer in Rome.

For a time, Nyal seemed to have been right. They'd had their hands full, with people coming to visit and pay their respects, once it became known that Nyal's cancer was no longer in remission. Also, there was the finishing work on plans for the ecological center. Nyal had been the lead architect, and this project had been his final passion. All else had been swept aside so he could concentrate his remaining energies. The strange Italian murmuring had become inaudible, all but forgotten. Now Hanson informed her that yet another letter had arrived, one which framed the complaint so aggressively, he suspected it was preliminary to a suit.

"We may need to get representation in Rome for the estate and for you as well, if she decides to press the matter," Hanson said. Emily tried to gauge the emphasis he was putting on the "if." Why was her lawyer so lackluster, such a practitioner of the uninflected? She could never tell where the meaning lay in his sentences. Since her husband's death, she had craved emotion in all her communications. This lawyer was an ongoing disappointment in this regard.

"Rome?" she heard herself saying, like a word spoken aloud in a dream. It was as well to say Jakarta or Bandar Seri Begawan. The only personal connection she'd had with Rome, other than her late husband's sojourn there, was having avoided the city while she'd traveled alone as a young woman in Europe. She had pointedly not gone to Italy when she'd heard that Italian men randomly and impulsively pinched women.

"Do you think I'll have to go to Rome?"

"It's possible," Hanson said. "But worse things have happened than a trip to Rome." Emily took note of a sound in the entryway and remembered the unknown man who, by now, must certainly have become restive. He might be deciding to go without having handed over the important, long-awaited envelope. She still behaved as if Nyal were in the house. Had he been there during the time prior to his illness, he would have heard the man at the door and come down. A mere two weeks had passed since his death, and the house seemed swollen and randomly eruptive. At times it pulsed with an absence that was a kind of presence, a hum of consciousness that ran parallel to her own movements in the rooms.

"I'm glad Nyal didn't have to bear this," she found herself saying to Hanson, as if Nyal could still somehow overhear. But what she really meant was that she was sorry she was having to bear it alone. "I have to go. There's someone here," she said, allowing a provocative edge to slip into her voice. They agreed to speak later. She paused a moment before hanging up, hoping Hanson would give a small reassurance that this trouble was likely to subside, but he gave none.

She hung up feeling betrayed by things beyond her control, as if some still trembling fiber of her dead husband's actions had brought them into an unfamiliar alliance. Why had he taken on the project of a house in a foreign country? This Riccardo—someone he'd known from his college days who'd married and settled in Italy—he'd involved Nyal, brought him in to solve an impasse on a project he'd begun. She only vaguely recalled. Nyal's expertise in the particular building materials had been important. But also something to do with an inflexible situation. Now some inflexible element had acquired another impetus. It was hardly conceivable that this had gotten so out of hand.

When she returned to the entryway she found the casually dressed, rather timorous man examining the quilt. Black arrowhead-like sets of V's dovetailed down the white fabric. There was something almost cruel about the pattern, but she identified with its pain-in-flight quality.

"It's the 'Widow's Quilt,' a nineteenth-century pattern," she said to the man. "But in the quilt books, the formal name is 'The Darts of Death.'"

"A lot of work there," the man said quietly, raising his eyes to her with what seemed a sepulchral gaze. He let the quilt edge slip from his fingers.

"I don't know quite where to use it. It's single-bed size." She felt at once she'd volunteered too much in speaking of a bed to a man she didn't know. She noticed him pull nervously on his jacket zipper, running it a short way down, then up toward his Adam's apple. There was a wedding ring on his hand. She felt herself drop her guard another notch.

"I have something to give you," the man said. The insupportable idea of the prize envelope fluttered tantalizingly again through Emily's mind. If it were to happen, it was a pity Nyal would miss it, she thought, characteristically undercutting anticipation with disappointment. The man definitively unzipped the jacket and reached inside to his shirt breast pocket. Next he extended a black leather holder the size of a checkbook and flipped it open to reveal a gold star on a dark velvet backing. It was a badge. It seemed the man was some sort of official.

"I'm a United States Deputy Marshal," he said, expertly returning the badge to his breast pocket. "And since you are Emily Fletcher, I have papers to leave with you. You'll need to sign, just to acknowledge you received them." He reached farther inside his jacket and brought forth a sheaf of official documents and handed them to her. She could see that everything, except the receipt form, was in another language.

"If you'd just sign here, please, Mrs. Fletcher," the man, said without the slightest doubt in his manner that she would comply. He now had the air of someone for whom these matters were beneath notice. He produced a black pen and handed it to her. She followed his index finger to a signature line, under which she saw her name typed. She was still quaking from having glimpsed the gold star. What exactly was a deputy marshal? She felt unable to speak the question aloud. To ask could invite a revelation as to the seriousness of the matter. Was she about to be arrested? She wanted to flee her own house.

She folded back the signature page and quickly scanned the

document for clues. It was in Italian, she confirmed from the legal address in Rome. Here, then, were the very documents her lawyer had feared were on the way. The word "press" came back from Hanson's characterization of what the aggrieved woman might do. She might "*press* on with things." A sexual verb, Emily thought. So here the woman was, indeed. Pressing on. It struck her oddly that the coincidence of her lawyer's warning had merged into the arrival of the process server. It carried an eerie resonance, as if something awful were masquerading as normal, a thought she had experienced most poignantly at the moment of Nyal's death, the way his breath, in its final rush, had been so cousined to a sigh.

Martin had said that when the woman telephoned three weeks ago, she'd claimed Nyal had once given her the number "in case I ever needed to reach your father." She'd informed Martin she would soon be taking the "necessary steps." Evidently it had not deterred the woman to learn from Martin that Nyal was terminally ill. Only after Nyal's death had Martin told Emily about having received this puzzling call. Maybe the woman, even now, believed and intended that her letters, followed by the serving of papers, would catch Nyal on the brink of his death. What sort of woman would do such a thing? She never wanted to become such a woman.

Emily held the papers and stared at her own name—again, the feeling of forces conjoining, of her consciousness swarmed with unsought intensity. She wanted to be rid of this man as quickly as possible. She moved her hand through the deft strokes with which she traversed her signature. During the days since her husband's death, she and their son had only once again referred to the woman in Italy.

"She can claim anything she likes, now that your father's dead," Emily had said. "She could claim they'd had an affair and that he promised her the moon!" The remark had flown out of her, and she'd reveled briefly in the absurdity of its fictional self-inflicted wound, or perhaps the wound had been meant indirectly for Martin. "To call you—she seems desperate," Emily said. Her son dismissed the woman as the sort of person who's delusional, who has nothing fruitful to do with her life, so she runs around, trying

to extort money and to get attention by threatening to sue. He'd
met this type, he said, in his job as an insurance adjuster. Martin
was forty-three, had a darling third wife and five children from
his two previous marriages. He loved to evaluate propositions,
buildings, objects, and the erotic parameters of any female with
whom he came into contact. Emily knew all this without surren-
dering affection for him. The more untrue he'd been to his wives,
the more attentive and solicitous he had tended to be toward her.
It consoled her now that he seemed to give no credence to this
woman's claims.

"I'm sorry," the bald man said, lifting the stapled pages to yet
another signature page. "Just here on the duplicate, if you'd be so
good." He pointed to a red X near a blank. Emily wasn't at all sure
she should be signing for these papers, but doing so was strangely
as simple as the fact that the pen was in her hand. She signed
again, then without replacing the cap, handed the pen back to the
man. His hands, like her own, were trembling. He was also finding the encounter stressful.

"Now," he said, and glanced pointedly toward the living room.
"Could you tell me, please, is Mr. Fletcher here?" He paused and
looked in the opposite direction toward the kitchen. "Or has he
relocated?" This second question startled her in the possibilities it
opened up. She thought of the woman's audacity in having telephoned her son, the invasiveness of her having insinuated a dis-
pute into such a time, when her husband's life had been reaching
its final days and hours. And now this woman, who should have
been in mourning, like herself, had propelled a process server
into her entryway. There had obviously been some delay in the
arrival of the papers, which must have been in the works prior to
Nyal's death. The U.S. Deputy Marshal probably did not read Italian and had no idea what this was about. He was restless and only
half-satisfied in his accomplishment. He tucked the signed re-
ceipts inside his jacket, allowing Emily to retain the sheaf of paper
in Italian. Then he regarded her, as if she were withholding something. He seemed precariously on the verge of becoming less
courteous. A set of undelivered papers still remained in his hands.

Emily's mind was speeding through the town. She could picture exactly where her husband lay—the freshly disturbed plot

which overlooked the town at its eastern edge. There was only a large evergreen wreath at the head of his grave with "Nyal" and "Beloved Husband & Father" in gold lettering on wide strands of velvet ribbon. It would be months before she arranged for the stone and decided what to inscribe on it, but there was a poem she already had in mind. It was a tanka by the Japanese poet Bashō—whose poem was modeled on yet another poem sent by a woman to a man after their first love-meeting. She might use only the first three lines:

> Was it you who came
> Or was it I who went—
> I do not remember.

She approved of the casualness of these lines, how they held a definitive absence in suspension, as some mere coming or going. The words would have yet another dimension, she realized, when her own remains eventually entered the plot beside her husband. It would be as if a conversation were still ongoing between them. Even while the poem subtracted their "remembering," it would insist on memory all the more for anyone who paused before the stone. But most of all, she agreed with how the words cast away life and death in one fell swoop. There was something at once simple and expansive in that motion.

"Yes, my husband *has* relocated," she said, bringing her attention back to the man. It occurred to her that although she had no control over the serving of these papers, she did hold sway over the exact moment in which she stood.

"Would you be so kind as to tell me where I might find Mr. Fletcher," the bald man said.

"Certainly," Emily said. She spoke clearly and decisively. "I'd be glad to help you find my husband." The man was clearly taken aback by her cooperativeness, as if he'd expected to be rudely dismissed. He shifted the remaining papers to his right hand and ran the hand with the wedding ring over the top of his pale head and let it drop. He then shifted his feet in a maneuver that brought him backwards and into contact with the widow's quilt. It was likely he'd experienced harsh treatment many times. His demeanor, she saw, had visibly softened when she said she would help. He did not smile, but dropped his shoulders, which had been held high and rather formally.

"There's a very nice view of the town where my husband has landed," Emily said. She disliked the casual implication of "landed" since she and Martin had carefully chosen the site. Nonetheless, she was determined to continue in this fashion, to reveal exactly where her husband was.

"Oh, very good," the man said. He resituated the sheaf of documents meant for her husband inside his jacket, then plunged a hand into his trouser pocket, jingling some loose change, no doubt an unconscious expression of delight at the surrender he assumed on her part.

"Go east on First, past the bowling alley and down Race until you come to Caroline," she directed. The man took a small notebook from a side jacket pocket and began to scribble. "Then turn right and continue past the hospital," Emily continued. "You'll approach some grassy fields, then go up a steep hill. At the top you'll find the development you're looking for." To call a graveyard a "development" would never have occurred to her, but she supposed death was a development. Still, her husband's death was beyond the word in such a physically challenging way that she felt an involuntary shiver run through her.

"I imagine there's a house number," the man said.

"If you need assistance to find exactly where Mr. Fletcher's situated," Emily said, "ask at the little white house just inside the gate. There's someone on duty until five p.m."

Emily thought she'd deflected the reference concerning the house number nicely. The man glanced at his watch, and Emily automatically checked her own. She saw that only half an hour remained for the man to get further help in finding her husband. He slipped the notebook with the instructions back into his side pocket.

"You've been most cooperative," he said, and glanced uncomprehendingly at the ferocious black darts of the Widow's Quilt which, as he brushed against it, seemed to be jutting directly into him. For a moment she thought crazily that, in his mute exuberance, he intended to embrace her. The idea made her quake, as when he'd flashed his deputy marshal's badge. She was relieved when he reached for the door handle and attempted to let himself out. She moved near his shoulder, turned the deadbolt, and moved back so he could pass through. On the steps he paused, turned toward her, and uttered some final sentence of courtesy, then crossed the driveway to his white Volvo. She was taking pleasure in the very fact of his going and that he would now be following her directions, this minion of the widow in Rome. He climbed into his car, then lifted his hand in a mild wave in her direction. She did not return the gesture.

She was thinking of her husband now, that he could not know these unpleasant things which had befallen her since his death, strangers who wanted to use his silence to beleaguer and ensnare her. Nyal would have enjoyed how she'd just acquitted herself. She imagined them laughing about the U.S. Deputy Marshal driving into the cemetery, hoping to be directed out of a wrong turn, asking the caretaker where Nyal Fletcher "lived." Well, the widow in Rome had misused Emily's husband, and now Emily would make use of her messenger. The man could stand before her husband's wreath as long as he wanted. Maybe Emily's circumstances would prick his heart. He might fully experience the weight of his actions that day. After all, they had each been reduced to functionaries.

She continued to follow the man in her mind as she gathered the quilt so the darts folded against her breasts and grazed her neck. She carried it upstairs to the queen-size bed she now occupied alone. She spread the quilt out on her side. With the pattern unfurled, the bed seemed to be sliced in two, but the quilt gave her side fresh vitality. Even though it was hours before bedtime, she unbuttoned her dress, stepped out, then lifted the covers and crawled between the sheets in her slip. The added weight was an unexpected comfort. She closed her eyes, then eased her hand onto her husband's side of the bed. It was cooler, and she realized that her cheeks, against the white pillowcase, were flushed.

She thought of the woman in Rome. What if? she thought, and Emily smiled to recall the moment with Martin in which she had cast her dead husband into the woman's arms, in a sentence uttered more as a challenge to the unlikely than a true possibility. But what would it change if her husband had sought the company of another woman? How casually the thought came to her. They had been married the same forty-five years. She believed they had loved each other beyond all others. She even recalled the exact site of her faith, her steadfast belief. One night before they were to go out in company, he'd put his arms around her at the door and said, "If I should ever say anything to annoy you while we're out, dear, ignore it, because I adore the ground you walk on." It was gallant and wide, and no one had said anything so beautiful to her before or since.

Death had added another dimension to that long-ago gift. Perhaps it was death, that ultimate release from belonging, which made even the idea of infidelity seem ludicrous. She suddenly caught a glimpse of a possibility she'd kept quietly in reserve. She wondered if all wives held aside a reserve of forgiveness for unrevealed betrayals, believing their husbands could, in some pull of opportunity, go astray, in fact, if not in heart? She had put aside such a reserve, she saw, without really having had to know it, until now. Yet: *so what?*

Prior to the Italian woman's intrusion, which had forced her to tremble in her own doorway, she'd had no idea of the degree to which she could still volunteer acceptance of all Nyal might have been. It was really in behalf of them both that she could manage this leap. At his death she had thought mistakenly that an end had come to the growth of their earthly loving, but instead she had stepped onto unexpected terrain, where what she held precious had become even more so. In these thoughts she was able to reach herself newly, and this both surprised and enlarged her sense of Nyal and of their life together. In her heart's reception of all her husband might have experienced, in and out of her knowledge, she saw with an ungaugable, onrushing force how deeply she'd loved him and loved him still. Would always love him.

"You're so very kind," the U.S. Deputy Marshal had said to her as he'd gone down the porch steps. Her throat tightened now as she recalled his words. She had not been at all kind toward this man, and by now he would be realizing this. What was there in being kind when life itself and the actions of others were often monstrous? Yet she continued to believe kindness was, when one could manage it, the ultimate checkmate, and beyond that, the one enviable gift. Yet could there be a hidden sleeve of malice inside too much kindness? Whatever else, she'd been true to her feeling.

Nyal's silence seemed more vast than ever, and she felt included there—allowing all things to be absorbed, to coexist—fidelity and infidelity, residence and grave, coming and going.

By now the man had likely reached his destination. He would have come to stand before the wreath. For a moment he might have studied the name on the fluttering ribbon. Then, deciding to go, he would have turned and begun to walk back to his car. Perhaps he was ruefully thinking of her this very moment, of how artfully she'd misled him. But maybe, if he hadn't passed too far into disgruntlement, he might pause and look back toward the grave, realizing that, on either side of the town, they could both be faintly smiling.

Fourteen

Kirby Dexter is forty-six years old, and for as long as he has practiced law, more than twenty years, he has thought of himself as someone who solves problems. He is a CPA as well as a tax attorney, and he is the person to call if you want something airtight. He is accustomed to an orderly cause and effect in his dealings with clients, and in his own life.

But lately this is less so. There are days when his clients seem crazy, their requests demanding and farfetched. And he cannot solve the cipher of his only child. Her name is Lizzie, and she is fourteen years old, and when she comes downstairs at seven-thirty each morning for her oranges—she eats two at breakfast every day, as if for survival—it is anyone's guess what she'll have on and what sort of mood she will be in. The only given is that she will be wearing a hat.

It is a Wednesday morning in May, and Kirby is in his kitchen, pacing. He wears what he wears most days: a Brooks Brothers suit and tie, oxford cloth shirt, and wingtips. He refills his coffee cup and stands at the sink, waiting for Lizzie and staring out at the golf course that his lot backs up to. They are running late. He splashes his coffee down the sink and is about to call her again when she comes into the kitchen.

"Morning," she says curtly, and she drops her backpack on the floor.

Kirby nods, looking her over. She has on a too-short plaid skirt, a denim shirt with the words "Property of Folsom Prison" stenciled across the front, black tights and combat boots, and a black bowler hat, a long way from what he would choose, but he is somewhat relieved: at least the important parts of her are covered up. He has lately developed a sympathetic understanding for Arab countries where girls are hidden away in veils at this age. He picks up his briefcase, old and battered and incongruous with his pressed suit, a gift from his wife fifteen years ago. Silver duct tape, which Kirby feels can fix just about anything, holds its worn corners together.

"Time to roll," he says.

"One sec," Lizzie says. She stuffs a pair of sweatpants into her backpack, then yanks the zipper closed.

He watches apprehensively. "Are you all right?" There is a steeliness about her this morning that worries him. And she looks tired; he heard her up during the night, but when he knocked on her door to see what was wrong, she only said she had leg cramps.

"I'm fine," she says matter-of-factly. She throws her backpack over her shoulder and takes two oranges from the blue bowl on the counter, then pulls the door open and flings the storm door outward. Lately it seems that everything she does is jerky and impatient.

"Lizzie," he says, "take it easy."

She is heading across the grass to the car, and she shoots him a *Yeah, right* look over her shoulder as she reaches his old Dodge. She pulls the passenger door open and makes a face as it creaks, then drops her backpack and the oranges on the front seat. "I have to check on Buick."

Kirby starts to say no, but knows it's useless where Buick is concerned. He sets his briefcase in the back seat and gets in the car and watches Lizzie walk to the ivy in the corner of the yard, Buick's spot, calling for the dog and clapping her hands, useless gestures in Buick's case. He is a mutt with traces of Labrador and shepherd, twelve years old and ghostly. Cataracts blur his vision and he is mostly deaf; the best way to get his attention in the house is to pound on the floor. Kirby thinks of him as Quasimodo's dog, the perfect companion for the Hunchback of Notre Dame. Lizzie loves him dearly.

Lizzie kneels in the ivy, then stands and leads Buick to the kitchen, her hand on his collar, as he stumbles alongside her. Once he's inside, she pulls the door closed, then hurries to the car. "I think he's sick," she says.

"He's old," Kirby says, turning out of the drive and heading toward town. "In fact, it's probably time—"

"He needs cortisone," Lizzie says. "Mom always—"

"He's more than old," Kirby says, and he hears the impatience in his voice. He has found it is not in him to talk about Sarah so casually. Not yet, at least. He tries again. "We have to start thinking about putting him down."

"My soccer game's at four," Lizzie says, her voice flat.

Kirby nods. "I know that," he starts, but when he looks at her, she is intent on peeling an orange, dropping the peels on the floor of his car along with the peels from perhaps a half a dozen other oranges that give his car a distinct, slightly bitter citrus scent that he somehow does not find unpleasant. He knows she can't wait to get out of the car, and he decides this conversation can wait.

He pulls up in front of the school, and has barely stopped the car when Lizzie pushes her door open. She leans close to Kirby and awkwardly kisses his cheek, her breath a mix of oranges and toothpaste, then she gets out of the car and is about to slam the door when Kirby sees a dark spot on the back of her plaid skirt. He looks at the seat next to him, and it, too, is stained.

"Lizzie."

She leans in the car. "Now what?"

"There's a stain on your skirt."

She looks at the seat immediately, then closes her eyes. "Oh piss," she says. She drops her backpack on the seat, yanks the zipper open, and pulls out a sweatshirt and sweatpants. She ties the sweatshirt around her waist, zips the backpack closed, and grabs the sweatpants. "Just go. I'll change in the girls' bathroom," and she slams the door and runs up the steps, and Kirby knows that he has somehow failed again, a feeling that has grown familiar.

It has been six months, and it happened like this: a Tuesday evening, Kirby and Sarah in the kitchen, her at the sink, rinsing snap peas, him at the table, reading the paper. She came and stood next to him and kissed his cheek.

"Hi," she said, and she smiled.

"Hi," he said, slightly puzzled. "You feeling better?" She'd been complaining of the flu during the week, only it never seemed to really grow into the flu; she said she just felt a little punk. She was holding a snap pea; she bit off half, and held the rest out to Kirby. He started to open his mouth, but for some reason took it in his fingers, then went back to his paper. It is a moment he regrets.

Then everything sped up; there was a thump, and Kirby thought Sarah had dropped something heavy, but when he looked to the end of the kitchen, she was lying on the floor, and the next few hours were nightmarish. The ambulance; the emergency room; the long night; the explanation of the aneurysm and its suddenness. When Kirby described the flu-like symptoms, the doctor nodded. "You see the symptoms in retrospect, but that's about it," he said. Kirby was staring at his old loafers, which were held together at the sides with duct tape. Lizzie was next to him, and when the doctor walked away, she held Kirby's arm tightly, but would not look at him. She slept at a neighbor's that night, while Kirby sat with Sarah, holding her hand. In the morning, when she died, Kirby sent the nurses from the room and closed the curtains, and sat quietly, stroking her fingers as he wept.

And now the only thing he can say is that time has passed. He has kept his practice going, and although he has not lost a client, it is not as effortless as it once was. He tries not to reflect that in his billing; no reason clients should have to pay for his distractedness. Lizzie goes up and down—her schoolwork has suffered, her appetite has decreased, she often sleeps only five hours a night—but they have no horror stories. As Kirby sees it, he's in a holding pattern, trying to bide his time until his life falls back into some kind of recognizable order.

It is a struggle to leave the office by three-thirty, which is what Kirby has to do to make Lizzie's game. He stops at Taylor's Pharmacy on the way and hurriedly finds the feminine hygiene aisle and scans the boxes lined up in front of him. There are more choices than seems necessary, but Kirby quickly settles on a box of Tampax Slender Regular Absorbency, throws in a bottle of Midol Teen, and pays.

Lizzie's soccer game today is a big one: her team is undefeated and is playing the only other undefeated team. Kirby parks and walks to the field, and when he is close, he spots Lizzie and Caitlin Porter, her best friend, their neighbor from across the golf course. Lizzie and Caitlin have linked arms and are singing a candy-bar jingle: "Gimme a break, gimme a break, break me off a piece of that Kit Kat Bar!" They are all show, laughing and kicking their legs in a modified cancan, as three boys hoot from the sidelines, boys who look, to Kirby, too large and too male to be watching his daughter like this. Lizzie's royal blue soccer shirt is tight across her chest, and while Kirby has known for some time that his daughter has breasts, the brand-newness of her curves and the attention from these boys are unsettling, and he finds himself brooding, fists stuffed in his pockets, as he walks.

He spots Caitlin's mom, Eve, on the sidelines and joins her. "Hi, there," he says. "I thought you'd be here."

She smiles at him hesitantly. "Hi," she says, and they look back at the field. The families used to be close—they live only a few houses apart on the golf course, and Lizzie and Caitlin are best friends—but they've grown apart lately. Eve and her husband separated a few months ago, and Kirby's found that no one knows quite how to act around him without Sarah.

He takes a folded paper from his inside coat pocket and hands it to Eve. "From your soon-to-be ex. It's a separate property agreement. Pretty straightforward, nothing that should come as a surprise."

Eve nods. "Thanks. Think this thing might actually be final one of these days?"

Kirby shrugs. "Stranger things have happened," and Eve squeezes his arm. Kirby looks at her, then at the field, where Lizzie is playing goalie during warm-up. He waves to her, and is startled when she glares at him in response.

"That was a look," Eve says.

Kirby shakes his head, baffled. "Where do you go to surrender?" he says. Eve smiles sympathetically and looks as though she is about to say something, but the game starts then, and they both look at the field.

From the beginning, play is fast and tough. At the half the score is tied, three goals each, and Lizzie's cheeks are flushed, her hair damp. She gulps cup after cup of water and pours it on her head and eats orange sections as though she's been starved. In the third quarter she is running for the ball when she is tripped by a player on the other team. She lands on her arm, and Kirby stares intently, trying to see her face. He combs his hand through his hair and touches his fingers to his lips as the ref glances at Lizzie, trying to gauge the seriousness of the injury. Then Lizzie is on her feet, and Kirby nods to her when she seems to glance in his direction, but she only glares at him again.

Fourth quarter, the score tied, and the other team is headed for the goal. Lizzie races toward the player with the ball, makes a clean tackle, and boots the ball away. But the whistle blows, and the ref calls Lizzie for tripping and signals a penalty kick for the other team. *Oh, now you call it,* Kirby thinks, frustrated, but he says nothing. Lizzie stares at her shoes, her arms ramrod straight at her sides, as the ref explains the call to her, and Kirby can see the anger in her face. He watches with dismay as she argues with the ref, who shrugs her off and starts to walk away from her. Then Lizzie says something else, and the ref stops and turns back, then motions to the coach that Lizzie has been yellow-carded for swearing. Four minutes remain; the penalty kick that results from the tripping call puts the other team ahead, and that's the game.

Kirby and Lizzie don't speak in the car. When they get home, he follows her inside, carrying the bag from the pharmacy. She heads upstairs, Kirby still following her, and he stops a few steps behind her, as they both stare at a streamer of toilet paper that leads to a wadded-up something stained with blood. He is bending down to pick it up when Lizzie clomps down the stairs, snatches the toilet paper before Kirby can reach it, and runs up to her room.

"Sorry," she says curtly. "Buick got into the trash. I'll clean everything up and put him outside, so please skip the lecture."

Kirby nods, remembering similar episodes with Sarah. "Fine," he says, slightly stung, "although there wasn't going to be one." But Lizzie has already closed her door. He follows her and knocks lightly.

When Kirby opens the door and steps into Lizzie's room, he feels as though he's entered a foreign country. The room's scent is a disorienting mixture of the gardenia shampoo she uses, her musk perfume, and baby lotion, and the room's order, if there is one, escapes him: clothes are draped over the desk chair, shoes litter the floor, silver bracelets and earrings glint on the dresser like currency. A coat rack in the corner holds Lizzie's hats: Mets and Yankees baseballs caps, berets, the bowler hat. A stranger could easily surmise that several people resided here.

Lizzie is sitting on the bed, working at the knots in her soccer shoes as though it is her employment. Kirby sets the bag from the pharmacy next to her. "I stopped at Taylor's. Thought you might need some things."

She doesn't look up. "Thanks. Sorry about your car. I'll clean it up."

Kirby waves her words away. "Already taken care of. That's what Clorox is for." He motions to the white corkboard that covers one wall, Sarah's idea last year. It has been empty for months. "I miss all that stuff you used to have up. The Grateful Dead. The Brazilian soccer team. I was just getting used to it."

"No you weren't."

"I was trying."

She glances at the empty wall as she pulls the first soccer shoe off and drops it unceremoniously on the floor. "I was tired of them."

Kirby nods, then he says, "Tough game."

She shrugs, but Kirby sees that she is fighting tears. "The coach yelled at me again. She says I don't pay attention, that she has to tell me everything twice. She said the tripping call was right and that I deserved the penalty." Lizzie drops the other shoe and looks at Kirby with an earnestness that he finds painful. "I do, though. I do listen."

He sees the image of his own cluttered desk, unheard of a few months ago, and smooths Lizzie's tangled hair. "It'll come," he says, but she shakes him off, and he knows he is being dismissed. He starts to leave the room, but something catches his eye, and he stops: Sarah's clock, Kirby's first gift to her, is sitting on the windowsill by Lizzie's bed. It is a small pale soapstone elephant, with the clock set in the middle. Kirby picks it up and weighs it in his palm. It is cool and solid and smooth.

"Where'd you find this?" he says.

Lizzie's cheeks redden. "In Mom's drawer," she falters. "I was looking for a comb."

"It's all right." He clears his throat. "I just hadn't seen it for a while."

He goes downstairs then. It's twilight outside, and the house is dim, but he doesn't turn on the lights. Lizzie said in the car she wasn't hungry, so Kirby just plunks frozen macaroni and cheese in the microwave, then eats it from its plastic container, only he's cooked it too long, and the cheese sauce burns the roof of his mouth. But he stands at the sink and stares out across the golf course and eats the too-hot food doggedly, as if to prove he can do it.

And then he sees Eve in her kitchen across the golf course. The lights are on, and she is standing at the sink, rinsing glasses, and all he knows is that he cannot stand his empty house and his daughter's silence tonight. He drops the empty macaroni and cheese container into the trash and finds Eve's number in Sarah's book in the kitchen drawer and does not allow himself to think about Sarah's handwriting, just punches the numbers.

He watches as Eve picks up the phone, and he says, "Hi, it's Kirby," certain that he sounds somehow foolish, but he forces himself to continue. "If you've looked over that agreement, I thought I'd pick it up and save you a trip."

Eve pauses, still standing at the sink, the phone held between her ear and shoulder, and Kirby watches as she rinses another glass, then holds it up to the light, inspecting it. He can hear water running. "I don't want to trouble you," she says.

"No trouble," Kirby says quickly. *No house,* he thinks, embarrassed at his relief at the prospect of company.

"Suit yourself," she says.

"I'm on my way," he says, and he hangs up. "Lizzie," he calls, intending to tell her he's going out, but she's right there in the doorway, glaring at him.

"How come you're going over there?" she says. She's holding a ball-point pen, and she clicks it a few times as though in warning.

"Legal stuff."

"I thought you weren't her lawyer." Click.

"I'm not. But I'm mediating, which requires that I talk to the woman now and then."

Lizzie nods, considering. "So I noticed." She pauses. "You know, you're not some bossa nova, some teenager."

"The bossa nova," Kirby says evenly, "is a Brazilian dance. I believe you mean Casanova, a reference to Giovanni Giacomo

Casanova, a notorious womanizer."

"Whatever," she says. "You know what I mean."

Kirby runs his hand through his hair and starts to answer her, but stops. *Choose your battles,* he thinks. "I won't be long," he says simply, and he leaves.

The night is cool and still as Kirby walks across the golf course. When he reaches Eve's, he steps over the small hedge and finds the yard painfully familiar, from picnics and barbecues and Easter egg hunts, but he forces himself to knock on the storm door, and Eve appears quickly and unlatches it. She's on the phone, and she mouths the word "Jay," then holds the door open for Kirby. She's wearing a pale peach kimono that Kirby sees her in when she walks her kids to the end of the driveway each morning, and he knows that she has just stepped out of the shower. He remembers that distinct female warm shower smell, and the way the steam seems to hover around a woman's body for a while. As she holds the door for him, the wide sleeve of her kimono falls open, and Kirby's gaze travels down the tunnel of that sleeve to her breast, round and lovely.

Eve hangs up the phone. "You coming inside?"

"Guess so," he says, feeling somehow caught.

He sits down at the kitchen table, and Eve pours him a glass of wine, then sits next to him, and Kirby wishes he could just sit next to her for a while, not even talking. She takes the folded agreement from the counter and puts it on the table. "Thanks."

He nods and puts the paper in his shirt pocket, then takes a drink, trying to remember the art of casual conversation with a woman. "How are the kids?"

She frowns. "With Jay tonight. Sometimes difficult, sometimes not." She sips her wine. "How's Liz?"

"Fine," he says. Then, "Difficult."

Eve is quiet, then says, "I miss you guys. I hear about Lizzie from Caitlin, and she comes over now and then, but it's awkward."

"We miss you, too," Kirby says. Eve smiles at him and smooths his hair, and then he says suddenly, "Would you like to have some dinner tonight?" surprising himself.

Eve shakes her head. "I have a date, Kirby," she says, but she leans forward and kisses his cheek. "But I'd take a rain check," and she smiles.

"Oh, sure, a date," he says, embarrassed, as though it's an unfamiliar concept he should have known, and he stands, almost knocking over his chair in the process. "I wasn't thinking."

"Well, like I said," Eve starts, but Kirby doesn't want the rest of the sentence, and he leaves as though taking flight and starts across the golf course toward his own house, which seems somehow less substantial from this distance.

In the kitchen he finds Lizzie's penciled scrawl on the Formica kitchen table: "Don't feed Buick. He threw up big time all over the kitchen." Kirby gets the bottle of Formula 409 from under the sink and wipes the table clean with the sponge, then calls to Lizzie that he's home. In the den he sits in front of the TV and flips between an old movie, a baseball game, and a program about open heart surgery, none of which holds his interest. The house feels vast and quiet, and at ten he hears the toilet in the upstairs hall bathroom flushing, water running, then Lizzie going back to bed. He goes upstairs to the bathroom cupboard he's so far managed to avoid and finds a box of Tampax and opens it and takes out what he hoped was there, a folded pamphlet provided in the box that he unfolds and smooths on the tile counter. He reads the fine print the way he would for a client, looking for something, anything, about the first time, the onset of menses. But there is nothing; only directions for inserting a tampon, nothing about what to expect, or what to do, or how to help. He starts to put the box back where he found it, behind Sarah's Neutrogena Body Oil and Chanel No. 5 and Chantilly Body Lotion, and he tries not to think about these things as he does it, to just close the cupboard door, but he cannot do it tonight. He takes everything out and holds the bottles and smells their contents, until Sarah's presence is so vivid that it hurts. And then he puts it all away.

He goes to Lizzie's room then. There is no light under her door, and he starts to turn the knob so that he can kiss her goodnight, which is what he does every night. But the door is locked, a first, leaving him standing in the hallway slightly stunned until Lizzie calls, "Goodnight, Dad. I'm fine," and he finds his way to his bed.

It is rare for Kirby to sleep through the night, and when he wakes at two in the morning, he mechanically gets out of bed, knowing that sleep will not return quickly. He goes to the closet and finds the pitching wedge he bought when he was in law school. Next to it is a cut-off plastic milk gallon that holds a dozen or so golf balls that Eve's son, Harley, gathers on the golf course and sells for a quarter apiece. Kirby takes the club and the makeshift bucket of balls and goes downstairs to hit from his backyard. He no longer golfs in the daytime—with friends and gin-and-tonics and the company of his wife and an occasional trophy. He is a middle-of-the-night golfer now: he has put up a floodlight that is aimed exactly toward the middle of the green so that it doesn't bother the neighbors and he can watch the ball in its course through the darkness.

He goes outside in his pajamas and robe, carrying his club and milk gallon. The night is still, the haze blurring the moon like gauze, and the trees look like cutout pictures. He is about to flip on the light when he sees headlights in Eve's driveway across the course. An unfamiliar car pulls into the drive and cuts its engine. Doors open, and a man walks Eve to her back door. They pause, and he holds her to him and kisses her. Kirby stands motionless, watching, until the man goes back to his car and Eve goes inside. And he watches still as the kitchen light goes on and Eve stands at the sink, her hands covering her face, and he knows she is crying. A few minutes pass, and she rinses her face with water, then flips off the light, and she's gone. As he hits ball after ball into the darkness, he aches.

Early the next morning, Kirby stands at the window, watching Lizzie haul her bike out of the garage and head down the driveway. She is going to the cemetery, something she does often. Kirby does not accompany her; he has not visited the grave since the funeral. He found the experience too much.

When he gets home that afternoon, Lizzie is not there yet. He leafs through the mail, sets the breakfast dishes in the dishwasher, looks in the refrigerator to see what there is for dinner, and comes up short; it will be pizza again. And then he sees Sarah's clock on the counter. He picks it up and holds it for a moment, and feels that if he holds it much longer, he will unravel.

He goes to the hall closet and gets an empty cardboard box. In the upstairs bath, he opens Sarah's cupboard and begins dropping bottles into the box, knowing only that he has to do something. This is only a start, he also knows that: he hasn't even begun to clean out Sarah's closet or her drawers. But it is something, and he is so intent on what he is doing that he doesn't notice when Lizzie opens the door.

"What are you doing?" she says, kneeling next to the box.

"I'm cleaning," Kirby says.

"These are Mom's things," Lizzie says, a discovery. She takes the bottle of Chanel No. 5 and sniffs. "This is Mom's," she whispers.

"They're not doing anyone any good here." He puts a bottle of sun block into the box.

Lizzie is silent for a moment, watching him, and then she says hesitantly, "Can I have them?"

Kirby stops and closes his eyes. "I don't know." He takes the last thing from the cupboard, a bottle of Johnson's Baby Powder, and places it in the box, acutely aware of Lizzie watching him all the while.

"It's like she was never here," she says softly.

Kirby cannot meet her gaze. "I'm only trying to get through the day," he says grimly, "and every time I come upon these things, I fall flat on my face." He shakes his head. "I can't do this, Liz."

"Why are you trying to get rid of her?" Lizzie says angrily. "You pack up her things, you start going after Mrs. Porter. You won't even talk about her. It's like, Poof! No Mom!"

"No," Kirby says tiredly, lifting the box, "it's not like that at all." He carries the box downstairs to the hall closet and places it on the floor; he'll figure out what to do with it later.

He goes to the kitchen then and dials the pizza place, no need to look up the number anymore, and he orders a small pizza that he knows they won't eat. When he hangs up, there is a knock on the door.

It's Eve. She's holding an open bottle of wine and seems suddenly shy. "From last night," she says. "I was wondering if you'd like to help me finish this off. It's been some kind of day," and she smiles.

Kirby nods. "It seems to be going around," he says, and he holds the door for her, then takes two juice glasses from the cupboard as though they do this every evening. "Didn't look like such a bad night," he says, watching her, and when she turns to him, he shrugs. "I've developed some strange sleep habits lately. I saw you come home."

Eve reaches for her glass, and her cheeks are flushed. "Sometimes things aren't what they seem," she says, and then her face clouds up.

Kirby hesitates, trying to think of something to say, but he finally just goes to her and takes her in his arms, and the feel of a woman's body against his is a forgotten pleasure suddenly remembered. When he kisses her and runs his hands along her back, everything is a rush. Still kissing her, he passes his hand over her breast. Her softness seems impossible, and somewhere he knows that the time and place are not right for this, but he can't quite let go of Eve.

And then he hears footsteps, and then Lizzie's voice. "Oh, great," she says, as Eve pulls away abruptly, but too late. Kirby turns, and Lizzie is in the doorway, glaring at them.

"Lizzie," Kirby starts, but she turns before he can continue, and he hears her pounding up the stairs, two at a time. He turns to Eve. "I'm sorry. I didn't mean to do that. I haven't touched—"

"It's okay," she says, and she starts to say something else, but there's a noise in the hallway then, a low whimper, and she stares at Kirby.

"Buick," he says. "He's sick."

Eve follows the sound and finds Buick lying at the foot of the stairs. She kneels next to him. "Oh, Kirby." Her voice cracks.

Kirby stands next to her, but cannot meet her gaze when she looks up at him.

"Kirby," she says again, more insistent.

He shakes his head.

She stands and looks him in the eye. "You're falling apart. You know that, don't you? Take a look. Lizzie's a stick; how much weight has she lost? Do you feed her at all? And this dog of yours should've been put to sleep weeks ago."

Kirby looks her in the eye. "Do you have any idea what you're talking about?"

"I just mean—"

"Do you?" he says again. "Do you have the slightest notion of what my life is like now?"

She leaves without answering.

Kirby and Lizzie don't do a lot of things that night: they don't talk while they don't eat pizza while they don't look at each other, and at eleven Kirby goes upstairs to bed, exhausted from the work of avoiding his daughter. There is no light from under Lizzie's door, and as he turns the knob so that he can kiss her goodnight, he finds the door locked again and feels a grim satisfaction; he knew it would be.

The next morning when he comes downstairs at seven, there is a note on the kitchen table—"Rode my bike. See ya"—and he has a fleeting but disturbing vision of the two of them going for months without talking, only these notes. He spends his day in a daze then, calling clients by the wrong names, searching for files, unable to finish even one small task—with the exception of calling the vet and making an appointment for Buick for the next afternoon—and when he gets home that evening, he feels ragged. Lizzie's backpack is on the table, and he guesses she's upstairs, but he doesn't go up there yet, knowing he can't quite face that locked door again. He finishes what's left of the orange juice, and when he goes to throw the carton away, the garbage is full. He mechanically lifts the bag and carries it to the trash can outside the back door. If he can just do these simple things, he is thinking, the evening will pass. As he carries the bag, he notices the plastic package from a doorknob stuffed on top. He starts to take it out to examine it, but hears a rustling sound from the corner of the yard where the lot backs up to the golf course. He follows it, and when he is at the edge of the ivy, he glimpses Lizzie's dark curly hair.

"Liz?" he calls.

"Yeah," she answers. "I'm here."

He cuts through the ivy and finds her digging, still in her soccer shorts and T-shirt and Yankees baseball cap. And then he sees Buick on the ground, a few feet away from the hole. "I found him here when I got home from practice," Lizzie says, her voice tight, "and I thought I should bury him. I called Dr. Mell. He said the hole has to be four feet deep."

Kirby nods, looking at Lizzie. Her eyes are swollen, her face streaked with dirt. She will not meet his gaze. "You didn't have to do this yourself," he says.

"I didn't want to ask *you*," she says.

He nods, stung, then goes to Buick and kneels and holds his fingers against the dog's neck and feels only the solid stillness of the dog's body. He stands, and Lizzie holds the shovel out to him without speaking.

Lizzie has gotten a good start on the hole, but the roots from the sycamore tree nearby make digging difficult, and he has to cut through them with the edge of the shovel. Lizzie stands a few feet away, watching. It is still light out, barely, and the air is warm. Kirby's shirt sticks to his back, and he feels sweat running down his face. Lightning bugs are beginning to appear, and the cicadas are loud as traffic. The last of the golfers cut across the course.

Finally, when he judges the hole to be deep enough, he stops and wipes his forehead on his sleeve, then kneels next to the dog and lifts him. It is an effort; Buick has lost some of his bulk over the last year, but he is still big, a good eighty pounds of dog. Kirby lays him on the old blue blanket that he's slept on since the arthritis started a few years ago, then folds the blanket over him and strokes his ear.

"Hey, Buick," Kirby says softly, "what a good dog you are." He wraps the dog up and lifts him and carefully steps into the grave and lays the dog in the earth. He wants to be done with this; the dog's body is already stiffening, and the air smells vaguely of decay.

When he has filled the hole, he smooths the dirt with the back of the shovel, and he and Lizzie walk to the house. He sees Eve watching them from her backyard, but he ignores her. As he follows Lizzie into the kitchen, he says, "I'm sorry. You shouldn't have had to do that."

Lizzie turns quickly, and her expression is anguished, but she says nothing, just hurries upstairs. Kirby follows, but he's not fast enough. She slams her door closed as he is on the last step, and he hears a sharp click as she locks it.

He leans heavily against the doorframe. "Lizzie," he says.

"Please go," she says.

"You need to unlock the door, or I'll get the key." He is trying to think where Sarah kept spare keys, and he looks at the doorknob and realizes that it is new and that he has no key. He tries it again, more to convince himself that it's real than to open it. It is cool and smooth and brand-new, hard as a weapon.

"Lizzie," he says softly, but there is only silence.

Kirby sinks to the floor then and leans against the wall. He has thought before that he and Lizzie have hit bottom, but from here, the floor by Lizzie's room, he has a new perspective on just how bad things can get.

It is dusk out. The streetlight outside flickers on through the hall window, and the doorknob catches its light, winking, a tease. He hears something downstairs, and he sees Eve standing motionless at the foot of the stairs. She puts a finger to her lips.

Kirby puts his hand on Lizzie's door. "Do you know what it means," he says, "to cop a plea?" There is no answer, and he takes a breath. "Say you try to rob a bank, and you're caught. You might confess to assault and get off on the robbery charge. You plead guilty to a lesser charge—in this case assault—to avoid standing trial for a more serious one." He pauses. "You'll say this is lawyer talk, but I'd like to cop a plea here. I miss your mom so much that some days I look at my watch three times in five minutes, and I can't imagine how the day will ever end. At work I need two hours to accomplish what used to take forty minutes. I don't sleep. I hit golf balls in the middle of the night. I do stupid, sense-less things, and I screw up, over and over again: if the answer's black, I'll guess white. But day in and day out, I tell people we're doing fine, all the while thinking that if I don't see your mom soon, I'll go nuts. It's like—" He clears his throat and lets his head rest on his folded arms. "It's like being fourteen," he says softly. "I've lost my bearings."

He looks at Eve then, and her expression is a mix of frustration and affection and worry, as familiar as breakfast. She stares at Kirby for a long moment, then mouths the words "Call me," and leaves without a sound.

Kirby smooths a place where the paint is chipped on the door. "I was at fault with Buick. He should have been put down, and I just didn't see how I was going to tell you that. And I don't know what to do about your mom's things." He takes a breath. "But I'm not trying to get rid of her. I just don't know how to do this."

He is quiet for a moment, listening to the silence of the house. "I'm worried about you. I need to see that you're all right, then I'll leave you alone."

He hears movement inside the room, then a quiet click as Lizzie unlocks the door. "Please don't be mad at me," she says.

"I'm far too exhausted for mad," he says, and he stands as Lizzie opens the door. "About this doorknob," Kirby starts, but he stops when he enters his daughter's room.

Lizzie's corkboard is covered—with jewelry, clothes, hats, scarves, photographs, letters, all of it Sarah's. Her blue and white pajamas are pinned up in the center, and the red bandanna that she wore when she painted or wallpapered is next to them, and next to that is the old straw hat she wore in the garden. The red dress she wore at Christmas is there, and so is the long black dress she wore on Halloween, when she dressed as a witch to greet trick-or-treaters. Her charm bracelet from high school is there, and her pearls—Kirby's wedding gift to her—and in between everything are photographs. Sarah and Kirby's wedding picture. Sarah pregnant. Sarah holding Buick as a puppy. Birthdays, Christmases, Easter Day. The wall is covered with his wife's belongings.

"Oh, Sarah," he says under his breath.

"Every morning when I came downstairs," Lizzie says tentatively, "Mom would say something nice to me. She'd say she liked my outfit, or that my hair was pretty, or that my smile was nice. A lot of times she'd tell me that my eyes were beautiful." She pauses and pulls up her socks. "I think she said that when she couldn't think of anything else, like when I wore stuff she didn't like or when my hair was wild. But I still believed her."

Kirby nods.

"I miss Mom," Lizzie says, and Kirby nods again, but he cannot take his eyes from his wife's pajamas. He remembers her laughing as he fumbled with the top's large white buttons when they were in bed. Lizzie was at a friend's for the night; it was the last time he made love to his wife.

When he finally turns to Lizzie, he finds her watching him

intently. He brushes her hair off her face, and it is as though he has uncovered something hidden: she is beautiful, and looks so much like Sarah that it is painful. He feels as though he's been struck, and he catches his breath.

"Are you going to make me take it down?" she says.

"No," he says, although he does not know how he will bear it. He looks at the pajamas again. There is something jaunty about them, as though their invisible wearer were joyful.

ANDREW SEAN GREER

Come Live with Me and Be My Love

Today is my fortieth birthday. I don't feel old at all. I've been sitting here for a while, on this courtyard bench, and if she's coming, then she's late. Married couples walk around, trying to interest each other, pointing to the faded pink walls and to the iron balustrades. The men tell the women facts from guidebooks, pretending these are things they know. Wind fans the blond hair of one young man as he takes a surreptitious photo of his bride. Photos aren't allowed here. She grins pinkly, arranges her white hat over an ear. I can see how happy this makes her—not the photo, but the consciously illegal pose. They'll look at the picture years from now and remember most of all the camera's secret whir.

I don't see anyone who looks like my wife, but then I'm not sure what she looks like these days. In college, where I first met her in the mid-sixties, she always showed up at places women never went—club theaters, professorial bars, psychology debates—and always entered late. It was her rule to be obvious. She'd show up in a brown plaid dress and blond hair curled in a neat cyclone on her head, and everyone would watch. They all would notice this strange thing—her eyebrows were painted on, and one was drawn in a hysterical, curious arch. That was what I first noticed in her: this painted expression.

We never talked until the day she grabbed me outside the refectory and insisted I go with her to audition for a movie filming in Providence. I refused until she intimated that my overbreeding showed in my lack of adventure. So I went, and I remember they wrote down on my card "handsome college type" and on Britta's "wild girl type" and we both got parts somehow. It was a terrible Rock Hudson movie, *Halls of Ivy*, and if you ever catch it late at night on television, you will see Britta's gigantic hat and laughing face emerge from Rock's shoulder. And even in that one second, the frame of action slows, drawn curling and enamored into the bewildering dream of her life.

So we dated for a while, the kind of formal dating set up back then. At least, that was how it began, but Britta wasn't interested in wearing a sweater across her shoulders and having me serenade her. I think she saw in me just enough reticence to be a challenge, just enough self-control, but also the kind of curiosity that, in spite of myself, made me smile and shake my head and follow her. The Rock Hudson movie, the greyhound races, the shop of occult necklaces and masks. She would try on a headdress of silver coins and turn to me, that eyebrow leering under the mail, and I thought here was a girl who could never come home to Kentucky.

Once in a while she went to my parties. There was one in 1964, a New Year's party in Boston held by a fellow I knew from the Jabberwocks, my singing group at Brown. It was a beautiful apartment, with an iron spiral staircase and brass Indian poppies littering the railing. It was Beacon Hill, and everybody there was Harvard or Yale or Brown; the rule was always *no Princeton ever* because they stole the girls. The Jabberwocks loved Britta, but you could see the other Pembroke girls in their navy woolen knee-socks and yellow oxford button-downs cringing, shocked sometimes at Britta's loud banging walk or clumsy maneuver with the matron's teapot. Britta embarrassed me, too, getting "clobbered," as the Jabberwocks liked to say, at cocktail parties and relating filthy stories to amazed young men, keeping us waiting forever while she searched a gutter for a Celtic necklace she had lost there—a hollow silver band which rattled at a touch, for inside were druidic talismans of hope. I bought her that necklace. She played an awful doubles tennis, but our opponents always asked for more matches because Britta's constant deep laughter was entrancing.

She and I walked into the upper room, and they had already run out of olives, so we had to drink Gibsons, which Britta pretended she preferred. A few men were in the corner singing a drunken "Aura Lee."

"You know where I'd rather be," Britta whispered to me.

"Do tell, darling," I replied, looking around at all the school ties.

"On an island."

"Any island, darling?"

She stared and me and clicked her tongue. "No no no. I'm very specific, and very serious. Saint Eustatius. It's Dutch, with a rain forest and a volcano and very mystical crabs..."

"Those islands are colder than you think. I've been there with my mother."

"But it'd be great. I wouldn't ever drink Gibsons, or listen to 'Aura Lee.' I'd be a pirate, a gilded white scorpion. Wouldn't it be wonderful?"

I didn't say anything, because I couldn't possibly imagine such a thing.

Out on the balcony, I caught my friend Marshall all alone, smoking a long cigarette and staring at a view he must have found tiresome.

"What kind of host are you?" I asked.

"It isn't my party, really. Sally wanted it." A Radcliffe girl he'd been seeing, and seemed bored with. He waved his hand girlishly. "You and Britta are my only friends here."

He must have said this for Britta's sake, for she was just then arriving through the glass door, saying something to a group inside who laughed suddenly and loudly. She turned to us, closed the door, and rolled her eyes.

Marshall blew smoke out and asked her, "How can you do it? Why does everybody love you, Britta?"

"Are you saying nobody loves *you*?" I broke in.

"Oh, that's no trick at all," Britta answered him, shaking her head seriously and pushing her dark lips into casual kiss. "You ask people about themselves. They go on and on and then turn and tell their girlfriends what a marvelous conversationalist you are."

I remember she smiled and turned away from him to go back inside, breaking her own rule to make Marshall think he had been let into some secret life of hers, a crueler one.

Marshall was new to the Jabberwocks, still a sophomore like me and slightly in awe of the secret ceremonies and histories of the group, though things like school and girls seemed not to interest him. He was tall, with curly red hair and nearly invisible eyebrows, but handsome and resolutely Irish in his chin and small, pink lips.

We had become friends only that Thanksgiving, when we were both invited to be on the Floor Committee of the National Debutante Cotillion in Washington. We took the train together, drinking Scotch the whole way, and met our stiff and beautiful debutante dates quite drunk, our hair messed up and our red sashes disarrayed. Presented on their fathers' arms on that giant stage, their escorts two steps behind, the girls were quite serious, but Marshall and I had a blast despite them. We had been to enough cotillions to be bored of the rituals. When the waltz came, and all the escorts were to tap the fathers' shoulders and release the girls into the world of men, we both took our dates into foolish jitterbugs, then waltzed off with each other to the bar. No one said a word, because Marshall's family was powerful—wealthy Washingtonian Democrats who had been invited to the front row of the Kennedy funeral. That night at the New Year's Eve party, I remember he wore a tie clip with a small photograph of Jack Kennedy under gold mesh. The tie was Andover. Mine was Kent School for Boys. Those things mattered to us then.

"Hey, Paul," he said to me. "Did Barick say you were moving up to tenor?"

"He's making me. He's crazy."

We were outside on a balcony, and it was cold. Yet we were drunk enough not to mind being alone out there. The only light came through the eyelet curtains, and it beaded on our backs like luminous rain we could not shake. The air was deep blue, and all in front of us, Boston spread out in a sagging post-Christmas carnival.

Marshall went on, "Oh, he likes the idea of a black-haired tenor. He's tired of us redhead Irish stealing the show every time."

"But I'm Irish. I'm Black Irish."

He seemed determined on this point, shaking his empty glass which glowed in the dim light like a deep-sea creature: "No, no. You, my friend, are Scotch Irish. You can tell from that nose you're a rogue clan. You have to have dominion over everything, especially women and horses. That's the South. That's your dear old Kentucky—every one of them rogue Scotch Irish."

"I've never thought of my dad as a rogue."

He turned away from me and lit a cigarette. "What does he do again?"

"He's on the radio."

"Runs the station?"

"No," I said, laughing a little and letting him pour me more gin from a bottle at his side. "He has a show. He's Mr. Social Security for Western Kentucky. They ask him questions, and he answers them. He's kind of famous."

"Wow. That's strange, Paul."

I pictured my family sitting in our living room in the summer, the electric fans blowing and my mother sorting her Butterick patterns while we listened to my father over the radio. He advised old, frightened Kentuckians in that countrified way of his about how the government would provide, always and forever. It was a government-sponsored show. "This is the Age of America," he always said to those folks, and they were grateful to hear it. Not long before he died, he told me he was proud to have comforted them, people who had lived through so much, their children always hungry, going to bed cold. My father knew all of that—his family lost a logging mill in the Depression. All of our money came from my mother.

I am proud of him now, but back then it was an embarrassment. I did not know why I was so anxious to impress Marshall, but there he sat, his hair gleaming from the apartment lights, that school tie, the beautiful way his white hand rose above his head to touch the brick.

"I have to go and host," he said, looking up at his own hand. His neck was thin and half-shadowed as it stretched.

I leaned to let the light catch my watch. "But it's almost midnight. You have to stay just a few minutes."

Marshall brought his face down, but his hand played with the brick. I remember he smiled drunkenly. "I should be inside," he said. "Sally will want to be near me when it comes time to kiss." I chuckled, sounding like my father in my false comfort.

"All right, you bastard." I stood up and felt the chill of the air. I turned towards him, and the light from the apartment's curtains dotted me. I must have seemed mystical in that pointillism, seen through a filigree. He sat for a moment, then needed a hand getting out of the chair, so I pulled on his wrist. He was very light, and his wrist was adolescently bony, and cool. Marshall was only nineteen. So was I. That was a long time ago.

Noises came from the apartment, foolish clacking noisemakers and bells and those shrill plastic horns. All of the cabs on the street began to honk merrily, and a whistling firecracker went off somewhere below.

"So I have to go," he said. But now there was something fierce in the air: he looked panicked, as if having to go were a frightening thing. His pale face became ruddy, fiery at the cheeks. He jammed his lips together.

I said the sort of thing we always said: "Well, give Sally a kiss for me, too."

But it wasn't the right thing to say. Marshall still stared around him, searching all the tiles of the balcony. He only said, "I will. Tell Britta I'll marry her."

Laughter came loudly from some men inside, and our singing group began to sing "Auld Lang Syne" in Scottish accents.

"I guess we should be inside," I said.

"No," Marshall said, giving a sudden look, bright and insistent. We stood there for a moment. As he stared, his cheeks burned away in the cold air. I know what the look was now. I suppose I must have appeared the same way. It was: *This is the word I've been searching for all day.*

"What is it?" I asked.

"Nothing, just let's not go in just now."

"All right." I put out my right arm to settle him, touch his sleeve, but it felt ghostly, as if it floated out by itself in the dark light. Marshall must have seen my hand palm-out to him. He grimaced at me and crossed his arms, and I put my hand back in my pocket. Or rather—the hand floated back to my pocket. We were both shaking with an uncertain shame, and shame was such an important part of our upbringings. It must have been that which made me smile, despite all my discomfort.

It was the most frightening moment of my life up until then, because somehow I knew neither of us wanted to be in there with our girls. We waited because it seemed someone had something honest and painful to say, but it was not said, so we stood half-shivering, amazed and innocent on that balcony, only nineteen and wearing the foolish ties of our boys' schools. Certainly in that moment I was loved by someone.

And then Britta walked onto the balcony. I turned my whole

body away from Marshall to face her.

"It's 1965," she said, then waved her hand. "So are you guys going to kiss or what?"

Marshall looked at me and laughed, then nodded and put out his palm. We shook hands—ridiculous—then he left through the glass door. Britta watched his progress through the room, the various stolen kisses I could hear but not see, then she folded her arms and looked at me, shivering. She looked radiantly happy.

"What?" I asked. She shrugged her shoulders. "What?"

I walked forward and kissed her for the first time. We had been dating for a while, but never had I kissed her because Pembroke girls were notorious for anger at such points. And Britta always laughed and turned away whenever we were close enough. She let me kiss her for a moment on that Beacon Hill balcony, then pulled away, and her face was as angry as I'd imagined. I thought to myself, *You did it wrong again.* But she patted my shoulder, as if the anger were about something else entirely.

"You're a puzzle, Mr. Robinson," she said.

"Not really."

"No," she said, smiling. "Not really."

Britta walked over to the balcony and leaned over the rail, thrusting her head up to catch the new wind. I stood behind her and watched her gold hairdo unravel.

I finally pulled out a cigarette and offered one to her. When Britta turned around, I tried to read her mind, but as usual it was impossible. I had dated many girls with wide expressions, but Britta was illegible. She took the cigarette and let me light it in her hand. She looked up into my eyes when she was done with the flame. She would always do that.

Near the end of sophomore year, I caught mono, which was a bad thing for the Jabberwocks because Marshall was sick, too, and we were the only tenors who could hit "How High the Moon." Also, Providence was warm and plush with magnolia at that time of year, and all the Pembroke girls would waltz down Thayer arm in arm, their Bermudas flapping and their capped teeth dazzling each bitter young man they teased. So I lay in my dorm room, my roommate having dropped out a month before and gone back to

New York City. I watched the fraternity men throwing footballs and shouting names of girls they loved too much.

Britta pounded the door in that way of hers to find me dressing for a Jabberwock cocktail party with the university president. I remember she was all in green lace, a dress and a vest, with a worn, brown leather bag thrown over her shoulder. She kept yelling at me to get back into bed, and when I wouldn't and stood delirious in front of the mirror fixing my Windsor knot, she offered me at least a cup of tea. I drank it all down, and within minutes I was dead asleep on my bed.

I woke up hours later to find Britta smearing cold cream on my face and humming faintly. She had tied her hair up and taken off her vest, so she was only in that green lace dress.

"Ah," she said. "You're alive again."

"God, what happened?"

"Oh, I drugged your tea."

I couldn't move, but sat there feeling her rub the cream into my skin.

"What?" I complained faintly.

"Don't move. I'm cleaning your face. Being sick makes you greasy."

"You mickeyed my tea? Are you a Communist or something?"

Britta wiped her hands off on a towel and knitted her brow. "I wasn't going to let you meet President Keeney feverish and strange, was I?"

"That's illegal, Britta."

She snickered at that and brought over a box of Kleenex to wipe off the cold cream. My view of her face was blocked by those tissues passing over me like clouds.

"How do you know," I began again, "that I'm not on some drug which would react strongly to sleeping pills?"

"Don't be a child, Paul," she said. "Sit back. I'm going to give you a dry shampoo now, so don't move."

"A dry shampoo?"

"You look awful." Britta brought out a bottle of baby powder and began sprinkling it in her palms. "Besides," she said, "I want to talk to you about something."

She dangled her fingers above my face, and some powder

snowed down on me. Then she slid her hands into my hair, rubbing at my sick scalp and cleaning me all over. I felt utterly helpless and ill, and she was cleaning me.

"What . . . ," I said, "what do we have to talk about that you must drug me?"

"I'm tired of living in the dorms, Paul."

"Yeah, really."

"You are, too, right?"

"Those frat guys drive me crazy with their boozing."

"So we're both tired of living in the dorms."

"I applied for off-campus permission," I said, closing my eyes as she stroked my head with powder. It was a lovely feeling.

I heard Britta say, "You know that won't work. No one gets off-campus permission except married couples. You have to be married."

"Right," I said. I sat there for a moment, eyes closed, until I realized she was staring at me. I looked up, and she took her hands out of my hair and put them on her lap. She sat very lady-like on my bed, the dainty dress, the neat green ribbon around her throat, her wide pretty face, the hair slightly wild piled on her head. She was expecting me to be wise at that moment.

"Oh, Britta," I said, "we've only been dating for a little while."

Then her composure dropped, and she laughed. She got up off my bed and walked to my door.

"We haven't been dating, Paul. You kissed me once, half a year ago." Britta closed the door and locked it. She leaned against it and widened her eyes at me. It almost looked like pity.

"What is it, then?" I demanded. "I spend every waking hour with a girl, and we're not dating? And now you want marriage?"

"Paul," she said, her chin to her chest, "we're not lovers. We're beards."

The men playing football began to sing the Brown fight song. It had a "Ki-yi-yi" in the chorus. "What does that mean?" I asked. The moment was entirely frightening to me. Britta seemed a nightmare creature of my delirium at that second, instead of my best friend.

"We're covers. We're false lovers, because we can't tell anyone who we really love, can we?"

"Who is it?" I asked, sarcastic and fearful. "Who is that I *really* love?"

"Paul, I've met your father," she said, walking towards me. "He would disown you. I know my father would disown me. They love us, but they'd kill us before they knew. And then what kind of life would we have? Not this one. I like this one."

"Who is this 'secret lover' of mine?"

"What a relief to just be married like they want."

"You've got mono," I said confidently. "You're the sick one now."

"No," she said, sitting on the bed and putting her hand over mine. "Marshall is. You and he have mono together."

I threw her hand from me. I felt nauseated. "What are you saying?" I said. I raged my fingers through my hair to get the filthy powder out of it. A cloud surrounded me, but Britta didn't laugh this time. She put her finger to her lips and whispered harshly:

"I don't want to talk about it. I have women lovers whom you need never meet nor mention. I'm not asking to discuss your love life. I'd rather we never discussed it. I'm asking for you to listen this once, Paul." She put her hands on either side of my chest, and a worried look came over her face. "We're unlucky. People are talking, Paul. Saying I'm a man, and you're a pansy. If we make a mistake, we could be ugly to the world, but we're smart. And we're creative."

I said nothing. Powder settled on her dress.

I will never understand how Britta knew everything I did or felt. It had only been a few months before, over spring break, that I had gone to Marshall's house on Long Island. I always did this— there was no special occasion. His parents were gone, as they usually were when he asked them, and we spent a few days getting cold in walks along the gray beaches. We became more and more silent with each other, and yet I was insistent that we take these walks. There was some kind of tea dance going on at Shelter Island, and that afternoon I suggested we go. I wanted to distract him from whatever was worrying him—I'm sure I needed distraction, too. There was a faint flurry falling outside, unseasonable, and Marshall had lit a fire. He was proud of the fire. There was something in his father which always made Marshall pointedly manly. So he stoked the fire in his thick gray sweater and, not looking at me, agreed. Then he suggested we arrive roaring drunk. Of course this idea came like a relief.

His father had a habit of storing half-drunk martinis in the freezer and forgetting them, so we started with those—there was no other gin in the house. Then we mixed drinks for each other. Not cruelly, though it began that way, but exotically. We made drinks like vodka and crème de menthe, which Marshall held up to his red hair. He knew doing that would make him beautiful. He made me drinks of blue-eyed curaçao. Soon it was dark, and we forgot all about the tea dance, perhaps had never really meant to go.

I remember watching him talk. I thought it was a trick of my heart. But there, just for a moment in his eyes, his parted lips, I could tell his mind was whirring. I saw the muscles twitch. But really, in the Yankee conversation and polite eyes, it was only a passing, deep, unordinary instant, and I thought it must have been the colored drinks he kept handing me.

Marshall played records for me, songs I didn't quite like then— modern jazz and odd, foreign classical—but we danced with invisible debutantes. We made false conversation to them, ridiculed them. We practiced shaming them with cool WASP weapons. Then we danced with each other, silent, not touching, and then, of course, wrapped warmly like an old couple near the end of the night. Then our heads tilted back, and I looked at him. Marshall's face was in a shadow, his stare at me the only bright thing there, but I could hear a tiny noise come from him, a kind of realization—*huh*—and then he smiled. And then, to make him close his eyes, I kissed him.

The bed we awoke in was two hundred years old, and it surprised me that nothing was different in the snowless morning. I began the lover's doubts: *Why is he not holding me? And there, now he's turned over as he wakes and he's looking at me. There, now he's holding my hand. What does he mean?* I caught his eye as seldom as I could, out of simple fear. And I almost bolted—only because I knew he was not going to leave.

"Think about it, Paul," Britta said to me that day of her proposal. "You're in trouble now, but this could make things very easy."

I turned away from her, out to the window where the other men beat each other on the back out of laughing brotherhood, which was also a kind of loneliness.

"I'm asking now because I'm getting scared for us," she said, getting up and pulling her brown bag off the floor. "And because that yellow house on the hill is for sale. Remember we walked by that house, with the white columns and the widow's walk?"

There was a knock on the door, and a look came over her face like a child caught burying her allowance. It was a lovely face, serious and innocent. Britta glanced at me and unlocked the door. Two boys from my singing group came in, with a Mason jar of chicken soup and a folder of dirty pictures. They were quiet around Britta, but after she left they told me about the Jabberwock party the night before and produced a note from Marshall, sick a floor below me, a note sealed in an envelope. They showed a boyish awe when I told them I was engaged.

Britta and I were married in October, in a small ceremony in Maine. She wore a band of daisies in her hair, and a white ribbon trailed down her back onto the ground. Marshall was my best man. I did not know the woman Britta chose as maid of honor, but she was beautiful and brunette and nice enough. The Jabberwocks sang at the reception, and Britta and I danced to "How High the Moon." Marshall sang the solo, looking at me the whole while I spun that grinning, ribboned young woman around the floor.

My mother bought us the yellow house on Meeting Street, and when Britta came wide-eyed into my bedroom with a photograph of a divan she'd cut out of *The New Yorker,* my mother helped us buy that, too. I still have that divan. The wood is deep yellow, and a sea of striped white silk covers it. We had an upright piano, a Baldwin, and acres of bookcases were built into the walls to house Britta's collection of foreign books and fairy tales. My bedroom was the "master" bedroom, and my wife slept in the guest bed draped in a ridiculous fall of mosquito netting, which she said made her feel exotic and safe. We were twenty, the same age as my parents when they were married.

The arrangements were unspoken but clear. Marshall came

over "for dinner" as often as I liked, but he never interfered in the time Britta and I had together. Sometimes I would bring out five ingredients and dare her to make a dinner from them, and she always took the dare. And her meals were always abysmal. Her frequent lovers came through back stairs and parked in the church lot. I rarely met them except late at night, when I crept downstairs for a book and found Britta and a woman, beautiful and sweet or harsh or distantly intelligent, whispering sincerely over sherry. Britta was never angry to see me. She always pulled her peacocked kimono close around her breast and smiled.

Britta often saw ghosts and haunts around this old merchant town, and sometimes sat in her guest bed throwing coins to tell the future of all her friends. She would yell out the fortunes to me, things that never made any sense: "A woman," I would hear through the wall at night, "crosses from a wide lake to a river," as if that explained it all.

We didn't live through the sixties, not the sixties everyone else seems to remember. I had Communist friends, but no one who would blow up the Supreme Court for a cause. They were Brown men who despised their parents' fortunes, wore only Salvation Army brown cotton jackets, but always their gold watches and rings gave them away. We listened to Dave Brubeck and not Charlie Parker, Tom Lehrer instead of Woody Guthrie, because what we sought was cleverness and not sincerity. None of our crowd stormed University Hall, and we watched with only mild interest as more and more colored boys entered our classes. It neither upset nor thrilled us. The change was utterly separate from the lives we had always led.

Marshall threw a party in my honor at our graduation in the spring of 1967. It was in the mansion of an old faggot professor we knew, a mansion down on Benefit Street with its cobblestones and brass horse-rails. A young Portuguese boy had been hired to ensure no champagne glass ever got below halfway full—he crept around handsomely, insistent with his bottle. Soon couples were dancing on the furniture, the Pembroke girls laughing in that silly way and loosening the tuxedo ties of my Jabberwock brothers. Marshall poured half a glass into my hair and messed it around with his hand. His own hair, I remember, was copper and curled from the heat of dancing, smoothed back with sweat as if he were from the thirties. He laughed and looked around for someone else to torment. It pained me that even at my party I couldn't simply reach over to this man I loved so achingly and brush an eyelash stuck to his cheek. Too intimate, too kind. He faded off into a crowd.

"I saw a ghost in our house," said my wife beside me.

I looked at her, and sadness must have been on my face, because Britta's smile fell for a moment and she lowered her shining glass. She wore blue-black velvet and luminous false pearl earrings in gold.

"You what?" I asked, breathless.

"Are you all right, Paul?"

"You saw a ghost? Tonight?"

"No," she said, then took a sip of champagne as a forty-five of the Kingston Trio came on to boos and hisses. "In our house. It was a man."

"Were you scared?"

"Would you ask that if it were a woman? No. It was a very old man, very tired, I think."

"Did he say anything? Where was this?"

"In the kitchen. Just before we came. He didn't say anything," Britta said, putting her hand to her chest. "He stood there confused as if it were an accident, the wrong house, maybe the wrong life to interrupt, and he stared at me not knowing what he was supposed to be doing."

"What did you do?"

"I stared at him the same way...I think...and then he was gone."

Britta looked at me, thinking to herself. One of the baritones asked her to dance, and she smiled back at me regretfully, flashing her marriage band, then giving a vampire face meant, I suppose, to scare me back into the party. I was thinking about other things, too drunk to separate the petty from the profound.

Marshall was caught up in this graduation. I think he was obsessively worried about his life after this, giving up all this to work for his father, or, perhaps worse, to go to law school. And maybe he was afraid I'd move away—I still don't know. But something made him shake me away when I grabbed his arm and whispered for him to be quiet—he was saying uncharacteristic things to young men. His glare wasn't just anger—he was sad, maybe disappointed in something, maybe in me.

The party went on all night in that old merchant house. I remember that the walls were striped with gold paper and that iron sconces lit up faces with flattering candlelight and shadow. Otherwise, the evening passed as many other evenings had in Providence, and even graduation did not frighten those of us secure in futures there and in wives. I passed out in a dining room chair, and awoke to someone telling me the baritone had kindly driven my wife home to bed. Britta was famous for never saying goodbye. I fell back to sleep with those walls of gold stripes papering my dreams.

In the morning, I was on the Oriental rug. I got up to go to the bathroom, and felt the left side of my face was ragged and burned from the carpet I'd slept on. I saw others asleep and drugged on couches, their jackets or wraps thrown over them by someone kind and sober, the sun reaching over them to light the paintings framed on the walls, all of willow trees. Outside, a radio was playing "Aura Lee." I climbed up the spiral stairs to the bathroom, but there was someone inside coughing. I thought maybe I'd try one in the master suite—the professor had already left, and the door was half-open. So I crept inside.

There on the green silk covers lay my lover, Marshall, and the Portuguese boy, drunk and dead asleep, shirtless and embracing with a harem of embroidered pillows fallen around them. I remember them well. I remember most of all how sweet they looked, how honest, really. Though he was a liar to me, my lover seemed so poignant with that dark boy clutched to him, as if they comforted each other the way young boys do when they have lost a thing together. I leaned heavily against the door and watched the room for a while. The light came in through sheer white curtains, slow as a tide. All around the ceiling, urns with wreaths were stenciled, and above the bed a blue cherub holding a bird. A common bird: a sparrow.

I remember the only thought that went through my head as I walked home in my rumpled evening clothes: *I have no claim on him.* No one knew I loved him. I assumed no one ever would, not even Marshall now.

When I came back to our house that morning, I called out Britta's name, and no one answered. The wooden floors glowed yellow with the May sun, and all the glass door handles sparked with light as if electric or releasing secrets. Perfume from some early morning bath still hung in the air—eucalyptus, I remember—and it scented the cold white walls, the framed maps of Maine and Rhode Island, made them intriguing, as if they trapped inside their surfaces unimaginable gardens. I remember it, of course, as beautiful and strange, and yet I am sure it is only memory because I know I slumped into an armchair and began to cry.

I don't know when I had ever cried before that, not since grade school, certainly, rarely in front of anyone and never in front of my father, but all alone in that warm wooden room, I wept, and because I was so out of practice, I wept loudly and badly. I panted and held my face to stop the pain there, speaking half-words to convince myself of a grief that needed no convincing, spitting long jeweled strands of saliva onto my lap as I bent over. My jaw shook, humiliated. The sounds I made were ghastly, but this was too much pain. I could not bear it. So I sat there childishly blubbering into the fabric, lost and generous at last with my pain, shipwrecking myself over and over against my old memory of love.

I felt my wife's hand against my shoulder. I was not alone at all. I could not look up, so ashamed with this fit, coughing up the tears. I was so ashamed Britta should see me prone over a red-haired dilettante. I leaned more into the nubbed pink fabric. I turned away. She should never see me like this, never, not this friend. But I felt her other hand against my arm, and then her cold face beside mine. She did not hold me but floated next to me, silent. We said nothing, and never spoke of it again, but with her gold hair stuck to my wet face and that smell of eucalyptus strong again, I knew there was a part of me, the greater part, which would endure.

We lived on Meeting Street long after graduation. In 1972, I was still working at the Brown Alumni Center. It was good enough, and Britta went back to school so she could open up a psychology practice. I heard Marshall went to Boston to work for his father for a while, but after a year he came back to Providence, bought a house near ours. A pink house—it showed how much he needed to be near, that he would buy a pink house. I know now he planned his day to run into me, just catch my eye outside the center, and after a while I spoke cordially to him. In those conversations he was confident, talking about law school at what we considered a lesser college in the area, applying to a better school, by which he meant a better name. And one day I took him back, and it was because the sky was bright around his face. I remember it made Marshall the focus of the air, with sky bent to his eyes like that eerie crème de menthe the night I kissed him.

And Britta had taken a more steady lover, a French woman named Nathalie who worked as a designer. I will admit I never liked her much. She was very quiet. She had a habit of sitting and listening to Britta and me jabber away, just sitting with the pink tip of her tongue sticking out between her lips, the way you see older cats do. But Britta loved something about her. I heard my wife laughing in her bedroom when Nathalie came over, but never saw this part of her lover myself. When Nathalie cooked her sacred cassoulets, Britta watched her from the kitchen doorway with a rapt, patient gaze, as if her lover were a book she read for pleasure. We never know what friends see in their lovers. We always expect they will see what they see in us, but it isn't true. What we hate in friends' lovers is a hoard of private moments we thought we would inherit.

She left Britta after some years. I forgot to say she was a married woman, and she decided it was her husband she really loved. Britta and I never spoke of it, but about a week afterwards, I took her to Boston to see her favorite place: the Isabella Stewart Gardner Museum. The idea of visiting an old dead woman's house just to see her paintings and her giant pink courtyard made me queasy, but I went for Britta. Marshall, visiting Harvard Law, joined us at the blunt medieval entrance. Britta said she wanted to see one particular painting, "The Birth of Athena," and we toured the balconied, decorated corridors until we came into a red silk room, silver chalices against the window catching sun, paintings all around us in leafy gilt frames, hung with wires from the molding, every one on them entitled "The Birth of Athena." Britta let out one throaty laugh, bending over with her hands clasped. Then she pinched her lips together and looked at me and Marshall wide-eyed. I think her loudness made me furious. That must have amused her even more, because she walked up to one of the paintings, dark foliage with a gleaming white god clutching his head.

"Now here," she said seriously, "here we have a Grecian forest, and what's happening is there's this crack in Zeus's skull, and who pops out of it is Athena." Britta walked to a painting next to it, bright green.

"This one's a little different," she said, considering it. "This one's about Athena popping out of Zeus's skull."

Then Marshall burst out in high laughter. I turned, surprised. Marshall was not one to laugh in public places, and I saw for really the first time that Britta and Marshall knew something I didn't. My lover pointed to a cartoon below the painting. "You should look at this drawing," he said, "because it's very unique. It's about this skull, you see..."

"Is it Zeus's?" she asked.

"And Athena pops out."

They snickered together, and a gold-buttoned guard came over. I turned away, delighted but ashamed to cause a scene in such a sacred place: a home, and a museum. The guard made us move along into the courtyard, my wife and lover arm in arm, unable to stop laughing at a joke I didn't quite understand. Britta wore a black jumpsuit and a wide black straw hat, which she held to her head as they strode past the yellow roses. There was a blueberry bush, and Marshall stood still as Britta moved slowly toward it. I don't know why he stopped—maybe he knew to let her walk on.

He did not look back at me. It was not our moment together watching her. It was his moment, seeing in her some loss he recognized. Something I'd never noticed, never thought of after years seeing her with her occult necklaces, batting at the mosquito netting of her bed, and giggling as if love could not be squandered.

So we watched her walk into the blueberries. A tulip tree shaded her there, and she stood inside that shadow, turning slowly and taking in the peeling pink on the museum's walls. I admired her, absorbed in the circle she was creating as slowly as a black-eyed Susan might spread its petals. The crowd around us was giddy with noise, but the main sound I remember was the clicking of her shoes and the buzzing of the heat that day.

I walked over to her. Marshall finally looked at me. I caught his eye, and he seemed to be examining me, the black-haired man, and not critically. As if I'd shown him some new talent in marrying such a woman.

"You all right?" I asked my wife when I reached her.

She stopped at once and looked at me. She smiled—her wide smile with teeth which I knew was her fake one, though it was beautiful.

"Why? Yes."

"You want to leave?"

She sounded oddly relieved. She took off her hat and looked up into that one tulip tree in this city museum. "No, this is nice. I was just thinking." Britta picked a berry off the bush and put it in her mouth. She quickly removed it and made a face. "These blueberries are terrible!"

"They're still green, darling."

She glared at the tiny fruit in her hand, then threw it away and blinked at me. "So they are, darling."

Marshall came up behind me. He put his hand in my coat pocket. It was one of our secret signs of intimacy, as if he were searching my coat, when really it meant: *Here I am.*

"She loved you, Britta," was what he said, and I still am surprised he said it. I didn't know he saw those things in people.

"No," she said. "You can only love one at a time. Apparently it's a rule. Like in chess."

"Britta," I tried, "Nathalie wasn't really right, and you know..."

She put her hat back on and interrupted, "No, it's fine. It's not a big deal, really. Let's go back and see the dungeon." She flicked a smile and walked past me and my lover into the sunlight.

"Britta..."

She turned around and faced us, faced me, both hands holding her hat against the wind. Her mouth broke down right then, just snapped in two like a twig. We all simply stood there, and she shuddered. I watched her pain pooling out into her face, her shaking hand moving to wipe her cheek, and she stared at me with the fear we had never spoken of except in that one silent moment when she held me, smelling of eucalyptus, on another bright, sad day.

"Here's something I want," she said, moving her head from Marshall to me. "If we never see each other again, we should still all meet every year right here," she said, tapping the table, "in the courtyard."

"No," Marshall said, glancing at me, "in the 'Birth of Athena' room."

Britta laughed and said, "Oh, yes, yes. But they only hang the paintings on off-years, so every other year, then."

"When?" I asked at last.

"Today," Britta said, raising her eyebrows, "on your birthday, darling."

"But we're not going anywhere, Britta. We see each other every day."

She put her hands out in honesty, and the hat got away from her. I ran out after it as it rolled around the hot air and into the yellow roses. I pulled it from the thorns, and Britta was laughing to Marshall again, arms tight around herself, eyes closed, face sideways to the light, which made her golden, valuable, alone.

Every two years we still met at the Isabella Stewart Gardner Museum. We did not go all together, of course. We pretended for that day (my birthday) we had lost each other in the span of years, the three of us who knew each other so well, we could imitate any of our laughs, and each loitered in the "Birth of Athena" room, staring benignly at a painting until someone finally recognized another and screamed their name aloud in delight (Britta recognizing Marshall the first time, Marshall seeing me the next). Then there would be more screams as I joined in the reunion, and for all the guards knew, it was really the most astounding coincidence.

And so it went for years. Those ridiculous meetings in the museum marked the time for me, much more so than the Alumni Center, which brought more and more of the same, well-brought-up men and, in 1975, women through my doors. I barely noticed the changes at Brown, either, except the one time a rally walked by my window. In that old brownstone building, the windows were drooping glass, so at first I couldn't make out the words on their signs. Then I saw one in pink: "Gay Is Good." I sat immediately back at my desk, looking to make sure my door was closed. I felt I had witnessed an obscene act, a prurient display shown to me without my wish or consent. I felt breathless and ill, and put my head on the desk. They were chanting something, too, which, luckily, the paneled walls muffled into a harmless rhythm. I concentrated then on that rhythm and tried to breathe along with it, get myself back to the man I had been five minutes before, and not until the sounds passed down the street could I bear to look up again. And I regained myself.

That was 1977. It was the year Marshall moved to Boston. He was finishing Harvard now, and had no time for Providence commutes. Instead, he or I drove to the other city on weekends, or met together on Cape Cod or Mystic at the Aquarium. These visits also meant my time with Britta was separate from my time with Marshall. My lover and I took more cold, stony walks on beaches. He was growing more serious as years went on. His father was already dead, and I saw something tempting him. It was not another man—that was past—but the temptation to tell his mother about me, his male lover, and let all this fall to rest. We never spoke of it, but I tried with every clench of his hand not to change things. I liked things as they were. I still like most things as they are—my father taught me this adaptability, this cowardice.

A hurricane came that year to the East Coast. They named storms after women then, so a female hurricane. Britta and I were bored with it at first. It distressed the routines we had developed, and I see we were turning slowly into those practical adults who hated the snow because of driving, hated staying out at night because it was hard to see in the dim light, hated most disturbances that were no longer new. So we hated taping up all the windows and pulling the shutters. She was particularly grouchy in the matronly, quilted robe my mother had bought her. But then, when Britta found a hurricane lamp and lit it, and the soot blew out and blackened her face, we laughed as we had as college kids.

I asked, "What is this, minstrel hour suddenly?"

"You are a racist, darling."

The lights flickered. "Clean yourself up. We have to get a fire going, or do you just want to go to sleep?"

Her eyes widened in shock. "Oh, no! Are you crazy? It's a hurricane night! We're going to stay up all night tonight, on a hurricane night."

I said we should read to each other. Usually she liked that. She shook her head.

"No. We're going to do what I want to do. This isn't Marshall you're with tonight. We don't have to arm wrestle to have a good time. You're a gay man, after all, no matter what you think."

She took me upstairs to her room and gave me her peacock kimono. She told me to strip down and put it on while she washed off the soot. She walked out of the room with the lantern, and I was left with just my dim candle there, in her room with Chinese coins strung along the mirror, striped masks on the walls. I stripped naked and put on her girlish robe. Marshall hated robes and girlish things on me. Shame, again, always that.

Britta came back, wearing a white nightgown. It was small and thin on her, and then I realized it wasn't a nightgown. It was her wedding dress. She put her hand to her mouth, then held it out as if to stop me. "Perfect," she said. "You look perfect. Now, just follow me." She grabbed a bag and a book from her dresser and blinked her glassy eyes for me to come.

Down at the fire, she made me rub sage oil in my hair and tie it up with a towel—I must have looked like a faggot then, but I was letting her control me that night. I made her wear her blue clay mask, and so we were both ridiculous. She was letting me see at last the kind of life we would have led if our hearts had been otherwise.

We read messages from a plastic Ouija board she had, and she swore she wasn't cheating when it spelled out names of men I'd had crushes on long, long before. Men who now were long married and buried in their children. These messages professed undying passion. They told of my innocence. Britta, or I could believe some ghost she found, told me stories I needed about myself.

She threw my I Ching. She told me a narrow river opened onto a lake, that I would cross the dam onto an open space. Her own fortune involved a girl with a package, and she read its meaning secretly to herself. She sat cross-legged before the fire. I could see more of her body than I ever had. She was gaining weight. But there was something newly compassionate in her larger body, the way her breasts now rested on her skin—I could see them beneath the thin fabric when she threw the fiery copper coins. I wonder what my older body looked like to her. Sometimes I wonder if she was in love with me.

She slept in my bed that night. It was in the corner of the house, safe from the hurricane. The lamp was on all night, but the glass blackened from the soot, and it might as well have been off for all the darkness in the room. Once, I woke up, and the kimono had come undone—I lay naked on my half of the bed, and she was turned towards the wall, so I let the green night glow over me and imagined this was marriage, this was love, and the person asleep, smelling of sage oil, was a lipsticked man in silk. A man who knew me naked, green in the night, listening. And that all this was perfect.

In 1980, a friend got me a job offer in the Alumni Center at Harvard. I hadn't even told Britta that I was looking around, and at the time I told myself I wasn't serious, anyway, so I needn't get her involved. But I told Marshall. Marshall knew about every step, every college I talked to in Boston. I think he knew what would happen, even then. Living in a larger city, a liberal one, he saw the changes going on in the world, changes that freed him after his mother died and that allowed him to live without pretense. And he changed. People at his law firm knew about our relationship, relatives, old friends. It was 1980, a unique moment in America. Those years in the late seventies when I was searching, he must have smiled to himself, thinking of my old-fashioned, ridiculous situation.

I finally talked to Britta in the fall, a rainy late afternoon. She was home from her practice and lay on the white divan, reading *Harper's* and eating potato chips from a garish bag. A white candle lay flickering next to her. Her hair was still feathered blond, but lighter at the temples, as if faded from so many years in sun. We were thirty-six.

"Honey," I said, sitting down in the armchair, "I have a great job offer."

She looked up, her face wide open. "Really? Oh, that's fantastic! Oh, Paul, that's great!" She threw a chip in her mouth, and it crackled.

"It's in Boston."

Her face considered this. She ate more chips. "That's fine. I'm bored of this place, really. We should have packed our bags years ago, and...," she said, pointing her finger, "you'll be closer to Marshall. This is perfect."

"Marshall wants me to live with him."

She closed her eyes and rubbed a finger over the lids, perhaps to be more awake. "Oh," she said as she did this. "So that's what this about."

"I was shocked," I said. "I didn't want to, I don't want to, but there's this part of me..."

"That really does. I know, Paul."

"And it's bigger than I thought." I leaned over and held my hands loosely together. "And maybe...," I said, wanting to skip past the next impossible sentence: "Maybe it's time."

She put her hand to her mouth, which was a movement I could not read. She wiped the crumbs from her navy skirt.

"It is time," she said.

I waited, saying nothing.

"We both knew this was to make life easier. And now it's silly, isn't it?" She nodded, agreeing with herself. "Being married? Isn't it?"

I couldn't nod, but I did smile.

She kept talking. These were not the exact words we said to each other that afternoon—my memory is never perfect. I don't usually remember her in quotations, anyway. What I remember is how we talked in this way, all that afternoon, as if it were a cocktail party we were canceling and not a life.

So she said, "Now I have to come up with something else to want. But that's okay, that's a good thing. We've been stuck."

"We have been," I said.

"Being stuck is comforting, isn't it?"

And I know I didn't feel that way at all. I was forcing myself to be sad and serious, but inside me I was thrilled to live with Marshall and change my life. I am ashamed to say I wanted Britta to smile and pack her things, to come up with something which would make this dull conversation end, so I said a common thing: "It's been wonderful."

She sat with her hand on her chin, looking up at the ceiling. She had long ago grown her real eyebrows in, and they were dark and thin. Her neck was half-shadowed, just like Marshall's on that night on Beacon Hill when none of us knew what our playful façades would make of our lives.

"It is time," she repeated, as if trying it on. "It's time I did something, too."

"What are you going to do?"

"Well," she said quietly. "I think once I wanted to live on an island. Didn't I? Wasn't there an island? What was that?"

Now she did make me laugh—it could have been relief. "You said you wanted to be a gilded white scorpion."

"Really?" she asked, staring grinning at me. "A scorpion? Right, be a wicked woman on a Caribbean island. Wouldn't that be something?" My wife looked at me and I could almost imagine it.

Later, she told me firmly, "But this is lucky. This is very lucky."

These were the kinds of things we said. But I can't picture us saying them. All I see is my wife talking in that dim, streaked light, leaning into the cushions and—I'm sure she didn't know she did this—drawing on her forehead with her thumb. Telling me stories of how she always knew this wasn't what I wanted, but sketching those invisible pictures on her skin. What I remember best is that. Not much, just that.

It only took Britta a month to pack what she wanted, which wasn't much. She quickly closed her practice and sent her clients to a friend, wrapped up the paintings she loved, only three, her clothes, some jewelry. I walked behind her, begging her to take things, but she told me, "Anyone who can't fit her life into two suitcases is stuck forever."

The day she left, I remember she took a long shower, and I tried to shove things into the crevices of her bags: my grandfather's pocket watch, my mother's diamond ring, a first edition Dorothy Parker. I wanted to give it all to her because I felt she was hiding behind this adventure, escaping the grief at my selfish act. I was so guilty at the thought of being happy up in Boston, living with my handsome lawyer, arguing playfully over whose china got put in the cabinet. But she must have known—there isn't much to do with friends who leave. Just these rituals of packing, but you can't say anything to keep him there. You can only repeat that once you drugged his tea.

My wife, Britta, came out of her room in her traveling clothes: black dress, red jacket, and, over her arm, the trenchcoat she claimed had always saved her. The hollow Celtic necklace lay around her throat, jingling hope, and she walked to me as she pulled on a silver bracelet.

"I'll send you a card from the island when I get there," she said confidently. "I think the phone's too expensive. Then you'll write to me."

"Of course I will," I said. "Are you crazy? Of course."

"And," she said, then let out a sharp laugh, "will you and Marshall still be in the museum two years from now?"

"You still want to do that?"

She pouted and shook her wrist to let the bracelet settle. "Anyway, I'll be there."

"Then I'll be there."

Britta started to put the trenchcoat on. Frost was on the windows that morning, and the last leaves on the maple tree looked frozen, thick as wax.

"I saw a ghost last night," she told me, one arm in the coat. "I think it must have been the maid or the governess. She was in the attic—what was I doing in the attic at that hour, even I don't know—and all green. A green ghost, can you imagine? I watched her for a little while, picking up invisible things and putting them back down, things that must have been here a long time ago. It was fun figuring out what they were, like I think one was a humidor." She looked down to pull her jacket sleeves through, and there they came, red and alive. "She was afraid she'd forgotten something. Afraid she'd left something important behind." I caught her calm look in the mirror.

I heard a horn outside, and the cab was there.

"Oh!" she said, frantically picking up leather bags with too many straps. "Case in point! I left my lipstick in the upstairs bathroom! I need it, I can't live without it. Put me on a desert island, and I'd trade the two books I brought for lipstick."

I put up one finger, then ran out and up the staircase, which creaked at each pounding step. On the sink was a gold tube of that garish red which had embarrassed me for years, the red of dirty stories and her Dutch island and of the silk-lined museum room. I ran downstairs with it and saw the bags were gone.

I glimpsed out the window just a tumble of trenchcoat into the cab, and then it sped off up the hill and over. With Britta, once again, no goodbye.

Today in the courtyard, as I wish myself a happy fortieth birthday, as I stare at the green blueberries, I know Britta might not be coming. It's been hard to contact her for two years now. She did go to Saint Eustatius, and she bought land there from an old dying man. She wrote lots of letters then, all about the insane things she saw there, the governor who was a tyrant, the rich white people on the hill hoarding a pile of wood, which on the island was like gold, her travails building a house of gingerbread and jalousies.

Marshall and I didn't show up here in 1982. There was so much going on at the time: living together became sometimes more unspoken hostility than love, and I changed jobs to MIT and had to go home to my father's funeral. That birthday passed unnoticed. Marshall still lives on Beacon Hill, and I now live south of there. Sometimes we meet and hold hands—you can do that now on the street—but I know his fright at middle age has brought other men into our old apartment. And the notes from Britta have been brief, businesslike.

That morning when she left our yellow house on Meeting Street, I walked outside in the October cold and saw the cab drive off, watched long after as the sun began to rise and make the brittle ice on the lilac bush glitter and break off. I sat down on that square wood porch, beneath the peeling columns, and could not think of anything to think. I'd given everything away and not even seen it. All the week before, I had been eager as a boy, excited to move up to Boston, experience the warm change my life would make, and never realized what I thought had weighed me down was simply love. I had sent away the one person I really loved, and made myself think it was a kind of freedom, and now I saw the empty space this freedom revealed.

I leaned against our house and cried, ugly as before, and there was no excuse this time for ugliness. I didn't coax the tears with self-pity or remembrance; they just filled me. A little boy wearing a birthday hat walked by, and he stared at me weeping with no consolation now. I thought he might give me the shining present he held, but he gripped it tighter and moved on. All my muscles gnawed at me and shook. I became angry with my body for betraying me, and I gritted my teeth as I trembled with more tears.

It did no good. So I let go. My hands fell to the cold white wood, and I let go, and the pain of losing all those years moved over me like a warm sun.

The courtyard here is skylit and warm, because it is spring, and damask roses, century plants, and palm trees grow here in their careful rows. All the rooms look onto this courtyard, and I'm searching one Moroccan window for a woman, middle-aged by now, pounding rudely past the guards in perhaps white island cotton robes, or a gold-threaded turban. She wears a hollow silver necklace and a kind of brave compassion. You'll recognize her laugh.

There's a red jacket leaning to the window. It begins a loud, annoying tapping noise against the ancient glass until a gold-buttoned man takes her arm and mouths irritation. A flash goes off nearby—someone taking a picture—and the guard leaves her again. The red jacket returns, slides open the lock, and swings out the window with a snow of black paint. I jump up at my wife's laughing face, and thank God, thank God.

About Fifty Band-Aids

The Ivy League is a short haircut. The sides and back are buzzed, and the top is just long enough to comb. It makes Kenny look like the boy in the school portraits his mother props on the mantle. Also like some California surfer our friend Missy fell in love with.

Lately, Kenny's been going for haircuts every Saturday, and I've been keeping him company. Soon we'll hear from colleges, and Kenny's hoping these haircuts will bring him luck. He's also hoping to play ball next year, and so Saturdays after the barber, we always look to hoop. Kenny can play—he practices—but he still can't make the high school varsity. He's just not the complete package that some kids are. Because no matter how good he gets, he's got no hops, and already that's a skill you need to play on the team.

We checked the Northwestern courts—locked. The church gym—closed for Christmas. And I wouldn't let Kenny run at the rec center anymore because too many busters there wanted to kill him.

We pounded on the emergency door at the Y until someone snuck us in. Games were running full. We recognized a big guy from our school named Charles Wormfeld, the type of cocky guy Kenny's always looking to beat.

Of course the trouble with Charles starts straight off. It starts because Charles is a hack, and Kenny keeps calling him "Charles the Worm Worm Wormfeld," and taking the ball to the hole. So first time Charles swats Kenny's shot, Charles goes, "Get that shit out of here," and pounds his hairy chest like the ape that he is. Kenny glares up. "Don't do that," he says quietly. "Not if you're going to foul me every other time. Don't talk smack, too."

"So what are you going to do if I do, little man?" Charles says, and that's when the oglers circle up, and I make for the closet where they keep the chairs. I yell, "Come on, Kenny, time to go."

But Kenny doesn't answer. Already he's got his arms spread, palms open, face right in Charles's face. Then Kenny smiles and shakes his head. Charles thinks that's it then, because he smiles and shakes his head, too, which is exactly when Kenny drops him—opens that can of whoop ass—and down Charles goes.

I don't know if any of the other guys are Charles's friends, but I throw the chair, anyway, just in case. People will clear off when you throw a chair, and it was getting so this was our routine: Kenny going wild, me throwing something big to get him out of there.

We jumped in Kenny's mom's black Beemer, and I was screaming, "The fuck are you doing? Always fucking shit up."

Kenny had us in drive and was looking seriously apologetic, swerving through the parking lot to make the street. "Sorry, man. Seriously, I'm sorry. He just pissed me off. I get so mad." And on the steering wheel I could see his knuckles laid out and flexing, the splits above his middle two fingers opening and closing like little pink fish mouths.

Two blocks later, Kenny broke left.

"It's his house over here, right?"

"Whose house?"

"Charles the Worm Worm Wormfeld's. You know, right up here, right?"

"Oh, man, Kenny, I don't know."

Kenny pulled in behind a garage with a hoop above the door. How he knew this was Charles's, I had no idea.

"Now just be cool now," Kenny said, and he dug the tire iron out from the trunk and balanced on the roof of the Beemer to pry Charles's rim off. Two minutes later it was ours—that is, Charles's pretty rim had ripped free—and we're bombing north toward Kenny's basement, Kenny raising the hoop up through the sunroof like a trophy.

Kenny's basement is mostly cement, and it's where his father used to see clients back in the 1970's. Now that he's set in his downtown office, it's become Kenny's unofficial bedroom, still sporting the black leather couch, orange carpet, and macramé wall hangings from when Kenny's mom redecorated the upstairs den. Most of the stuff we've somehow managed to break, or scorch, or in some way mar—there's silver duct tape on nearly everything—but Mr. and Mrs. Sharf never snoop down here, and it's funny because just above us, the Sharfs' house is full of these really nice rooms where it always feels like the cleaning lady's just been.

I squirted Bactine on Kenny's knuckles, and he bit the neck of his shirt, even though I didn't think it could hurt as bad as he was making it seem.

"Okay," I said, "you're good to go."

Kenny smiled. "Ready for Christmas," he said, and we watched rap videos and did bong hits until Mrs. Sharf called from somewhere in the yard.

"Kenny, your father wants you to rake the leaves up. Kenny, can you hear me?"

Kenny made a face, didn't bother to stash the pipe. He yelled, "Mom, it's gonna snow."

"Kenny, your father says he'd like you to rake the leaves. We're having company. Kenny?"

"Fucking Christ," Kenny said to me. "Like, no kidding."

So we raked, squinty-eyed and mellow, and in the middle of raking, the snow commenced to filter down.

"You see," Kenny said, ripping at the leaves with his rake. "This is exactly the shit they pull all the time. Do you see what I mean? It's snowing. I said it would be snowing."

"So let's stop."

"You can. I'm fucking raking these leaves."

And so that's what he did—raked through the flakes—and I helped him, both of us just in our thin sweatshirts because Kenny wanted his parents to feel bad for making us cold. And just to make sure they noticed, Kenny lit the leaf pile on fire instead of bagging it, and we stood around the smoldering little heap just waiting, a wind cutting through us, tiny wet snow crystals melting on our skin.

Nothing changes, I thought. When Kenny was ten, he torched the upstairs den, and his parents didn't even yell or ground him. They just gave him the basement, his own space, a move which, I guess, I can understand. The basement isn't too flammable. It's got access to the yard. And it's a place for Kenny to be instead of picking fights on basketball courts after school.

My mother brought my good clothes over along with the salmon pâté she brings to this party every year. I had to wheel upstairs where the adults were milling with drinks. My mother met me in the kitchen, eyes bugging like she'd never seen me before in such ratty gym clothes. She turned to a withered lady in a shiny green dress. "Honestly," my mother said. "From the look of him, you'd think we didn't have money to buy him clothes."

I took my things to the upstairs bathroom, and by the time I was dressed in what my mother thought appropriate—blue Dockers with too many pleats, white oxford, red sweater vest—most of the other kids had arrived. I could tell because I saw their parents. Saw my father, too, in a pack of other fathers by the bar. He raised his drink and motioned me over. I played dumb, waved once, hustled back down to Kenny's private space.

Some nights, maybe after a fight, or a car crash, or a particularly bad loss by the Bulls, you could find ten kids down there, guys and girls, passed out or hysterical, depending on the event. Terry Mayday shot Brad Grinnel's dog. Richard Hoffman smacked the clerk at 7-Eleven. Who knows if we were any different from any other groups of friends. But people were always showing up. Everyone knew the way.

This holiday thing was like a reunion. Kenny, Missy, and Betsey Nelson—back from Skidmore College with a bouncy new hairdo—were playing slap-n-flinch when I walked in. Big, Lumpy, Hollywood, Billy Boo the millionaire bike thief, a guy called Dish because of his big ears, and a few of the other clowns from our school were swilling champagne on the sofa. My man Ross Meyers and his girlfriend, Naomi, showed up—first time ever—and Ross was walking around nodding, going, "So this is Christmas, yesss, I likes, I likes, I likes." And up above you could here the grown-ups shifting chairs and slurping eggnog and munching ham to the tune of "White Christmas."

Missy was so wrecked. Eyes half-closed, she kept getting her hands stung every time she settled them on top. So now Kenny was concentrating on Betsey, who, at the moment, was examining his knuckles. "Do they hurt very much? Was it a very bad fight?"

Missy stepped between them. "I want to hit," she said and stuck out her lip.

"You have to win first," Kenny said. "You need practice, you really do. You're not at all fast. In fact, you're slow. Merry Christmas and all, but you're slow."

Missy spun in place and careened toward me, mouth glistening, hands held out. Her perfume smelled like maraschino cherries, and I rested my big paws on her soft palms and let her go off, huge drunken slaps to the backs of my hands. I'd known Missy since ninth grade, when she moved here pregnant from San Pedro, California, and Kenny, even though he wasn't responsible, sold stolen Polo shirts from Marshall Field's to pay for an abortion. You weren't supposed to talk about it.

In the middle of the room, Kenny and Betsey kept playing, hands lifted so that if you didn't know better, you'd think they were rehearsing for some formal dance. Kenny looked so clean-cut over there, khakis cuffed just above the scoop of his shoes. I could see what girls could see in him. He had a presence, and he had this room. Missy pressed against me. I wrapped my arm around her and patted my pocket.

"Got a card for you."

"You're sweet," she said, still paying attention to Kenny and Betsey. "You know I don't owe him anything," she whispered. "I don't care if it is Christmas." And then she stalked off in her tight little skirt, with her short shapely legs, into the room where the lights don't work and where Kenny's father keeps his unused tools. From the sofa, Billy Boo offered a toast, "To all the many fine babes here," and he winked and nodded toward the tool-room.

"She's not like that anymore," I told him.

He waved his hand at me, knocked back his champagne, and went after Missy, the thought of which—the two of them tanked and slobbery—made me sick.

I wandered out the storm door and into the backyard, where the new slushy snow lay barely an inch deep and the blocks of light stretched from the Sharfs' kitchen windows across the pale muck. Missy hadn't asked for her card, and now it felt heavy enough to drag my pants down. The air was turning colder, and on either side I could see inside Kenny's neighbors' lighted homes. On the left you had the O'Donnells in their hardwooded den, cocktail city, the whole clan seated before a huge, gaudy tree. On the right you had Mr. and Ms. Berkowitz in the kitchen with their three slouchy sons, everybody snarfing, heaps of food. And with all these neighbors so close, not a one of them suspected I was out there or had any idea of what I felt capable of doing.

I made a snowball, squeezed it tight, then added more snow and squeezed again until I had a fat, hefty ice-ball. I edged around to the front of Kenny's house, leaned in the shadow of the porch, cold pinching my lungs and stinging my fingers, not a single thing moving on the sidewalk or street. The first car that passed, I blasted it, fired a strike, and then listened for the hollow smack as I bolted back to the bright lights and red faces of my best friends.

Kenny was in a corner, flashing bills, probably giving away money, which is something he had a tendency to do. Ross was imitating a fight ref and doing the rules for Christmas dinner: "No turkey football. No drinking from the baster. If you gotta gnaw from the bone, you take it outside."

As for Billy Boo, he was back on the sofa, nodding and laughing at whatever Hollywood was saying. I saw him sniff his fingers and then let Hollywood sniff his fingers, and I felt sick all over again. Where was Missy? I didn't see her anywhere. Then I looked to the toolroom, and there she was, stumbling out of the darkness like a horror-film lady, hair mussed, big breasts hanging free, thick, ugly blood bubbling down her left wrist. She threw a dry-wall knife at Kenny and Betsey and streaked past us, out and into the snow.

We had to tackle her and cover her mouth to keep her quiet. Kenny squeezed her wrist and held it up while me, Ross, and Big dragged her back downstairs. Then Kenny held her still while I pasted on about fifty Band-Aids. She'd made a mess of her arm, mauled the skin up, but not too deeply and not vertically along the vein the way her friend Julie Fisher had. I squirted Bactine on top of the Band-Aids and helped Kenny dress her. He raised her arms, and I had to lift each of her heavy cold breasts, one at a time, to get them set in her bra. Her blouse went on easier. Naomi smuggled down a bright red sweater—from where I didn't know—and we put that on her, too, just in case some blood leaked through at church. The whole time, Billy Boo kept shaking his head, mumbling, "Sorry, Missy, I'm sorry, I'm sorry."

Finally Kenny just snapped, "It's not your fault already, Bill, so just shut up."

Missy smiled then, and I wondered if she knew what was happening or who was involved. She never once opened her eyes. And when it came time for midnight mass, we all rode with our parents, in separate cars, except for Kenny, who said he'd ride with Missy and her mom.

The priest called out, "By the light of the redeeming love," and we all answered, "Fill our hearts with hope and peace," just like it told us to say in the program.

We were sitting in back, or at least near the back, and we'd downed so many drinks that even with Missy there leaning woozily on Kenny's shoulder, looking faded, we somehow felt loopy and ready to giggle. Everything was just so ridiculous: all our trim, good-hearted parents in bright outfits, every last one of them clueless and loaded to the gills. You knew it soon as you stomped in, soon as one of the dads took your coat and pumped your hand, smelling of pipe smoke, green Tic-Tacs, and underneath it all reeking of gin.

The thing that fucked us up was Kenny's tie. We were standing to sing, and when we sat, Kenny's tie flopped over the pew in front of him, and a fat lady leaned back against it. Kenny was pinned. He had to bend forward and turn his head, and everybody had to bite their lips to keep from laughing. I did, too, bit that lip hard, but then strange sounds started to jiggle out of me, and I squeezed fast toward the aisle.

A minute later, Kenny met me down in the gym, where we rolled on the floor and laughed so hard we couldn't make noise. The backboards loomed like friendly ghosts. Kenny kicked his shoes off and balled his socks.

"Quick game of sock ball?"

"I'll kill you."

"I don't think so."

"I think so."

Just then, Kenny's father flicked up the lights.

"Is there a problem here, Kenny?" he said, squinting into the new new brightness.

"No problem, Dad," Kenny said, loudly.

"Well, then, what are you two doing here? I mean, your mother and I were wondering about you upstairs."

Kenny shrugged, and Mr. Sharf looked sad to have to be asking us stupid questions. After a minute or two, he just sighed and walked off.

Kenny twisted his mouth into a grin. "Think I made him mad?"

I stared at the floor, Kenny's bare feet, and then the next thing that happens is Kenny's peeing. It's the gym in our church.

"Why, Kenny?" I said. "Why?"

I walked home with Ross and Naomi so I wouldn't have to face my parents or Kenny or anyone else that would set me off. Out on the street, our footsteps crunched, and the air smelled of pine smoke, and all the big homes winked with tiny lights. So we were walking. Ross and Naomi said they thought mass was cool—so much incense! so much singing!—and now they wanted to try hanging an actual ornament on an actual tree.

"I don't know," I said. "You have to do it just right." I was trying to goof on our whole situation, trying to forget about Missy's bloody wrist and Kenny's twisted grin and all the grotesque statues of Christ on the cross. I just wanted to enjoy who I was with and what we were doing. But it was hard. Like we had to walk past so many familiar streets, so many houses of the friends we'd known forever, and especially past Missy's mom's dinky flat with the two-step porch and the dark spooky windows that made me worry. Missy's card was in my pocket. "Hold on," I said. "Can we . . . I mean, do either of you have a pen?"

Naomi patted her pockets and searched her coat and came up with a red felt-tip. "It'll do," I said. "Two minutes." And I hustled up to Missy's and stood there shaking while I ripped open the envelope and took out her card. It was just a silly Hallmark on which I'd written, "Love, Santa." Now I x-ed out the Santa part and penned in KENNY. The porch wood groaned. I slipped the card through the mail slot, and that was that.

My mother was up waiting when we reached my house. I didn't have my keys. She was in her nightgown, and she had a champagne bottle in her hand. She pressed her face to the door glass and said we couldn't come in.

"Mom, come on." I was embarrassed in front of Ross and Naomi, embarrassed that this was my mother and that this was Christmas. "Mom, they just want to see the tree, and then we'll go out."

My mother waved the bottle and shook her head. "Nooooo. I'm in my nightgown, pumpkin."

I apologized to Ross and Naomi and ran around back. "Mom, open the door. Mom! I'm serious, they just want to see the tree. Five minutes. Seriously. We're going to leave in five minutes."

"I'm in my nightgown, sweetie."

"Mom, no one cares."

"Philip, I don't want a whole herd of your friends traipsing through my house in the middle of the night on Christmas Eve when I'm in my nightgown. Now, don't make me wake your father."

"Mom. Let me. The fuck. In."

"No, Philip."

I ran to the front. Ross and Naomi looked scared. I didn't care. I climbed like a madman—up the small pine beside our porch, up the porch roof's slanted shingles—toward the window. Down the hall, I could see my mother flying toward me, flimsy robe billowing out behind. At the window she locked the lock and stuck out her tongue.

"Fucking bitch," I screamed, and I put my foot through the glass to kick her teeth in.

She shrieked. A light popped on in the hallway behind her, and I wrung down the tree, scraping my hands and bicycling my feet. A dog was barking. Houselights were coming on next door. I hit the ground running, but then I fell and scraped my palms and just waited, kneeling, for Ross and Naomi to catch up.

We were all breathing hard. Naomi gave me a tissue. Ross made a soft, low whistle. "Merry Christmas?" he said, and we all laughed a little and then walked on, in an awkward silence, breathing dragon smoke, sliding and skittish, heading for the best place we knew to go.

A flaming meteor had landed, and aliens had stamped down the snow around Missy's blood.

"Something's burning," Ross said. "A bonfire."

And he was right. All this crap from Kenny's basement was piled in the backyard—a heap of flames—smelling of melting plastic. We could see the flickering shadows from the alley, and we hurried past them, past the black leather couch growing soggy, and down through the storm door to Kenny's big room, where the lights were blazing.

Kenny had cleared the place out. He'd pulled down the shelves and ripped up the carpet, and the walls were stripped clean except at one end, where he'd tacked up Charles Wormfeld's hoop with huge spikes, right into the foundation. A sledgehammer lay on the floor, and the wall had a lot of crumbly holes in it where you could see Kenny must have missed what he meant to hit. The basement ceiling was low, and the hoop was even lower, and Kenny was running back and forth, sweating through his church clothes, sprinting from one end of the room to the other, sprinting, planting, leaping. He had a deflated basketball that he could palm. He was jamming. And for a minute we just watched in awe while Kenny rattled the rim with windmilling monster dunks.

He saw us, smiled, took off again to tear the house down.

I said, "Come on, Kenny, let's put this thing out."

Kenny's eyes looked feverish, and he swept his arm out to cover the room. "There was blood, man, blood everywhere. I couldn't clean it up." He was leaning under Charles's hoop, squeezing the ball.

"Okay, whatever," I said. "Come on now, Ken. I mean, I mean, this is some shit."

Naomi tugged gently on Kenny's arm, and Ross held the door open, and after some head-shaking, Kenny let himself be led up the slippery wet steps and into the yard, where the flames were still flaming. Nothing seemed obvious. We had to huddle together and stare while we wondered about exactly what to do. There was this smoldering mound, our problem, this circle of light, and then just beyond it, at the edge of Kenny's yard, there was this dim blackness. We couldn't stay warm. Kenny kept stamping his feet and turning to look up at his parents' dark window. Meanwhile the snow had stopped falling, and God or someone had shook the stars out, and I had to wonder what we looked like, what the neighbors would think if they noticed us, four kids standing together before a stinky blue flame. Would we look like we were roasting chestnuts? Would we resemble, in any way, a small family?

Search Bay

At night the wind sometimes woke him as it sliced across the tin roof of the cabin, and he would open his eyes in darkness to find his hands gripping the bedframe. Thirty-five knots, forty knots—it was impossible not to gauge the speed of the gusts in his mind. He felt, too, the chastened shudder of a hull and the inevitable way his bones prepared themselves for a hard roll to port. The lake was a quarter mile away, beyond two ridges feathered with birch and spruce, yet he could hear her, feel her. The wind might eventually shift to the south, or it might blow itself out. Still, he never again found sleep on those nights—a cruel, honest fact of his body. He lay alert on his thin mattress, boots and slicker hanging so close he could smell them, completing his watch as he must.

November. A month of change, a time of vigil. The last of the leaves flared and fell away, scouring the withdrawn horizon. Winter almost always broke over the bay like a green sea this time of year, this far north. It happened quickly, without much warning even to him, and he'd lived on this stretch of the eastern peninsula all of his life except when he'd been on the lakes, or tramping the Atlantic. He cut wood. He laid in kerosene and dry goods, reorganizing supplies on the shelves of the cold porch until they made sense only to him. He repaired the roof, suffered a bitter night's rain, repaired the roof again. He visited his sister in town, took her a face cord of mixed hardwood even though she hadn't asked for it. He turned back the deer hunters who wandered east from the state forest. He studied the patterns of the crews from the power company as they did their last work of the year in his territory. It was a season of reckoning and recognition, one he liked to mull over. He was old. Preparation was the only rule left to live by.

On most days he walked down to the shore. It was the one aimless routine he allowed himself, and it was far better, he thought, than being part of the union flotsam that washed up on waves of coffee or worse along the gangways of the Soo locks. Those were the men who couldn't break their habits, or didn't know they had them to begin with. Not that he avoided every laker he ran into. He did not. He'd taken his nephews to the locks once or twice, shared some stories with the jaw gang there. And he saw the old pissers in the Indian casinos when he went, former oilers and bosuns and mates exchanging their pension cash for lightweight tokens, their dark deck clothes replaced with golf shirts that made no sense on their bodies. He had little need for their sort of commerce. It was enough to come to the edge of the bay. Sniff at the nearly odorless water, utter the old names that gave character to its waves and the ranging grays of its skies. Mackinac, the queen island, stood some miles offshore, her bluffs a charcoal slash of shadow and spume. Often there would be a ship clearing the straits as well, and he would eye her as carefully as he dared, knowing there was a good chance he'd recognize her, that she'd been plying her trade when he'd been scrambling at his. Seven hundred feet long, a thousand feet long, riding high on ballast or filled with grain, phosphates, maybe ore. There was a great deal he could tell from a glance. Yet all he really found himself studying was her silhouette and her motion, knowing she held desperate men. November, and the ice was not here yet, the gales were still howling their chorus to the north. A walk to the rocky, wind-whisked shore of the bay. A savored cigarette. The rest of the day for the simpler, bracing tasks he now asked of himself.

He had the bulldozer out of the shed the day the boy came. He was lubing the blade lifts and half-tinkering with the engine, which was how he explained his unreadiness when it needed to be explained. There was a locked gate between his place and the state road two miles west. No one was supposed to bother him except the Sandhursts, who used his track to get to their cottage, and maybe the Mahans, who owned a few acres along the shore to the southeast. Even his brother, Otto, didn't come out here. Too far from town, Otto said. They could talk at the shop if they needed to talk, or at their sister's. Then the boy appeared, on foot, moving like he knew where he was going and why. He was startled and felt surprise flutter across his face like a dusky wing just before he went spiteful.

If the boy said hello, he never heard it. But the boy did stop walking, waiting for a moment on the wet leaves of the path, which allowed him to cut the grind of the bulldozer's diesel to silence. It was as though the afternoon went dead when he did that—no noise, no heat or vital stink from the engine. The boy was dressed in a red plaid wool coat, jeans, a beaten felt hat, no gloves. He looked warm enough, though he wasn't wearing any blaze orange, which made him a damn fool. Dark eyes and skin, flattish nose, wide jaw. Chippewa, maybe, though it wasn't a face he recognized. If the boy was poaching, he'd gotten half-smart and stashed his gun. If he was just wandering, he'd made a considerable mistake.

He laid his crescent wrench in the toolbox bolted behind the seat of the dozer. It was the boy's place to get nervous and speak.

"Came for the beaver." The voice was quick and casual, though deep enough to make him believe the boy was older than he looked.

"Don't look like you came ready for much of anything." He waved at the boy's empty hands and began a controlled laugh, wondering if the boy had heard any bad stories about him and the lonely way he lived in the woods. He hoped he had. "You shouldn't be here."

"I got the permission." The boy swung an arm down the track past the cabin. "Man called from Lansing, having trouble with too many beaver."

He understood then, enough of it. A portion of Sandhurst's land had been flooded all spring and summer; they'd had a helluva time with the road. He'd been over there a time or two himself to clear the dammed culverts. Once he'd spent part of a morning taking potshots at the animals as they swam across their new pond, but he hadn't hit anything. Beaver learned fast. He'd told Sandhurst he'd trap them out if he wanted. Sandhurst, it looked like, had decided to do it right. Indians had unrestricted rights to trap beaver. The boy was definitely Indian.

"You know what you're doing, go on."

"I know what I'm doing." The boy shrugged his wrists up into the sleeves of his plaid coat. "My uncle said to come out here and look it over. He also said to come to you, let you know. His legs are bad today."

"You walk in from the gate?"

The boy nodded.

"Sandhurst plan to send you a key?"

A shrug again like that didn't really matter. The boy lifted one foot, then the other, restless. The boots he wore were too large for him and cracked along the soles. They'd be wet and awkward in the bogs.

"Who's your uncle? He know me from somewhere?"

The boy stepped back like he'd been cut loose by the question. "He didn't say to talk about it." A straight look, black-eyed. "Just said to tell you I had the job. If you knew that, he said, I'd proba-bly be all right."

It made his chest burn in the old way to watch the boy walk off like he did, easy, preoccupied. He'd be a better man, he thought, if he didn't want to bust everybody like they were on his crew. Yet it was the truth that he sometimes lost his taste for people for weeks at a time. It always came back to him, a doglike understanding of companionship. But as warm and viscous as the feeling was on its return, this desire to tolerate others, to congregate with them, it remained fickle within him. It made him a disappointment, too—he knew that—but he hadn't decided to live any other way.

The boy's face came back to him when the day was done. He hadn't left by the road, choosing to hack through the under-growth instead, or to follow the rocky hip of the lake. That was how he imagined it, anyway—the boy's evasion. But as he fried his potatoes and onions in a skillet, the broad face with the angled, assessing eyes came back to him. The boy reminded him a little of Henderson, that was the only connection he could make. Henderson was an Indian, too, from somewhere up in New York state, and he'd been a cook on the *Pontiac* for a while. Reasonable cook, reasonable man. Not much remarkable about him, though he never ran short of coffee, ever, which was a good trait in a gal-ley man. Most of his people walked steel in Pittsburgh or New

York City, that's what he said, but he'd signed onto a freighter out of Buffalo after his stint in the Army and never looked back. Henderson told some good stories, as most cooks did—he remembered that. The man kept his hair braided, he told stories while he worked both messes, officers' and crew's, he stayed out of people's business. It was funny he even recalled Henderson; he'd worked with hundreds of men on a long line of ships. But this was the *Pontiac,* old and cranky even when he hadn't been, running coal up the dark spine of Lake Erie, her every inch, he remembered, stinking of black dust and hurry. Henderson had never been able to cook a meal that didn't taste of it.

Later, when he was on his bunk with the radio turned low, a hockey game from endless Canada, he believed Henderson hadn't been on the *Pontiac* at all. It had been the bad luck *McCurdy.* Memories lagged and heeled, and he understood he'd hoped to fool himself. Yet even as he closed his eyes, he found he could clarify little more than the smell of burnt anthracite and onion. Henderson would have laughed to hear it. No ship's cook he knew had ever been so bad he ruined onions.

He turned off the radio and lay square on the bunk. It seemed as though he ought to prepare himself for something that was as yet out of sight, beyond guessing. The thing he called his storm sense was tracking a disturbance; he felt the fine tingle in his skull. A low pressure system, maybe. Illness. Maybe ghosts. He'd have to bide his time before he knew.

The snow came. Not enough to plow but enough to blanket the ground, quilt its mineral smells, leave him to feel like his season had begun. Most of the years he'd sailed on the lakes, they'd made it into December, the ice of Superior would hold off that long, so he wasn't home to see the tatted crystals begin to fringe the bay or to taste the air's last flavor of earth. He returned to a world already insulated and hard. There were the years he'd bunked in Toledo, of course. Not so cold there, or easy. That was when he'd been married, had a house, aimed to study his way off deck and onto the bridge, a foolishness he'd undertaken for Mary and her sad, pleading face, though it had been a good thing in the end. Officers served two months on, two off. Able-bodied seamen worked as many voyages as they could hustle. Mary believed she wanted him home in that gum-green cottage above the scudding Maumee. So he studied when he could and parlayed his long years aboard into favors. Made himself into a third mate from nothing in the days when such a thing could still be done. Then he lost Mary.

He gathered half a sack of Idas from the cold porch and set off down the track, his head soon clear in the still, dry air. He took the apples up on a knoll he knew, one that had the black trickle of a spring at its base. The deer would find the shriveled fruit by sundown. He fed them most of the winter if he could—carrots, apples, acorns—not so he could hunt them, but so he could know they were there and that they would stay there, in his woods, because of him. He hadn't taken a buck on his own property in several years. Foolishness, no doubt, but it was a foolishness he could afford. His family had owned this land above the bay for more than a hundred years. They'd logged it, fished it, trapped it, hunted it, tried to sell it to rich people from downstate who didn't stick. Now they held it because it was easy to hold and righteous to claim. He stayed there because his brother and sister didn't care if he did otherwise, and because it was good for him to be plant-ed, safer. It made him pay attention to himself—this place that expected little of him, which needed even less than he gave. The lakes had not been like that.

He'd nearly ruined the memory because he'd dragged it out so much, the one about how he got his start on water. He'd been young and crazy and skittish, enraged by his father in all the usual ways. So he hitched rides on mail boats and farm trucks, made his way to Leeland, where there was damn near nothing to do, and lied himself onto a leaky, jury-rigged vessel named the *Alma L.* They wanted him on the black gang shoveling coal, but when he convinced them he halfway knew how to navigate and that he'd skidded his share of logs in his life, they put him on the deck crew instead. It was merciless work, yet he loved it in ways it took him years to understand. Weather and exasperation, water and break-down—he went at it all.

The captain was an arrogant drunk who used his instruments and charts when he felt like it. The mate, soon satisfied that he couldn't buffalo the new boy, gave him half of his own job to do, and he lasted at it as long as the *Alma L.* did. The captain ran her across a bar near the Manitous in a spunky summer storm; the mean pounding they took there snapped the chain to her rudder. Another vessel answered the captain's obscene distress call and was able to put a line across *Alma*'s bow, but it was clear they'd need to jettison cargo if they hoped to be pulled free. The old man went into a blind rage when he heard that, calling for barges to take on his pulpwood, then for a breeches buoy rescue, though they were too far from shore for that and no one but the captain himself was old enough to have ever seen such a thing. He helped the mate cut loose a level of logs, but the captain ordered them to stop and struck them both across the face with a leather lanyard. It was the first act of shipboard madness he'd seen.

Since they weren't allowed to rebalance her load, the *Alma L.* listed starboard and eventually heeled over in the waves. He later heard that she was salvaged and that she and her captain made hell and money in those waters for many years after. He, however, disappeared as quietly as he'd come, heading south until he found deck passage across Lake Michigan to Wisconsin. He'd been told that the place he needed to be was Duluth. Freighters reigned both the Iron Range and the big waters up there, and there was a belief within him, even at sixteen, that some men were meant to labor their way toward extremes of their own choosing.

He walked until he couldn't think about that version of himself anymore, then he turned back. He skirted the thicket of the cedar bog, passed close to a bear's den he knew about, eyed the empty trees. On his way to the cabin, he saw a speckled scatter of feathers near the splintered stump of a pine and realized that there was a thing he would miss until spring, the shy occupation of the loons on the bay, the full sound of their inhuman laughter.

Some days later the boy left him a note on the ground near his door. *Set 3 traps,* it said. *Uncle still sick.* The note was written in pencil on a large, silvery square of birch bark. Its letters were careful and upright. The boy had even signed his name. Frank Andrews. When he walked out to the track, he could see the muddy, bowlegged wells made by the boy's misfit boots as he labored under the weight of his traps. A stagger coming and going, and that was all.

That night he awoke in his chair near the stove only to realize that his deck crew had not run short of paint and primer, that his boiling anxiety about a young wheelman was phantom vapor and heat. He thought about taking a drink. He thought about going beyond solitude toward something dark and squatting entirely. He believed he'd been talking in his sleep, though to whom he couldn't say.

His sister, Frieda, liked him to come for Sunday dinner, so he went when he felt like it or guessed she could use a little money or help around the house. Cecil, her husband, was a long-haul trucker who did what he could when he had the time. Frieda had been talking for years now about how good things would be when Cecil finally got a job at the prison. But prison jobs were hard to come by; they paid damn well. People waited a long time.

Frieda never said much about the money he slipped her when he visited. He told her to consider it rent, since he was living on property that belonged to all three of them. She kept the books for a gift shop in town and made a few things to sell there her-self—wood-burnt plaques and Snow Island table runners—but she mostly stayed home with the boys. She'd take the money from him, her big brother, and thank him for something else, firewood or a door he'd rehung. They both knew if they stooped to talking about money, they'd end up discussing the years he'd traded most of his for liquor.

This Sunday they had sauerbraten that Frieda had marinated, and mashed potatoes, and a salad thrown together by the boys. He was in the kitchen smoking the one cigarette his sister allowed; his nephews were watching football on the TV in the den. Somehow it came about that he told Frieda of the boy's visit to the beaver ponds. Nothing else had happened to him in the last few weeks, unless he counted finding a gut-shot doe near the north edge of the bog a piece of news, and Frieda didn't like to hear about things like that. Ravens had led him to the doe, the heavy way they croaked and gathered in the treetops attracting his attention more than usual, and he'd cut the doe's throat with his knife, though she was nearly dead, anyway. Frieda wouldn't want to hear about the ravens, either, or the raucous bald eagles, or the chipmunk which desperately wanted to hibernate on his porch. His sister liked to hear about the human leftovers, snapped saw blades or rusted drag chains, implements that proved the Hansens had broken their backs and spilled their sweat out there in the woods like any other family with an honest history. She also liked him to talk about how things were along the western shallows of the bay where they'd built teepees of birch saplings and bark when they were children, the three of them, and their father took them camping. She loved that place, she said, how the yellow sun fell off behind the spiked fence of the pines, the way grilling fish smelled, and she would never forget it. She wished Cecil would take the boys there, just pitch a tent and forget about the motorboat for one damn day. But she never suggested he take his nephews instead, as though it would not be the right favor to ask, as though his choice to live the way he did now, just like his choice to sign onto a steamer thirty-some years before, was the wrong combination of impulsiveness and love.

"You say his name is Andrews?" Frieda scraped hard at a crusted pot. "Paula Andrews's got a son still in school, and I know you know who Paula is."

Frieda didn't bother to turn away from the sink after she spoke, but he understood he was about to be punished. "Chad," she shouted, "get your butt in here."

There were groans and the padded sounds of a scuffle before his oldest nephew appeared in the doorway with his forearms folded across his black T-shirt. He felt Chad look at him neutrally, the one houseguest he didn't have to behave for. They'd had a short conversation at dinner about his Venezuelan tattoo and how much it had hurt, and they'd talked about the Lake State hockey team. It had been enough for both of them.

"Frank Andrews go to school with you?"

"Not no more. Dropped out." Chad lifted his arms above his head and mimed a jump shot. "Chip kid. You know how it is."

"I know it's tough for everybody." Frieda dried her palms on her skirt, looked at him, then away. "Take the garbage out, will you, then go on back and behave. Leave your brother alone."

Chad headed toward where his boots were sprawled on a rug by the door. "His mom's the one works at the bar."

"I know that," Frieda snapped. "I better not find out you've been over there."

Chad clomped out the door without his coat, and his sister turned on him. "Get what you came for, Johnny? I could have hooked you up with Paula without feeding you a good dinner."

He spun his glazed coffee mug between his hands. There were lots of Andrewses between here and the Soo. He hadn't really thought about the boy belonging to Paula. "I haven't been in there in a long time," he said. "Not since before I retired."

Frieda sat opposite him at the table. Her fair skin was smooth and pretty, flushed with the anger she'd stirred up, but still pretty. He was more than ten years older than she was, and there'd been times he'd taken care of her as well as any parent could. "I guess I'd be the first to hear otherwise, since the place is still packed with tattlers and assholes. I'd like to keep Chad out of there. He takes after Cecil's side, too slow to stay out of trouble. Not like his uncle."

He listened to her voice, careful and parched with forgiveness. Cecil ought to be around more, he thought, or somebody should. "Paula Andrews just poured the drinks I ordered," he said. "And it's all over, anyhow. I don't have time to drink."

Frieda laughed then, raising her chin and flexing her shoulders just as their father had when things were right with him. "You got time to do nothing *but* drink, so you give it up like a stubborn bastard. John Hansen, always cutting his own trail."

He stood, the trill of her chuckle running through him. Frieda closed things up between them; she always had. She flattened her hand as he slipped a fifty-dollar bill from his pocket. "Take the leftovers with you, do that much," she said. "And thank you for the wood. Chad and C.J. stacked it like you taught them. It's worked out good."

He drove like he was in a hurry until he reached the blinking yellow light across from the grocery, where he turned toward the water. He drifted past the house of a childhood friend who was on disability from his job with the road commission. Two doors down was the brown, asbestos-shingled bungalow his own family had lived in during a good stretch. The lake was in front of him, broken up by the gaunt reach of a few docks and the frosted cluster of Les Cheneaux Islands. The water here looked black, but common, polished into a series of pathways that led from shelter to shelter.

He parked, but it wasn't until he was out of the truck, his fingers working at the large horn buttons of his jacket, that he realized he was just up the block from The Chinook. He'd been thinking about Otto and how he was going to drop by the shop to say hello, and his fidgeting had driven everything else from his head. Everything except muscle memory. He walked across the damp, deserted street and looked in the storefront window of the bar. Closed until four. Chairs upended on the tables like spindly carcasses. Pool table in the same naked place. There were plastic garlands strung with Christmas lights nailed inside the window frame, though the lights weren't plugged in, and he could see a pall of fine dust on the sprigs of false holly and cedar. There was a tiny crèche nestled in cotton wadding on the varnished windowsill as well. Touches of Paula. Sweet. Well-meaning. Incomplete. He reopened the top button of his coat and began to search for his gloves. He'd lived a piece of his life in The Chinook, fighting, paring down love, filling his core with the false heat of bourbon. Then he'd moved on. The building felt no different in his mind now than the small dog-brown bungalow hunkered just out of sight on this same hill. He would swear to that.

He knew Otto would be working, even with the marina shut until spring, because that's what Otto did. His brother had repainted the building that fall, and he'd put in double-paned windows and new barn-red awnings. But he hadn't changed the name of their father's business. It was the same. *Hansen and Sons. Boat Builders. Docks. Storage.*

He knocked on the bolted front door, though he had a key to the lock on his own key ring. Otto had never been one for surprises. He waited, then heard a motor fire up just as he was setting his face to meet his brother's. The engine sounded muted and sluggish in the cold. He stepped around the corner of the shop, across the old launch ramp that was now boarded up, and toward the quay. His brother was casting off in the Chris-Craft, his face a putty-colored mask above his coveralls and the thick, speckled scarf done up for him by his wife, Marge. The gunwales and windshield of the boat were glazed with ice, and the inlet was curdled with slush. Boxes and bags crowded the floor of the boat behind where Otto stood at the wheel, his movements stiff but sure as he throttled into the channel. He was running groceries to widows and shut-ins out among the islands, stern and charitable with his yellow Labrador braced against his legs, her nose raised in the slapping air. That was his younger brother, as able and Lutheran as they came. He watched Otto take the chill breath of the lake across his face, watched him handle himself as any good wheelman might as his wake spooled and crimped the dark water. Something about the sight made his neck feel bowstrung, but he conquered it. Then he worked his way back to his still warm truck and the narrow, patchy roads to the bay.

The boy came when the girl got hurt, and it later seemed to him that the boy, Frank Andrews, had guessed that they'd be shut up in a room together one day, that he was somehow prepared for it. He was patching the wall behind his wood stove with metal cut from a wrecked panel truck because it's what he had for the job. There'd been a wet five-inch snow the night before; he didn't feel like plowing his way toward town. Besides, he liked an ugly repair that called on him to be resourceful.

The cabin door was open a crack for fresh air, but the boy knocked on the jamb, anyway. The noise of the knock pivoted him against the stove, crouching. Then he saw it was the boy from the brownish slash of face, the drained color of his hat. "Yeah," he said, standing with the hammer still in his hand.

"It's Frank Andrews." The boy laid out each syllable like it was stolen. "Got my beaver, but had a accident with a trap and wondered if you had a bandage. Just till I can get to my car."

He went to the door with purpose then, knowing that cold and shock could make a bad thing seem not so bad at first. A man could break an arm in one of those traps. The low, marbled sky was spitting snow which had begun to dust the boy's sturdy shoulders with flakes. He took in the boy's eyes first, which were black and even and undeluded by pain, then he saw the sleek carcass of a beaver cast into a pocket drift near a corner of the shack. It was bloodless as it ought to be since the traps were made to drown a beaver and never tear its pelt. It took him a moment to register the girl standing half-shielded by the boy. She was the one who'd been hurt. One of her hands was cupped beneath the other like a bowl, collecting the run of blood.

"Get in here," he said, "get on in," and he didn't take time to say what he wanted to say about the cramped way he lived. The blood he'd seen was bright red, but there wasn't much of it. There'd be more in the heat of the cabin, but if she hadn't nicked an artery he supposed he could handle it. Otherwise, it would be compresses and blankets and a damn crazy dozer ride out to the road. Neither kid did anything more than cross the threshold, though the boy reached for the girl's elbow, as if to offer her rivuleted skin as evidence of some sort of sincerity. "I got a first-aid kit," he said before either of them could start with an explanation. "Sit her in my chair and lay that hand where I can see it."

Coat and cap off, hands washed, kit opened on the table, which was scoured smooth and clean because he kept it that way. He'd never served as purser onboard, but he'd cleaned up his share of sailors after fights or mishaps with winches and snapped lines. He'd doctored himself plenty, too. He placed a towel under the girl's blood-mapped wrist. Her eyes were a shiny tannin brown, contracted some with pain and worry, though her cold-flushed mouth flitted with a smile that was part embarrassment, part apology. Indian, too, he decided, though not as full-blooded as the boy. Her hair was pulled off her face and hung down her back in a smooth, water-beaded hank. It was easy for him to see that she was pretty. Of course any son of Paula's would be used to that, fine looks in a woman, though whether he'd come to expect it, to search for it, was maybe another matter. He laid his own toughened fingertips at the base of her hand, felt it quiver, yet coaxed her without words to open her fingers. She shivered all over then, and he remembered what little he'd seen of her when she'd been standing on his doorstep. She was wet to the waist, soaking wet, like anybody might be who went after beaver dressed in jeans and cheap stay-in-town boots. He nodded to the boy, who was hovering at the edge of the table. "Build up the fire, will you? Or the hypothermia will get to her before I do."

The cut was ragged and ran from the crease of her ring finger across her palm to the fleshy base of her thumb, which accounted for the good amount of blood. Her thawing hands ached and stung; he could see that, too. And before he thought about it, he was massaging them some with his own, carefully, his skin feeling husklike to him against the raw damp of hers. She was small-boned, trembling. He daubed at her palm with a corner of the towel, then looked into her eyes, which gave him nothing. Without wiping his own fingers clean, he began to irrigate the wound.

"I can fix this good enough to get you to the clinic. You going up to the Soo?"

Neither of them answered him at first, though the girl dropped her head so he could see its delicate oval crown, the pale scar of her part.

"St. Ignace," the boy said from where he was squatting by the stove. "She's from there."

"They got a Indian clinic there, somewhere she can get stitches?"

"It'll get taken care of." The boy's voice was harder than it needed to be, and he wondered if they'd both been scared out there, truly afraid they were up against it, and that was what was holding them in so tight. Then again, maybe he'd made some kind of mistake. Maybe the girl wasn't Indian at all.

"Good," he said. "You take care of it. Because I can sew it up here and now if you're planning on getting stupid on me, or lazy."

The girl flinched so hard her knuckles knocked against the tabletop. The boy, Frank, stood halfway and took on a look that read mad-as-hell, which made him feel solid to see because he knew how to deal with an angry man, whereas this other, this unprepared for ministering, had brought a floating feeling to his stomach and beneath his words that he did not care for.

"Don't do no more." The boy moved up against the table again. "She's all right. Shelley, you all right?"

She nodded and began to push away from the heavy oak table, her hand stained orange with disinfectant but unbandaged, gaping. She seemed caught in the swift stream of the boy's assurance. Her legs failed her, though, faster than even he'd foreseen, because they'd been half-assed, all of them, and hadn't stripped her of her wet boots and clothes. She sank toward the chair, faltered, fell against the boy. He caught her under the arms and lifted her as though he'd cradled her before, then carried her to the bunk without asking. That was fine, though, he thought. It was the right thing to do.

"We need to get her dry," he said to the boy, aware that his voice had gone solemn and whispery, though the girl was very much awake. "I've got some clothes. See if she'll undress." He went to the place he kept his chest and flipped open the smooth brass latches while they spoke in low voices behind him. Everything in the chest was neatly folded and held the warm, powdery scent of cedar. It was easy to find what he needed.

"She wants to dress herself," the boy said, and the girl, who was sitting upright now on his scarred bunk, swung her head in blank agreement. "You...we...," the boy half-coughed, "we make her nervous. Could we leave for a minute, let her take care of it?"

"Yes," he said, and that was all. He scooped up his cap and coat from the floor where they'd fallen and headed out the door. He'd forgotten to expect modesty from the young.

Frank Andrews closed the door behind them, and the clean, diffuse light the snow carried with it made it seem as though they'd stepped into a white, high-ceilinged room, one just large enough to handle their talk and commotion. He stepped over to the plump carcass of the beaver, knelt next to it. Its dead eyes and yellowed teeth were invisible, buried, yet he thought he could smell the oily, musky taint of panic.

"You planning to haul it out yourself?" The beaver was big, sixty pounds easy.

"She's strong," the boy said, tilting his head toward the cabin. "That's why I brung her along."

He laughed until the boy showed his well-spaced teeth, and then it was in him, fast and mean, to give his laugh an ugly twist. A girl like that shouldn't be out here, though he thought he understood why she'd come. The boy was rocking on his feet again, rippling with the unguided energy of a young man, an unbeaten one. Women would follow the stream of that energy as long as the boy had it, he thought. Follow it and try to drink it down.

Before he knew it he'd reached into his pocket for two cigarettes and a lighter. It amazed him, the way two people could
make headway without words. He thought briefly of the girl dry-
ing her small, cold-clenched body with his bath towel, the live
tinge that would come to her skin, the darkening smears of her
blood. Then something about the way the boy handled his cigarette, his whole body sheltering the lighter's blue-whipped flame,
brought a question to mind. "You play some basketball?" He
tapped his own smoke on a thumbnail. "I think my nephew
talked about that."

The boy narrowed his eyes as if he were measuring something.
He raised one hand, cocked it at the wrist, then flipped it forward.
He could see that was all the answer he would get. It was over.
The boy had left it behind. And even though his body remem-
bered the moves, would forever remember them, he'd stopped
tunneling into that game with his mind.

"We can stand out here and freeze, then, just standing here. Or
we can load that beaver in my truck." He bent over and scythed
the snow off the glossy pelt with the edge of his hand. "I'll take
you out to your car."

The boy squinted at him through a scrim of smoke, then
shrugged the way he did.

"Check on her first, maybe," he said. "Make sure she's using the
blankets."

The boy grabbed at his frosted hat and stuck his head back
inside the cabin. He could see that the boy's hair had been cut
since he'd last seen him. It fell in a smooth, blunt line along the
flat muscle of his jaw and the coppery nape of his neck.

"She's all right," the boy said, fitting his hat back onto his head.
"Dressing."

They squatted as a pair and shared the beaver's weight as they
lifted. He glanced up the track and made a guess that the Ford
would get to the road all right; it would be a lot easier if they
could travel in a heated cab. When the beaver was laid out in the
truck bed, he found his fingers spidering through his pockets for
more cigarettes. The boy seemed impressed that he had two
trucks in the shed, plus the dozer and a good canoe. He wanted to
know about the machines, if they all drove well.

"Used to know your mother," he said to the boy instead, and right away the words hung from him like brittle ice from a branch. He felt foolish. The boy probably knew all he wanted to know about old Hermit Hansen. He had no business trying to make himself out to be another kind of man.

"Everybody knows my ma." The boy ran a hand along the searing green flank of the Ford, admiring the tires, the roomy bed. "Everybody from around here, anyway. Long time she's worked at The Chinook."

"I shot pool in there some, when I wasn't shipped out."

"Thought you hardly ever left this place." The boy blew some air into his hands, kept his eyes on the truck. "Guard it like a damn Doberman or something."

Hearing that strangled the bland words he'd aligned in his throat, and he stepped out of the shed into a dervish of snow that whirled off the roof. He tried to lock his mind onto the idea of the half-dressed girl, how she needed to be wreathed in warmth, gotten home.

"Hey, you want to tell me about my ma, go ahead." There was swagger in the boy's words now. "I've heard it before. One million times. So don't think you know a story that'll get to me. You don't know a story like that."

He turned on the boy, headed back to where he stood in the shelter of the shed. But he couldn't get his head to go all silky like it needed to be before he went into a fight. He couldn't even bring Paula's smooth, silent, commiserating face into focus, her sympathetic neck. He stopped, letting the wind split at his back.

"I guess now you're gonna tell me Ma's the reason you keep women's clothes way out here." The boy had his arms away from his sides, hands flexing. "Do it, then. Come at me with your weird-old-man shit. Cause no woman would ever come here for you. You can't tell me that."

It had been a long while since he'd been where the anger took him, riding roughshod through nerve and vein, howling within him louder than the words in his bitten throat could howl. Yet it came easily enough. He didn't bother to wait for the boy, who became like a broken-winged bird to him, clucking and fluttering in outrage. He went straight to the cabin, burst inside with his vision blanched by fury and the ungiving glare of snow. The girl was slumped on his bunk, drowsy maybe, wilted by comfort. He grabbed her where her shoulder met her collarbone, bent on flinging her to her feet, which he did. She gasped, and he felt her warm, shocked, caressing breath but didn't hear it. Didn't hear the boy tear into the cabin, either, though he knew when he was behind him, exactly there, and was able to meet him with a solid punch to the gut when it was time. He flung the girl's short-waisted coat after her and her false-furred boots and her wet, crumpled clothes. He flung them both out, into the world where they could keep their messes to themselves. The girl began to cry, but he was deaf to that also. He did see the boy's face, though, and he knew what it meant, the black line of brows, the jagged, uncentered glint in the eyes. It meant the boy had been cornered for the first time. That he'd just about found a new edge to plunge over.

He barely heard the bleating curses and the crude battering of his truck as they tore at the tailgate and took their beaver back. They would have stolen the truck if they could have, maybe even wrecked it. It's what he would have done. He watched them hump up the track with the beaver bowing the boy's infuriated young body, the girl stumbling along behind. He noticed that the girl had left her soaked garments strewn between the cabin and the shed, and he thought he could either burn them or fold them into his sea chest—that it wouldn't matter which he did. He saw, too, that she'd wrapped her hand with the gauze he'd laid out for her. There was the blankness of a bandage on her, just as there was the resin color of corduroys on her legs, the noon-blue print of a turtleneck on her slender torso and arms, the musky linger of her sweat. What he didn't know and couldn't give a good history to were those vagabond clothes, what she'd taken from him. He did not recall who they'd once belonged to or whether he'd known her name at all.

The nights became as long as they ever get, and as stark, and the wave-etched ice shelved itself around the bay and out into the lake until the shipping channels were closed. Snow came in sheets and squalls and perfect geometric drifts. On clear days he hauled wood in the restless company of crows, skidding pallets of poplar and deadfall oak in from the far-off places he'd stacked them. On days when the sky seemed no higher than the treeline and the smoke from his chimney fumed at his door, he stayed in, flipped cards, listened to the insistent radio. He spent some complicated hours with a T square drawing up plans for a sauna, but he did not keep at it.

One night he pried open a carton of cigarettes and thought about the boy. He hadn't been back for his traps. It was no way to run a line, but laziness of that sort was up to the boy and his uncle, if there really was an uncle. He considered how he'd once connected the boy with Henderson and what a mistake that had been. Henderson had a sense of humor and a bolt-tight sense of himself as a man. Henderson had never thrown anything in another man's face, which was where the boy's weakness was, in his impetuous, assuming pride. Good sailors withheld almost all there was to withhold aboard ship—it was how any crew avoided murder—and if a sailor was smart, he behaved much the same way when he had to be on land. Surviving. Two legs to stand on.

Henderson on the *McCurdy*. They'd been aboard together, hauling a capacity load of taconite out of Duluth, running to make St. Marys River before she froze. On his first watch they took white water across the bow, and some of the vessels ahead— especially the empty ones—heaved to in the lee of Keeweenaw Point or short of the river, where thick fog was said to be mother- ing chunk ice and sleet. The *John C. McCurdy* steamed on. He had little trouble driving her into the black, foaming swells and keep- ing her trim. At next watch, though, things were different.

The old man was on the bridge by then, sleepless, thin-lipped. The wind screeched through the gangways, and the water they took across the bow began to rivet itself into a crystal armor of ice. Radio reports put them on the near side of a full-blown gale. The captain was an able man, overly cautious but never stupid. He ordered a change of course designed to run with wind and current alike. But *McCurdy* began to wallow under the extra weight of the ice. Two hours later the propeller gave way, unable to take the strain of being pitched into open air, then slammed into the mad roil of a twenty-foot crest. They all felt it, the wrench and give, and they hated the loss of momentum, the wheezing surge that had been the one force under their control. The captain radioed the Coast Guard and prepared for a merciless wait.

A twin-screw freighter from Canada offered to backtrack and give *McCurdy* a line to keep her off the shoals. But the captain told the freighter to tend to her own needs; he was nearly far enough east to be safe. And this was how Third Mate Hansen left things when he climbed from the bridge. Square-shouldered men not thinking ahead. Stoic.

He came into the officers' mess dripping and swearing. The air in the galley was stale with breath and sweat and the soggy smell of food no one wanted. He coughed into his hands, tasting the layered man-stink while he exhaled the arctic swipe of the storm. He noticed there was a passenger in the galley, a smallish withered man who was trying to read a magazine. It bothered him that the man was not in his cabin puking into his steel bowl and staying clear of a crew that had trouble on its hands, but he said nothing.

"Sandwich," he called to Henderson, and he shed his rain gear behind the chair that was his. Sloppy, irregular, but he did it, anyway. The ship fell off into a trough; each man braced himself for dive and recovery. Devil's pride, he told himself, all of them pretending that this cork-tossing was normal.

"I got some fish and some ham," Henderson said, his dark arms crossbarred in the doorway. "Your choice, sir."

That made them both laugh. "Make me four hams to run topside with some coffee. I can't stay here."

"Sure you can. No man is that everlasting important." The words came from the passenger, sudden and taunting. He glanced at Henderson for confirmation of the man's impertinence, but Henderson had turned to his work, bowed and uninvolved, so he angled his body across the long, tilting table toward the stranger.

"Maybe I don't care if I'm important. It's my job."

"No, it's not, Mate Hansen. You've pulled your watch. You were off at twelve bells."

"This is a bad time, sir."

"This," the man said delightedly, "is what a freshwater sailor would call a bad time."

The old fellow, he decided, was crazy with worry, or simply crazy. He yanked his slicker from the floor while the *McCurdy* balanced atop yet another wind-shorn crest. He moved into the galley as she paused, looking for a place to steady himself because he didn't like the way she felt, bovine, resigned. The ship plunged hard, then submarined. He found himself pressed next to Henderson in the tight space below the ovens. The Indian showed clenched teeth. The passenger, it sounded like, was flung against a wall. Seconds later the bow pulled free of the water, and they were afloat again. They'd need worse luck to lose her—he knew that—but the captain would want him to ready the boats just the same.

Henderson went to help the passenger while he tucked his pockets full of sandwiches and a thermos. He listened as the passenger insisted he was unhurt. "I am fine," he chided the cook. "You men have been through nothing if you can't chin up to this." Henderson said something inaudible, and the passenger began to cackle, then cough. "I've been washed ashore bare-arsed twice in my life. You ever sail Torpedo Alley off Cape Hatteras? Ever hear of the bloody hell called Dunkirk?" He paused long enough to hear the man's hollow accent become more British than it had been before. The captain had passed along a name at one point— Burley? Billingsley?—a joyrider, the captain said, with plenty of money. He fastened his slicker and made his way to the corner, where Henderson had propped the man upright.

"Ready to take to the boats, are you?" He leaned into the yellowish, translucent face that up close seemed shrunken by illness. He hadn't seen that before, or the blood dribbling from a split lip, and he felt pity mix with frustration in his gut, a blend he didn't like. "If that's what you're after, I'll make it my business to see you don't get it. Not on this ship."

"You don't give the orders." The man bared his pinkened teeth for a laugh.

He grabbed the man's throat, sank his fingers into slack, wattled flesh, and shoved until the galley wall banged, then banged again. "I give the orders needed, you bastard. Go back where you came from and do it while you can."

He stood and wiped the spit from his lips. The *McCurdy* chose that moment to slither and spasm beneath them. He could sense the massive torque along her keel.

"There it is, Mate Hansen," the voice at his feet wheezed. "You feel it. You'll be my man before all's well and done."

He struck the man outright. With the flat of his hand at first, then his rapid fist. The old fellow closed his eyes, and his head went loose on his neck, as though he'd been beaten before and knew how to take it. Three punches, maybe four. He stopped when the cartilage of the thin, arrogant nose gave way beneath his knuckles.

It was Henderson who surprised him. The cook looked like he planned to drive his own fist into the man's sunken gut. Yet he somehow fell away from the scarecrow collapse of the passenger, every glint of irritation and resolve drained from his eyes. His grim mouth moved in silence. He watched Henderson hard until the cook gasped as if he'd just discovered air. It was the ship, he thought. The damned strangling ship. Or the garrote of the storm. Henderson had caught something in the confluence of the two, something chill and speechless, and he had not.

It wasn't long before the cook came back into himself, ran his blade-nicked hands across his white apron, and offered to haul the passenger to his quarters, clean him up. Henderson's voice was low and easy, as always. Neither of them mentioned what had just yawed between them. If they spoke of it, they'd do so after the *McCurdy* had docked and unloaded and the time for stories had come. He left the galley in silence, turning his thoughts to his stubborn crew and what he would ask of them. The lifeboats would be frozen hard to their tackle, and the one on the bow might not be there at all. They'd have to go out—on lines or not—and see. And he would go out among them.

Some days later he found himself back in Frieda's kitchen, feeling browbeaten for reasons that were mucky in his own head. He hadn't been in touch with his sister for almost a month, a fact he registered when he emptied his box at the post office, searching for his pension check and finding letters from charities and colored flyers for the Christmas craft fair. He'd missed the holidays. He stopped at the hardware store and bought his nephews gifts. It would be okay, he thought, to give Frieda money as he usually did. Perfume, a sweater, a scarf—it wouldn't feel right to buy something like that for her. He planned for them to handle one another as they always had, without decoration.

It was the middle of the week, so Frieda put coffee on and allowed him his cigarette, but there was no food. The boys were still at school. The Christmas decorations, which his sister lavished on every surface of her small house, were gone, stored for another year. The brown paper bag that held the unwrapped gifts for his nephews mocked him from the kitchen countertop. A stupid idea. Weak. He smoked in silence, trusting he could hold fast longer than the nervy glimmers of his embarrassment could. The boys deserved something. He watched Frieda take things out of the refrigerator and the pantry. She stooped and bent, but even in a sweatshirt and purplish jeans, she didn't appear old to him. She was nimble, still concerned with the visitations of failure or success. He was the one who'd aged. He'd run from so many things, he'd pretty much run his way to the end of his life.

"You talk to them?"

"Marge and Otto? Oh, sure. They were here for—" She shook her head in disbelief. "We all got together for the holidays. Just once, but it was nice. Marge brought the ham, and the girls got along all right with C.J. and Chad. Otto complained about the government, as usual, and the bank, too, if you can believe that. He's on the G.D. board there. I thought Cecil would just bust."

They laughed, both of them, at the vision of Otto preaching about money. Their good brother, so sure of his restraint.

"Sorry I missed the party."

"No, you're not. And I'll tell you again what I told you last year. We've got so we don't miss you. Don't even bring up your name." Frieda was behind him, sweeping the floor. He could hear the hasty, scritching strokes of the broom.

"Makes it easier."

"Yes, it does."

He stood and drifted into the den, into the crabbed and narrow hallway that was so much like the hallways of his youth, drifted into the yellow-tiled bath looking for something to tinker with. When he asked Frieda where he might find replacement screws for the hinges of the clothes hamper, she handed him a shoe box of junk—buttons, paper clips, hardware—and told him to get on with it. He wanted to thank her for taking him up again, but he didn't. He thought about the jaundiced bathroom instead. How his sister never had anything unspoiled or new. He was sorting nails and scrap when his nephews charged into the house, faces stung red from the cold, their cheap, oversized parkas flapping.

They launched into competing stories about teachers and bus brawls before they saw him. C.J., the young one, clammed up at once. Chad dropped his backpack on the table and took up as much space as he could between his uncle and his mom.

"Did you tell him yet?" Chad pinned him with a squint, like he was studying long words on a sign.

"No." Frieda gathered the coats, knocked the slushy boots into a corner. "Hasn't come up."

"Well, I'm bringing it up. Everybody's talking about it."

"Just to be gross," C.J. said, edging out of the room. He was a large-eyed kid, and shy. "You like to think about him underwater all winter, down there with the pike and stuff."

"That's enough." Frieda waved an arm as though she was good-humored and tolerant, but he could see the creases around her mouth deepen and how she wouldn't look his way. "Out of here, and keep it down. Uncle John and me are talking."

"Then talk to him, will you?" Chad strode into the den. "It's like he lives in the desert or something."

He did a calm inventory in his head. The family was fine—he knew that. Something local, then. A thing spectacular to people who decided to share their tragedies.

"It's just one of those sad messes kids get caught up in because it bothers them. Maybe it'll bother you, too. It was the one you know, Paula's boy. He was running hay out to Mackinac, for the horses there, and the ice broke in a freak way. He's so far down, they can't even dive for him. Driving a Sno-Cat. The guys on Ski-Doos are all fine."

He looked at her, reacquainted himself with the wrinkles around her eyes.

"Plain bad luck is what they say. A squall got them off-track, and they say one of the snowmobilers—some relative—was drunk, but they didn't do anything stupid. People make that run all the time."

"Been making it for years," he said.

"Yeah," she said, looking at him like she couldn't quite bring his hairline into focus. "Horses have to eat just like the rest of us. Some guy in St. Ignace has the contract, and he let this kid, what's his name, drive the Cat because he asked to. The paper said some nice things."

"Same as dying in a car wreck," he said.

"Maybe so. All the way to the bottom, though, that's different. Feels different to me."

She went on then—to a salting and pounding of meat, stopping once to ask if he wanted to stay for dinner. He didn't. He stood and rinsed his mug, emptied the green glass ashtray into the trash, found his hat and gloves on top of the refrigerator where he'd left them. Only when he went to put on the gloves did he realize his left fist was clenched. When he opened it he saw two wood screws pressed deep into his callused skin, so deep they ought to hurt.

"I'm sorry," his sister said. Her arms were folded tight over her chest, but her face was elongated, soft.

"About what?"

"You know what I mean." And she moved after him to shut the door, sealing her house again from the cold.

When he pulled in across from The Chinook, he realized that his mouth was wet and drooling for a drink while his throat was wrung dry. Divided up, he told himself. Same old story. He went inside, nodded to the men playing eight ball, then slid onto a stool at the bar. He ordered a Coke, and the bartender, a red-haired guy he didn't know, brought it to him right away. He left a good tip and moved to an empty round table against the wall. A stuffed salmon bucked on the wall above him. The air smelled of fry grease and sleep.

He finally thought to slip his coat off so he wouldn't look like he was on the run. Chewed on the ice in his Coke and watched the pool players circle the table like boxers, high-shouldered and flat-faced. He didn't have to wait long. She brought him a second

Coke in a highball glass and sat down across from him.

"Hello, John." She'd always said it the same.

"Hello, Paula. Thought I'd come see the sights." He took in her face, which was thinner; he looked for gray in her hair or any bad sign of grief. What he could see right away were diamond-chip earrings and lipstick and the way she hid her hands.

"New jukebox. We got that for big dancers like you. And the kitchen's been redone. You want some food?"

"No," and he shook his head as her wide-set brown eyes smiled. He'd been puke-sick in front of her in the old days, there was that humiliation. He'd touched her some as well, as much as she'd allowed from an earnest drunk, since she had three or four kids already. That had happened maybe half a dozen times in ten years of drinking, shipping out, moving on. What he'd kept with him most was what hung before him now—her lovely, unassailing face.

"I heard about your boy."

She sat back in her chair and brought a hand up along her neck and ear. Her nails were still short-bitten. "I knew you were here because of that. You remembered, didn't you? That time with the puppy. It's good for me to think of times like that." She began to cry a little, even while she was trying not to, and the tears ran alongside her small, blunt nose. "I didn't see much of Frankie lately. He was living with his father's people. Wanted to do for himself."

He looked down, saw that his distant fingers were shredding a napkin.

"He loved when you sent me home with that crazy pup. Thought it was pure German shepherd and told everybody that, bragging. He was gonna train that dog, too, but it got killed on the road."

All those kids, tangled shapes of her kids, tangle of what she said about them, and him never bothering to sort them out by name or size or worry. No one in The Chinook had. And one of them was Frank, into his life then out of it like an ass-whipped bad dream. He sat there knowing he'd never given any kid a dog.

"He shouldn't have been on no Sno-Cat," he said. "That was plain stupid."

Paula tensed, looked at the wall next to them, then back.

"He was stupid about laying his traps, too. I could have told him if he listened one damn—" He choked up on his loud words as he realized the redhead bartender was watching him, and Paula was watching, too, but not in the right way.

"You come in here for whiskey, I won't sell you whiskey." She wept openly, with the light of temper rising in her eyes. "Don't talk down my boy, neither. It was an accident. Nobody meant no harm."

"I knew him." He felt terribly hot under his clothes, like he needed to tear them open. "We got along, and then we didn't, and I tried—"

"Say you're sorry, John. Then move on like we both got to. I'm marrying Pete Norlund." She sniffled and drew her arms tight to her sides. "Frankie hated I was with Pete. And now I don't got that battle to fight."

He took hold of his riptide mind, grappled and thought about Norlund, a barrel of a Swede older than himself, made rich off timber and real estate. There'd been a stout wife around, last he'd heard, but something had clearly been done about her.

"Maybe it'll go good, Paula. You deserve it if anybody does."

"Still know how to make sweet, do you? I didn't never forget you or the things you did." She stood and covered one of his hands with hers while she reached for his empty glasses. A brush light and warm, but he could feel it go deep just before it left him. Saw her ring, too, set with hard, permanent diamonds. Norlund had a big glassy house on the lakefront. He would work to imagine her in there.

"Sorry about your boy."

She swung her head as if she could fling it empty of tears and walked from him. A black, sleeveless blouse that was more modest than it needed to be. Good boots, tight jeans. Her long, thick hair fanning out from a silver conch clip that he immediately recognized, so like the ones he'd almost brought to her after his trips away, the ones he'd fingered and never bought in those smiling, jostling marketplaces far from home.

He took note of the ragged cuticles of snow left by the plows. Of the snapped-off tree branches. Of the convoyed clouds to the south. There was a way to carry on that every sailor learned after his first few watches—a way to remain alert but separate, never mesmerized or confused by the shape-shifting of fool water or the sky. Peering ahead, looking for decisions to make—that was the way a man remained clear.

He parked on the track, leaving room to swing the canoe out of the shed. He looked her over carefully first, eyeing the seams, checking where he'd patched her in the fall with a square of cloth from a shirt and some ambroid glue. She rested cleanly on her braces, a beamy wood-canvas shell. He'd bought her from an old steam-tender who'd foulhooked the end of his luck, gave the man a sluggish Grumman and a hundred dollars in exchange. The steam-tender said she came from Minnesota and was made the old-time trapper way, to last forever. Whatever the truth, she handled well in light water and was easy enough for one man to portage. He slid her off the braces, flipped her, then worked her up on end until he could yoke up between the varnished, seat-worn thwarts. The snow was crusty and deep. It would be a long, panting carry.

By the time he could see the wide silver scuff of the bay, he'd begun to sweat through his second shirt.

He took the canoe to the place he always took her, next to a great smooth log that had washed ashore in a spring storm not long after he'd moved into the shack for good. In summer he chained the canoe along the far side of the log, but he did not chain her now. He merely nestled her into her accustomed place, protected as much from wind and weather as she could be. He was months early. Porcupines or others might do her some mischief, though it was not a possibility that bore thinking about. He'd make up a special buoy before long, get together a good anchor and plenty of strong line. What he needed to consider now was when he would next be out on the water, stroking through the rocky blue shallows of the bay into the lake.

He made his way downshore to a natural cairn of porous, fossil-etched stones, swept them clean of snow, leaned against them. Mackinac Island was a tired mirage beneath the translucent clouds, a smudge of dirtied crystal. Winter had leveled it, as it leveled them all. The boy he'd known had done nothing but take on a few jobs, try on his shifting attitudes. It hurt Paula plenty that he'd died, more than anything had ever hurt him. He knew he wouldn't set foot in The Chinook again, not even to recast his words to her, the ones he'd meant to say better. If he took up liquor, he'd go to the next town to drink it, or drink it in the hidy-hole of his shack like he was expected to.

The sun drifted west until the snow on the lake was shadowed in lavender and blue, and the trees drew themselves into a phalanx of darkness at his back. He had always cared for this, the way the lake sealed itself off, flat and silent and hidden. There was nothing practical to be done about the boy. He could walk the ponds and try to locate the beaver traps, though the uncle would surely come after them before long—maybe he'd come with the girl—and he had no business pretending he was a help to anyone. He was not.

His sweat cooled but did not dry, and there was a chill against his skin. Then the vast hush of an unhindered night brought Henderson back into his mind. Strong, private Henderson, who should have been a cook on the lollygagging, sweet-tempered *Pontiac* with its simple runs to Buffalo, but who kept manning the slipshod *McCurdy* in his mind. It had been Henderson who'd done the visceral thing.

He'd run his gang out along the decks, captain's orders, as they needed to know how bad things were with the boats and hatches and rails. Most of them went on safety lines—the decks were slick, the air burned with sleet—but he and Quillian, a true New-foundland bastard, went footsure and unfettered. They'd discovered the worst, and he was on his way to report to the captain when he saw a man peering at him through a scleric portal. Henderson. Broad and searching in his foul weather gear, face pressed against the murky glass. He feared the cook wanted to volunteer for his crew, and he did not want that to happen.

He took his tidings to the old man on the bridge. The bosun would need a look at the number three hatch; he'd take him there. There was some relief in the orders that followed, the risks, the sleight of hand it would take to get through the remainder of the storm. There was a kind of march to the whole thing that he relished—a sailor's muster and charge—all done to the drumbeat of weather and damage.

Quillian was waiting for him below deck, his face and cap beaded with melting sleet. "The Indian's gone out there. I told him not to." Quillian spoke with neither urgency nor judgment. Narrow talk, the speech of an islander.

"I'll get him. He has some crazy idea about helping."

"Don't know about that," Quillian said. "Had his duffel with him, like he meant to leave."

He pushed his way out then. The deck lights flickered in the thick spray and wind, teasing his sense of balance. He clutched a rail as the *McCurdy* bucked through a shallow trough, water spewing green and black across his face. They'd been spared by the genius of the chief engineer so far, but if she caught beam seas again, caught them hard enough, the decks would be carried under. He looked midships for Henderson, thought again of the blackjacked look in the cook's eyes when the passenger had sworn them off, and made his way down an accursedly icy ladder and aft. Henderson was on the fire crew. Maybe he was crazy enough to take his drill station. If he was still onboard at all.

He found him leaning over a beaten section of railing, sweeping his arms above the frenzied leap of water. Madness. Or an Indian thing, maybe. Or just madness. He'd ask him to come back with him, to the galley for coffee, but if he wouldn't come, so be it. The lake knew her business. He did not move, however, when he saw Henderson lift his duffel—stuffed and heavy—onto the rail. A clumsy shove, and the bag went overboard, and while he waited a pitiless moment for Henderson to follow the duffel, it did not happen. The cook turned and saw him through the dim shower of spray and nodded, his rain hat tied tight beneath his squarish chin. It was as though he'd known he was being watched. Henderson then passed by and made his way up the ladder with slow purpose. He followed the cook until he met up again with Quillian and the hard-pacing bosun. There were no words exchanged. They all went on with their jobs.

He didn't hear about the passenger until the next day. Awake for thirty hours until the weather broke, out dead for four hours' sleep, then back into the crowded mess for some breakfast. He didn't hear about it from Henderson, who was preparing a sherry soufflé for the captain, his apron starched flat, his black hair drawn into a neat, foreign-looking knot at the base of his skull. He heard it from the chief steward, who'd been to the passenger's cabin with clean towels and linens. The fellow was gone; the cabin as tidy as a commander's. They were looking for him in every bunk and locker, knowing how panic could make a rat out of any man, but some who'd met him or seen him walking the decks before the storm did not expect to see him again. This was what the steward said, working the tale slowly around his soft Caribbean vowels, savoring it for the drinks that a longer, more lush version would someday buy.

He knew. And could feel the knowledge loop about him like a fresh manila line, connecting him hard to Henderson and that damnable yakking man. To Quillian, too, no doubt, though the Newfie would never speak of what he'd seen, as he lived ancestrally in the gap between what he witnessed and what he needed to act upon.

Now, standing on a plain of sharded dark and light, at the edge of water and his land, he could not remember what it had been like to look Henderson in the eye after that moment. He could not recall what they'd said to each other, though he knew they must have spoken—each of them—and let the words wrap the shroud on tight. Had they ever gone that far? He knew well how the *McCurdy* had been towed back to Duluth by a Coast Guard vessel with a belligerent crew. He knew Henderson had left the ship, as all the crew did, off to sign onto other freighters while the *McCurdy* underwent repairs. Henderson in his massive pea jacket, his oft-healed hands, a neatly packed duffel like a rolled sail across his shoulder. They had said goodbye to one another in the usual brief way, as there were always things left unspoken when a man passed by another man. He remembered that he never questioned Henderson's reasons. The passenger may have died on that pitching galley floor, or, good Christ, he may have begged to taste the saltless water of their particular sea. There *had* been a reason, he was sure of it—one that meant everything to the assembled heart that worked inside Henderson.

He walked onto the ice. First to where it laced around the lifeless rocks. Then to where the water of the bay deepened and he could have fished if he cared to and speared his share of whitefish and pike. Beyond, the ice grew thinner and might have groaned and pealed beneath him, but it did not. He went on, to the point where his canoe would begin to feel the draw of the great lake, its deep currents and cold logic. He would plant a hand-painted buoy when the ice broke, pay his delayed respects. The boy was out there, open-eyed and washed and preserved, a victim of risk and channel water, but all he could see were the pitiful man-lights that necklaced Mackinac and adorned her property. He turned back only when the wind rose from the black distance and drove into him, squalling with snow and bitterness. Only when he could be driven ashore like a sail with no good hull or keel beneath him. It was a motion he understood, for it was how his watery heart now worked within him.

LESLIE McKENZIE BIENEN

The Star of Africa

There were two women I thought might be able to help me, or rather help Lance, and that night, sitting on the bus on the way home from the hospital, I vowed to find one or both of them the next day, even if I had to cancel a couple of my afternoon classes to do it. There was always Sammy, of course, but I was anxious to keep him out of it because every hand up you get from Sammy today is one you won't be getting tomorrow. It doesn't matter whether the stuff is for me, Lance, or Santa Claus—I'm the one who's asking so it's going straight onto my balance sheet. Sammy shares the house with me and my son, Adam, and the Old Lady, the maid/nanny we pay to watch soap operas.

I should have been using the two-hour trip to grade papers, but I couldn't face it, and the bus driver was weaving through traffic as though he were maneuvering a motorcycle, cranking on the steering wheel so the back of the bus swung wildly across the lanes, making the passengers grab for the tops of seats to avoid being pitched into the aisle. With the kung fu movie blasting above my head and all the blank faces staring up at it while they spooned the dinners someone had prepared for them into their mouths, it was like being in twenty living rooms at once. I couldn't wait to be inside my own house and enjoy the hour between getting there and going to bed that my home life had dwindled to since I started going to the hospital after work. I had barely laid eyes on Sammy in weeks, between my coming in late and him keeping stranger hours than usual, but I was just as happy to avoid him. I owed him a few baht for an advance he'd given me—only an ounce or so—and he was pissed off about a deal with a friend of mine who, he said, had screwed him over. I've never met the man who could stiff Sammy, but when he decides he's in the right, that's the end of it. No further discussion.

That left Sister Michael as my first choice of savior. She's a nurse at the Seventh Day Adventist Hospital, where I'd done one of my detoxes. I had long suspected she had a little thing for me, which wouldn't hurt. It would be tricky, though, because she was a toughie, the only ex-nun at Seventh Day who retained her male saint's name when she went AWOL. Second and last resort was Noi, an ex-student of mine, but she would involve money changing hands. Since Angie left, I hadn't been with anybody (of course I can't properly say I was ever *with* Angie, but that's a whole other story), but occasionally, when the money situation loosened up, I visited Noi down at Soi Cowboy where she worked. Noi had wanted to improve her English so she could actually converse with her customers beyond "You want hand fuck? . . . How much you give me?" so she'd signed up for my class. She even paid for it herself. We never actually did it, but I liked to share body heat with her, have her slip me the tongue. It was nothing serious— she usually didn't even take out her chewing gum. Anyway, I knew Noi had connections and might be able to get me some prescription pills—stuff Lance wouldn't consider too low for him to stoop to—if she could skim a little off the top without her guy realizing.

I needed a wide variety—painkillers, barbiturates, Valium, whatever—since you never know exactly what's going to work when they're so far gone. The best would have been junk, but I knew Lance would never take it, even if I fixed him up, so it was useless to try persuading him that it would make everything feel better. It was an image thing—shooting just didn't fit in with his vision of himself. Lance saw himself as some other kind of person, the kind who would never ever do that. As if that's how people who do shoot primarily define themselves: *Well, here I go again, because I'm a junkie, and this is what we do, this is how we see ourselves.* Give me a break. So far I'd resisted the temptation to say, Are you the kind of person who imagined himself rotting in a scummy hospital in a slum outside of Bangkok? Held hostage in a filthy bed at the mercy of a bunch of snotty nurses, the recipient of everyone's scornful pity, a body that others avert their eyes from because it's too painful for *them* to look at *you*? Why screw everything up for someone who's dying, anyway, all their years of hard work down the drain?

I say work because you could tell right off when you met Lance just from the way he carried himself—before all this happened, I mean—that he had a very definite idea of how to present himself, *Lance,* to the world, and that it had taken him a very long time to construct who that self was supposed to be. I have a certain admiration for people who can do that, even though I don't necessarily like them, and usually even *dis*like them. Here I am, a blind blob of something, a clam or an oyster that someone has torn from his shell—not necessarily to eat, possibly just for the hell of it—then tossed back into the water, where I bob along for all the world to see, waiting to be swamped by a wave or gobbled up by any old predator that comes along. And there those other people are, the Lances of the world, with their million layers of protection and self-definition, unreachable and impenetrable. It wasn't until Lance got sick that I saw the slightest crack in his persona; and even then he managed to keep up appearances for a good while.

One of the first, and one of the few, times I saw him lose it was about a month after he'd been hospitalized. I'd gone on a Saturday, which was rare because Saturday was my only day off. Usually I'd take Adam on some outing, but the Old Lady's niece and her spoiled kid were coming for the day, and I decided to clear out and pay Lance a surprise visit. Sammy was gone already, God knows where. Relations between me and Sammy had been deteriorating, which worried me a little, but I figured I'd deal with it later, when there was more time. I knew he didn't like me visiting Lance so often, maybe just because it was a change and Sammy doesn't like changes. Or maybe he had some Sammy-logic that was known only to his brain; whatever the reason, he was out more and generally chillier when he was home—doing the crossword without me just to make a point, stuff like that. Anyway, since there was no patching up to be done that morning, I thought I'd keep Lance company, bring some work with me, see how things were going there, and maybe if he felt good enough, we'd play a game of chess. That was before I realized he was hopeless at the game—in the hospital, at least, he had no heart for it. Maybe it was too reminiscent of the fact that he had no move to make for himself now—whatever control, at least by legal methods, he could have had over the situation probably evaporated as soon as they got him into that hospital.

The hall was empty, per usual. Lance was in a ward the staff worked hard to avoid. The receptionist had nodded me in, recognizing me by now, although she rarely looked me in the face. He didn't have many visitors; even the other gay men in our office couldn't bring themselves to come more than once or twice.

I knocked and then opened the door gently, so as not to startle him. He looked at me through puffy eyes, like he'd been crying for some time, and his cheeks still had sleep crinkles from the coarse pillowcase. Both activities were so recently represented on his face, he could only have been crying in his sleep.

"Rough night?" I said.

He looked at me vaguely, then, after a few seconds, like he knew who I was. "Did you just get here? What are you doing here? It's Saturday."

"I know." I put my papers down on the floor and sat in the only chair. There was absolutely nothing to look at in the room but each other. "Thought I could inveigle you into some chess." His face looked so distraught, and was such a contrast to his normally composed features, that I had to look away; staring at the floor was preferable, despite the presence of a metal bowl next to his bed that he had vomited into during the night and no one had come to take away. I was about to get up and rinse it in the sink, so I wouldn't have to smell the odor, and to make myself busy while he got under control, when Lance said, "I was dreaming, but the same dream I had once a few years ago—the worst dream I ever had." His mouth looked like he was going to cry more. He must have become conscious of his lower lip trembling because he chewed on one side of it for a second. "It was a dream that I had AIDS, and I was in the hospital, and no one would come visit me. And if they did come, they just stared at me through a little glass window in the door of my room and wouldn't enter. No one would touch me."

I muttered, "Oh, no, that's not...I'm sure...," something I thought would be comforting, but he spoke over me, which was probably for the best because I had launched into a sentence without really having a plan for where it was going.

"I lay in bed, and I could see different people's faces at the little window, my brother and my parents, and then random dream people like my Italian teacher from high school, and I was crying and crying, saying over and over, *I'm so lonely, I'm so lonely.* But you know what the worst part was?" He was talking so quickly, a ragged breath every now and then obliterating a word entirely, he wouldn't have heard a response if I'd made one. "When I woke up, I couldn't remember if I had it or not. I lay in bed not know- ing for about ten minutes, before I figured out that I was perfectly healthy. And that's what happened to me this morning, too. Only I woke up in this shithole instead of my bed, which was my first tip-off. But I still wasn't sure, I thought maybe I was really here for something else, you know like a hernia operation"—he almost laughed, but it was swallowed up in a sob—"and a bad night in the hospital had given me an anxiety dream. It took me a few minutes to realize that it's not just as bad as my dream, it's worse."

I was silent. Any words of comfort would have sounded fatuous and artificial, and I was a little caught off-guard seeing Lance weep so openly. I had barely even seen him scowl, before the hospital. Of course he wasn't the same since, essentially, being locked up to die, but most of the time he managed to carry off an almost collu- sive air, as though it were all happening to someone else. Like he was on the side doing the pitying, and the pity-ee was a third, invisible party in the room that we had to be careful not to allude to in any way, lest we offend him. I got up to put the bowl in the sink, hating the noticeably heavy footfall of my bad leg as I crossed the room and how the tap of my cane on the linoleum gave a syn- copated rhythm to the sounds that were coming from the bed.

With a name like Lance Potter, you almost have to go in one direction or the other: millionaire snob or all-smiles-apple-pie- boy-next-door. Lance was striving for the latter but fell short, headlong into that middle ground, which is where you run into trouble. His natural tendency was to be a little snarky, but he tried to disguise it under a patina of false good will. It wasn't just that he was insincere, it was something physical; even his good looks were fakey. In fact, it was the day I ran into him at Bobby's Arms, when he was still healthy, or at least still looked healthy, that I finally figured out what about him had been nagging at me ever since I'd first met him.

I was surprised to see Lance at Bobby's—the place wasn't his style. Bobby's is musty and moribund, full of *farang* doing their best to escape the crud of Bangkok: the heat and glaring sun, the choking fumes. Bobby's was one of the few places that catered to foreigners but not tourists, which meant bar girls weren't constantly thrusting themselves in your face to get a few hundred baht off you. Still, Lance claimed to avoid *farang* ghettos like the plague, though I'd heard he frequented some of the raunchier boy bars in town—places like The Saloon, where patrons could fire blanks at little boys onstage whose job it was to duck for cover behind cardboard horses and saguaro cacti, and Club 21, where teenagers were led around in chains. The rumor mill also had it that he lived with a young Thai kid. Then again, I'd heard gossip that I went down to Klong Toey and hustled with the drag junkies, so who knows, maybe it was all bull.

I myself went to Bobby's to play chess, but Lance preferred games like go-fish and gin, where you could bluff, not the all-out war that chess involves. What most people fail to understand about chess is that it isn't a game. Even the most minute weakness of the opponent has to be immediately exploited, until he's backed into a corner, trapped, and killed. Lance tried to negotiate his way out of bad situations, making little détente moves that were the end of him. The men who played at Bobby's were almost all vets from Vietnam or Korea, so they understood this aspect of the game. Most of them had married Thai women, ex–bar girls who now ran little export businesses or restaurants, and the men still talked and acted like they were on leave, kind of a permanent R&R.

And Bobby's was quiet. Even the cacophony from the street didn't seep in there—it was much quieter than our house, where punks on motorcycles roared by at all hours and vendors screamed up and down the street, until you went out and bought something just so they'd shut up and move on. The door at Bobby's was four-inch-thick wood, and there were only a couple of tiny thick-paned windows, set way up high in the wall like in a dungeon.

The afternoon I saw Lance there, he was sitting at a table reading, his head bent and chin resting on his palm. A shaft of light fell on him from one of the little squares of glass overhead, making his hair shine. I remember thinking he was probably reading one of the incredibly trashy books he favored—he had the worst taste in entertainment of anyone I'd ever met—and then I recall noticing, as I watched him unobserved for a few seconds, that he had colored his hair. I was very surprised, shocked almost, because he was only about thirty-five and his slightly pudgy baby face, always completely hairless—not even the shadow of a beard—made him look even younger. His brown hair was darker around his ears than on top, and in the soft beam from the window, it had a brassy red overlay, a metallic sheen that could only have been the product of a dye. Suddenly his fresh-faced health looked like something that was perfectly fine on top but, when you turned it over with your shoe, was all rotten underneath.

Just then he looked up from his book and waved me over, polite as always. He kicked the chair across from him out from the table so I could sit down. "What are you doing here, Francis?" he said, cracking the spine of his book gruesomely so it would stay flat—fortunately it was only *The Bad Seed*. I stretched my leg out and leaned my cane against the wall.

"Getting out of this heat, maybe pick up a chess game. And you? What are you doing here? I come here with J.C. all the time and we've never seen you here." J.C. was one of the other teachers who couldn't stand Lance, and Lance knew it.

"Just reading. I haven't seen J.C. in weeks, I thought maybe he'd been fired." He smiled one of his noxious meant-to-please-but-not-really smiles. "I'm teaching at the Daiwa Bank tonight, on Soi 4. It's right around the corner." Daiwa was one of the plum jobs the Institute tossed us—teaching English at night to a bunch of bankers. Good money, eager students—a breeze. I'd taught the course a couple of years ago, but after the whole fiasco about my contract, they'd given it to Lance. I didn't know if he was the one who had ratted to our department head, Achara—also known as the Viper—about my little habit, but I had a strong suspicion. He knew that piece of information would get him a perk somewhere down the line. In the end, nothing much came of it except that I had to produce a doctor's certificate saying I was clean before the university would renew my teaching contract. An Australian friend of Sammy's did it for five hundred baht, but I resented everybody knowing about it and having to spend the money.

"I know where it is," I said.

Lance laughed nervously. "Oh, right." He picked up his book and waved it enthusiastically. "Have you read this? It's great—really gripping."

"No."

"I'll lend it to you if you want, when I'm done. I got it out of the AUA library—"

"That's okay," I said. "I'm in the middle of a few things."

We chatted for a few more minutes, and then he rather awkwardly got up to leave. Maybe he felt bad about the job. "Can we play chess sometime?" he said. "You can teach me. But you're probably really good, right?"

I shrugged. "Sure, if you like." I was hoping I'd never have the opportunity. What I really wanted was to come out and ask him directly about the Viper, but then I decided with a liar as smooth as Lance, you'd never know for sure unless he was ready to tell you. He was waving goodbye before I had a chance to change my mind, and I was glad to be free of his babble about what he had watched on video the night before—ten episodes of *The Golden Girls,* all at once. His favorite was the one where Betty White asks one of the other old girls how long she waited after her husband died to do it with another man, and she says, "Till the paramedics got there." I was to hear that countless times in the next few months, and it never amused him any less. No matter how often he told you, he'd slap his leg and laugh, the corners of his mouth wet with saliva.

Lance left for the bank, and I stayed and played a few hours of chess before going home to the kiln that was our house in summer. I tried to stay out at least until the sun went down. When I pulled open the heavy wooden door to leave Bobby's, it was dusk and as hot out as it had been at noon. I've always loved twilight in the tropics. It comes and goes quickly, and then it's dark, not that lingering murk you get farther north. The light everywhere was soft and consistent, padding Bangkok in a thick gray blanket streaked with purples and pinks. I felt as though my eye could see inside the light itself, see it changing wavelengths, speeding up and slowing down as it passed through different media—metal, glass, air. An upstairs room across the alley looked like it was deep under the ocean where the sun penetrates just enough so that you can make out shapes but nothing has edges or shadows. There was a mobile with angelfish on it hanging in the window, and the evening breeze was moving the fish around so it looked like they had taken over the place—flooded everything and kicked out the people.

For some reason, that twenty minutes at Bobby's with Lance had allowed the thought into my head that it might be possible, under the right circumstances, to get an honest answer out of him, and I wanted to know badly, irrationally, if he had been the one who had gone to Achara and violated the *farang* solidarity in our department. Maybe noticing that he dyed his hair made him seem vulnerable to me for the first time. Later, when I thought about it, which was fairly often while I sat by his bed and graded papers or read to him, and sometimes even tried to let him beat me at chess, I realized that I hadn't asked that day at Bobby's because I couldn't stand to hear him lie about it. That was the beginning of me wanting Lance to tell me the truth, even if I had to wait a long time for that to happen.

Lance lied by second nature. I didn't believe most of the stories he told when we all sat around the teachers' lounge swapping anecdotes. In the hospital he seemed different, but then again, why would he lie to me about his childhood, about people I had never met and never would meet? Sometimes I wondered, though. Before he got sick he was often sarcastic, but not openly like the other expats, which was for humor or to tease. Lance's cynicism was slyer, masquerading as an overly polite veneer that mocked by its very inappropriateness. His manner put off the other Americans most of all, his attitude of having everyone fooled, as if he actually thought *you* believed he was for real. It was hard not to stop him in the middle of one of his archly delivered jokes and say, *Don't pull this on me. Some putz from Perth or Liverpool might fall for it, but I know your kind, and there's millions just like you where you came from. The suburbs are oozing with Lance Potters.* But I'll give him this. Now and then, when he laughed that ironic laugh, not the bogus hearty chuckle he forced for the Thai teachers' sake, the name *Lance* seemed perfect for him—undercutting not just everything that touched him, but himself, too.

He must have actually succeeded at being the boy next door when he was a kid—hell, he probably believed it himself—at least until it became apparent his interest in the other boy next door was outstripping his interest in the girl next door. Even then, Lance was smart enough to know that wouldn't sit well with the good folks of Chippewa Falls. Rather than destroy the vision of him held so dear by his parents and neighbors, he bided his time till he could escape, and once he was gone, he was gone for good. There are probably little old ladies in Chippewa Falls who still get a warm glow when they think about the boy from church who shoveled snow off the walk so they wouldn't fall and break their brittle backs, maybe freeze to death inches from their porches on the outskirts of Chippewa proper. That was the image Lance had been trying to project, at least at first, as if that could save him, as if even a disease could be disarmed by boyish charm. Later, when there was no hiding how sick he was, he couldn't quite give it up completely, which was why I think he never let me contact his family. I don't know if they would have come, or tried to get him sent home, or what. Instead, I was the last person he was with—me, someone who only a few months earlier he couldn't have said with confidence even liked him.

The bus driver craned his head backward so he could see the movie, too, and the bus narrowly missed swiping a telephone pole. Packages that had been balanced on laps went crashing to the floor around me. I thought that this night was probably one of the last times I'd visit Lance. He was going downhill quickly, and I wasn't sure how much more he could stand; pharmacological intervention was definitely called for. It would be doing us both a favor. He'd been pretty out of it for about a week and was barely speaking at all. When he made any noise, it was usually a moan of pain, though he still looked at me and seemed to follow if I said something. The last exchange we'd had that could be called a conversation was three days earlier, when he'd woken from a restless sleep, bathed in sweat from his dreams and the oppressively dense, unmoving air in his room.

"Francis?" he had whispered. I was surprised he knew my name. For the past few days he'd been calling me Joey, his dead brother. I said, "Mm-hmm, I haven't left yet," though I'd been thinking that I should get going—I was falling asleep over my papers and I had a full load of teaching the next day. "Did I tell you, when I was a kid...," he went on, in such a weak voice I could barely understand him, "I had a paper route. My favorite thing was to deliver the paper on holidays or Sundays, so early that everyone was still asleep. I'd get on my bike around quarter of six, and I felt like I was the only one who was awake and on top of things. Like I owned the whole town." He stopped and rested, wheezing audibly, and I waited for him to go on. This was the most he'd said at one time in days. "I used to throw the paper, this took me months to learn, so it landed on the doormat perfectly square, so when Mr. or Mrs. whoever came out, the paper would be exactly parallel to the door."

"That was nice of you," I said. "Very thoughtful. Quite the perfectionist."

He raised his head slightly to look at me. I could see a big wet spot on the pillowcase where sweat from the back of his neck had dampened it. "Can you believe that shit?" he said. "I actually cared that the paper lay just right on the porch."

I shook my head. I'd had a paper route for a little while, but got fired because one too many irate husbands called and complained that the paper wasn't there, or it was late. I always swore to my boss I'd delivered it on time, but after a while he canned me anyway.

"You tell me," Lance said, letting his head fall back onto the dingy pillowcase, "how I got from there to here. You can't, can you?"

I said no, I couldn't. Somehow Lance's not knowing how he'd gotten there seemed preferable to the line that led so directly between my getting the axe at *The Beachcomber*, the weekly newspaper, and my present situation.

"I was saving up," he said, "to buy the Star of Africa. I was going to be known as The Man Who Owned the Star of Africa, and everyone in Chippewa Falls could say I had been their paper boy."

I didn't tell him I had no idea what the Star of Africa was, and that if I didn't, you could bet no one in Chippewa Falls did, either.

The hospital they'd moved Lance to was about two and a half hours north of the city, and by the time I reached home, it was almost eleven, and I was exhausted. The Old Lady had left some unidentifiable mush out for me, and there were flies all over it, trapped under the insect screen she had placed over the bowl right before she went up to bed and after the food had evidently been sitting out long enough for the flies to really embed themselves in it. I gave it a miss and ate a piece of toast with bananas and butter.

That day, I'd had a big fight with one of the nurses because she wouldn't change Lance's IV often enough; instead of switching it when the bag was almost empty, she'd slow it down to the tiniest drip—the least amount of fluid you could allow out without letting any air into the vein. I found it difficult to eat after staring at that bag all evening. Although at least when Lance was on IVs I didn't have to worry about his food source. Before, when he was still eating solids, the nurses refused to bring his tray into the room. They left it outside the door until I got there, so whatever it was to begin with had congealed and been covered with dirt kicked up by people shuffling up and down the hallway. I started having the Old Lady make extra so I could bring it in to work with me and go straight to the hospital when I finished teaching. The Old Lady was crabby about doing more cooking—if you could call it that—and she took it out on my son, the Gripper, who cried more, so Sammy was crabbier, and the result was that my life at home was a living hell.

The nurses let Lance sit in a dirty bedpan for hours, so half the time I cleaned it—and him—myself rather than smell the stench. He'd turn his head away, embarrassed, but it didn't bother me much. I've seen junkies do the same to themselves, and worse. The rare occasions anyone else from our office came to the hospital, they didn't stay long. You could tell from the expressions on their faces—suddenly they were all such fastidious creatures—that the sights and smells were too much for them. They were thinking that they'd rather be dead than sink that low, but it's a crock. In the same situation, each and every one of them would be begging and praying for another day to live, just the way Lance was.

Of course, they resented me for making them look like cowards and spread malicious rumors about me to make themselves feel better. Everyone in the office had one ally who told them all the crap everyone else said about them; after Angie left, mine was a young thing from Maryland who never wanted to upset me, but I usually managed to wheedle out of her the rumors that had been poured into her perfect little shell of an ear.

This particular set of slanders, however, was even worse than I'd imagined, and she repeated them to me in a shocked whisper, as if my hearing them at a lower volume would make them less hurtful: that I was a voyeur, that I had tested positive already and I was preparing for what was coming, trying to figure out how to get around in that hospital system—that I was in effect considering Lance's death some kind of dress rehearsal for my own. As if I'd ever be stupid enough to let myself fall into the clutches of the people who'd gotten their hands on Lance. I guess it made our colleagues feel better about their own behavior to see mine in that light. The gay ones were probably scared shitless the hospital would grab them and lock them up, the way they'd gotten Lance.

First, Lance had gone to a regular hospital, a ritzy private one, to check out a cough that had been hanging on for weeks. After the pneumonia diagnosis, they tested him without telling him, and next thing he knew, he was being strapped into an ambulance and whisked away to a special "high security" hospital up-country, even though he said he felt fine. After all, he'd had only a mild bout, but there the ward doors were locked and they wouldn't let him leave.

When Lance called me that Sunday morning, after spending the weekend in the hospital, he didn't let on that anything was amiss. I was surprised to hear his voice, partly because no one in Bangkok relies on telecommunication, so the phone hardly ever rings, and because Lance wasn't one of the few people who called me at home. I'm still not sure why he called me particularly. I guess he knew there were certain things about my lifestyle that precluded me judging other people's.

When I put the phone to my ear, the background was crackly, and I could hear high-pitched giggles coming over another line we'd intersected. "Francis? It's Lance," he said in his self-confident way, emphasizing his name in case I didn't know who he was. "Lance Potter." As if he were a salesman and he wanted to be sure I remembered him later.

I said, "Yeah, I know. Hi, Lance. What's up?" Our conversation sounded more stilted and awkward because of the voices laughing over it. I wondered if they could hear us, too.

"Yeah, right," he said after a long pause, while he tried to figure out if the laughter was coming from my apartment. "I guess there aren't that many Lances in Bangkok," he said, and chuckled a little too heartily.

"Just enough," I said laughing a little as well, but not very enthusiastically. "So...what's up?" I didn't want to be rude in case he had called just to say hello, though I knew it was improbable, but I wanted him to get to the point.

"So, I need a favor. Would you mind?"

"Depends what it is, doesn't it?" I hadn't forgotten about that whole other thing, with my doctor's certificate.

"Oh, it's no big deal," he said quickly. "Can you just tell Achara tomorrow morning that I won't be in for a few days? I tried to call her at home, but her phone must be out."

"Sure," I said. "Where are you? Stuck out of town? Did you suddenly fall in love with a village beauty?" Lance wasn't really out at work, though everyone knew he was gay, so sometimes I liked to give him a little jab about it, to keep him on his toes. He humored me with a dry snort. In the background I heard an announcement paging someone, and then I knew instantly Lance was in the hospital. I think I even knew why, though nothing in his voice betrayed it.

"Oh, right, *that's* what I meant to tell you. I'm quitting! No, I'm in the hospital, in Siriwan. I had one of those intestinal things, and they're running some tests to make sure they got it all. Must have been one of those crabs they fish out of the sewers and dish up at the Goethe Institute Sunday brunch." He lied without missing a beat.

It wasn't until I visited him myself, a week or so later, that I realized how difficult it must have been for him to feign cheerfulness on the phone that day. After we'd hung up, he'd called his boyfriend to tell him he had been involuntarily removed to a different hospital, and on top of that, they weren't letting him go home to get clothes and books, and could the boyfriend—I never heard Lance say his name or mention him except to tell me this— please bring Lance a few things he needed, and he never heard from the guy again. By the time I went over to Lance's place to get some of his stuff, the boyfriend was long gone. He'd cleaned the place out—Lance's expensive stereo, the microwave and American blender a friend had brought him, his VCR—but there was no point in telling Lance. I knew he'd never get back there to find out for himself.

By Monday afternoon, the whole office knew because when I told Achara that Lance was in Siriwan Hospital, she put two and two together immediately and called them up. So much for patient confidentiality; I guess the place already had a rep to Thais as a containment vessel. I don't know if Achara had the clout to get him out, but she didn't seem too inclined to try. So much for him ponying me up in return for everlasting favors from the Viper. Maybe she thought that's where he belonged, or at least as much as any other poor bastard who ended up there.

Lots of the other patients were bar girls and boys, and junkies into the bargain, since rich people or ones with well-connected relatives knew better than to entrust themselves to any government hospital. If one of them got *it,* General somebody-or-other's eldest son, say, who'd made a few too many trips to the cathouse, well, he was kept at home, with private nurses. At Siriwan, people with lethal infectious diseases were all lined up next to one another in the same room, on cots a few feet apart, hacking up sputum and God knows what into bowls that sat by their bedsides. Thanks to a high level of xenophobia, Lance had his own private cubicle with a door and everything. Then, AIDS was still being treated as a *farang* disease, so any foreigners who had it were despised as bringers of death upon an innocent people.

When I finished my toast, I went upstairs to look in on my son. The Gripper, as I call him, had strewn toys, books, tin cans, all over the floor in the hallway separating his room from Sammy's, but I was too tired to do anything about it, even though I knew Sammy would give me hell about the mess. The Old Lady had nothing to do now that the kid was in pre-school half the day, but that didn't seem to result in the house being any cleaner. I opened the door as quietly as I could and saw the Gripper asleep, one little hand, still wet from sucking his thumb, curled up on the Old Lady's wrinkled, sagging breast. It seemed like I hadn't seen him awake in days. After Suchada, Adam's mother, left, the Old Lady started sleeping with the Gripper because his was the only air-conditioned room in the house. I still slept downstairs on the mattress where I'd been sleeping ever since Suchada kicked me out of the bedroom when the Gripper was born.

I borrowed Sammy's radio from the kitchen and put it next to my head to listen to the BBC world news hour, then fell asleep still dressed but minus my boots. I was so wiped out, I dropped off without my last fix of the night, but into more of a nap than a deep sleep, where I was half-awake and knew I was dreaming but couldn't put a stop to it. I dreamt I was looking at a picture of myself, and the picture was of me looking at a picture, and *that* picture was of me, and on and on. Then in my dream I woke up, and I knew, more clearly than I had ever known anything before, that history *is* the present; but what is recorded of every thought, every act, is pure chance. Evolution only creates a series of altered appearances, a catalogue of ever-changing symptoms.

Still dreaming that I was awake, I looked at the picture I held in my hand, and the face in it changed from mine to Lance's, and I knew he was dead. My body filled up with a fear so palpable, it seeped into my lungs and turned them into two smooth oval stones, dense as diamonds. In the picture, Lance began to yawn, and his mouth became a gaping black hole stretched across his face, into which some invisible hand was pouring his death, a dark liquid which surged down his throat with a power all its own, like a black horse running, then disappeared, to wait and hide inside us until it was ready to come out. A British man's voice was saying over and over, *The Star of Africa, the Star of Africa,* and when I awoke for real, my head snapped up suddenly and peeled my sweaty cheek off the vinyl of my sleeping mat. The newscaster's voice was buzzing tinnily in my ear about an uprising in South Africa, and for a disoriented second I thought there was someone in the room with me. The air was still and roasting, and I was soaked, but the premonition had turned my lips cold and my skin clammy. My hands were shaking so much I could barely get the needle in. Poor Lance. His crumbling body was proof of what no expat likes to admit: no matter how far away you get, it's never far enough.

I was sure when I set out the next day after work that when I got to the hospital, one of the slaggy nurses would tell me Lance had gone during the night. I stopped by Seventh Day anyway, just in case, hoping to catch Sister Michael as she was getting off shift. I figured I could always use the stuff myself if it was too late for Lance. Most people would probably hate to spend their time going from one hospital to the next, but I've never minded hospitals; maybe because strange behavior is barely noticed in them, or is explained away by strange circumstances. In fact, I find them vaguely relaxing. In hospitals, nobody stares at me because I walk with a cane and a limp. It makes me feel at home, as though I were there for rehabilitation.

Sure enough, Sister Michael was at the main registration desk, filling out her paperwork. She looked up when I cleared my throat, then smiled when she saw it was me. She seemed genuinely pleased.

"Hello, Francis," she said. "What brings you here? Pleasure, I hope."

"Business, I'm afraid," I said. "But not for me. I'm fine."

"Fine in what sense?" she went on in the same tone, as though we were exchanging pleasantries. "Still alive and working eighty hours a week to support your habit? When are you coming back to try again?"

I never knew how she could tell just by looking at me that I hadn't quit. Maybe she still had some connections to the powers that be, left over from her nun days. I nodded to acknowledge her position, the worthlessness of my present life, etc., etc. It's not that I disagreed with her, in the abstract I agreed entirely, but principle and practice are two different things. At least I wasn't in Lance's shoes.

The last time I'd seen her was several months earlier, when one of my friend Patrick's smuggling schemes had backfired and two condoms filled with junk burst in his colon on the way to the airport. Inferior Thai rubber, I guess—couldn't stand up to those intestinal enzymes. He was probably spared years in jail, because he looks exactly like the kind of person who would try a scheme like that. The taxi driver saved his life; when he checked the rearview mirror and saw Patrick slumped against the window, ashen-faced, with drool running down his chin, he turned around and took him straight to Seventh Day. Sister Michael was the one who phoned me—she figured anyone in Patrick's condition with a Bangkok address in his passport had bumped into me or Sammy somewhere along the line. She was becoming kind of the matron saint of the Bangkok junk circuit.

"I have this friend . . . ," I said, getting right to the point and seeing immediately by the set of her face she didn't believe me. "He's really sick." I also knew she knew "sick" meant "I'm not getting enough, and I need something else to take up the slack," and I let her think it was for me.

Sister Michael sighed. "Will you promise to come back before the end of the year?" she said. "If you do, I'll see to you personally."

"I'll try. But—" I rubbed my thumb and first two fingers together. "There's the cash problemo. I just don't have any. But I'm working on something. I'm putting something together." Seventh Day was one of the only places that had a real detox program, not the kind where they rope you to the bed and leave you there, but it was also the most expensive. I'd gone through it once, when Suchada was pregnant with the Gripper, but she had paid for it. That was the agreement, she wouldn't end the pregnancy if I would straighten up. About three months before Adam was due, not long after I got out of the program, Suchada came home one day and found Patrick at the house and lost it completely. I wasn't supposed to hang out with my old friends, the ones who were still using. After calling Patrick all sorts of names and kicking him out on his ass, she left, and I didn't hear from her for two days. When she returned she was pale and silent and spent a lot of time doubled up over the toilet bowl. But she had the baby anyway, and he was fine. I knew she'd gone to one of her mother's herbal doctors, but what could I say? She would just scream that I hadn't kept up my end of the bargain, and there was no reasoning with her. After those fights I usually had to rescue my books and papers from the sodden heaps on the lawn they accumulated into when Suchada threw them out the window.

Sister Michael stared at me evenly, as if she were reading my mind and knew I was thinking about spells and hexes and other things I should be leaving to forces she considered to be marshaled on the side of good. You couldn't put anything over on that woman. Her cheeks were pink, skin perfectly clear—she practically glowed with health. "Hold on," she said. "I'll be off in a few minutes."

When she reappeared in her street clothes—perfectly ironed, surprisingly close-fitting jeans, a maroon silk blouse, and thin-strapped leather sandals—she was carrying a small green plastic bag with a Styrofoam carton in it that could have held her lunch. She waited until we were outside to hand it to me. "This is the last time," she said. "You understand that, don't you?" The look on her face let me know I had pushed her far enough.

I didn't peek in the bag until we had parted and I was on the long bus ride headed toward Lance. I felt like I had just gotten off that bus, and there I was right back on it. Since this was the last hurrah, as it were, Sister Michael had gone all out and arranged a whole sampler. There were at least twenty-five pills inside the carton, all different shapes and colors, even a few I didn't recognize. I emptied them into the bag and ditched the Styrofoam, then folded up the baggie tightly and put it into my pocket. It was all I could do not to skim a couple for my own rainy day, especially since there wouldn't be any more coming down the pike from that direction, but I knew I was warm and dry compared to Lance. There was also a piece of pink phone-message paper folded in the bag, and I opened it and read in her perfect, Jesuit-school handwriting:

I am a follower of Jesus Christ but I know I have brought shame to His name many times. He doesn't ask that I be perfect, but He does want me to be honest about my mistakes. And then, farther down the page, *And I saw as it were a sea of glass mingled with fire: and them that had gotten the victory over the beast, and over His image,*

*and over His mark, and over the number of His name, stand on the
sea of glass, having the harps of God.*

I refolded the paper and put in my breast pocket. No need for
Lance to see that. He'd grown up as an Episcopal altar boy, and it
still haunted him, that vision of himself carrying the cross down
the aisle, holding it overhead, bearing the burden for the entire
congregation while the priest intoned the week's reading.

I stopped by the reception desk and said Lance Potter, fully
expecting the receptionist—a new one I'd never seen before—to
shake her head, meaning it was over, but she gave a bored nod
and gestured with her chin for me to go ahead. On the way down
the hall I saw Vini, my least favorite nurse. She must have gone
into the profession to escape some terrible fate awaiting her as a
beautiful young Indian woman, because she didn't have an ounce
of compassion in her body. At least, not for humans. She did like
animals, though, and was hiding some orphaned, worm-ridden
kittens in one of the supply closets, feeding them and giving them
medicine she'd pilfered from the hospital. I had to pass the closet
on my way to Lance's room, and sure enough she was holding
something carefully in her hands—a bowl of milk with bread
floating in it, I saw when I got closer—which she placed in front
of two mangy little tabbies with infected eyes swollen shut with
pus. Vini hadn't heard me. As she put the bowl on the floor, she
said in, for her, a cheerful tone, "Eat, you blind fools!" I'd hung
my cane over my arm and tried to walk lightly, but she finally
realized someone was there and straightened up quickly, tugging
her uniform down over her lovely hips and turning around with
an annoyed scowl.

I wasn't totally convinced the staff would even know if Lance
had died, so I opened the door slowly and peered around it. His
body was still hooked up to the machines and the IV drip-
dripped away, stingily as ever. His eyes were half-open, and his
teeth showed where his upper lip was pulled back a little, as if he
were thinking about something slightly amusing.

"Lance...," I said, leaning over the bed. "It's me." I patted my
breast pocket with the green baggie in it. "I have something good
for you in my pocket. Truly."

I reached over and touched his face, just to make sure, and his cheek was hot and dry. He opened his eyes the rest of the way and looked at me then, and even tried to smile a little. "Can you swallow?" I asked, but he made no response.

Lance had all his teeth capped when he got to Bangkok because, he said, it was so cheap, and afterward he showed them off with toothy grins and silly crude little jokes that the Thai teachers didn't quite get but laughed at anyway, not realizing he was making fun of them. He never said Thailand, but always "The Land of Smiles"—the slogan the Government had used to kick off the promotion for the Year of the Tourist—and when he said it, he oozed that grin in your direction. "Oh boy," Lance would say, shaking his head in supposed sadness, "another factory burnt down; two hundred workers incinerated in The Land of Smiles!" Cluck-cluck went his tongue. *What a shame. Tsk-tsk.*

Lance was neat and clean-shaven and every day his shirts were ironed and bleached—he made the rest of us look like vagabonds when we came in with razor stubble, wearing the same rumpled shirt and tie as the day before. That and a lot of ass-kissing ensured him the best courses and the most profitable outside work. Most of the Thai teachers were on somewhat shaky ground as far as their English was concerned, even though we all taught in the Language department, and they badgered the foreign staff all day with minute questions of grammar and usage. When one pretty young Thai teacher asked Lance shortly after the Reagan polyp disclosure, "Could you say *Ronald Reagan is a cancerous president?*" and he took it, it was too much—even though we'd all voted absentee for our favorite write-in candidates. Most expats don't see a contradiction between their rabid patriotism and the fact that they can't even stand their home countries enough to spend more than two weeks a year there. Lance was the exception—he had no loyalty to anything or anyone, as far as we could determine. He started to answer, but Paul, a seventy-year-old Irish Republican pothead from Chicago, leaped from his chair and said, "Yes, you can, you can say that because in America you can say whatever you want about our leaders no matter how degrading or insulting it is, because it's a free society," and stomped out of the teachers' lounge. A few days earlier, some lowly P.M. had been thrown in jail under lese majesty for saying he wished he'd been born a prince. When Paul was gone, Lance lifted his perfect eyebrows and shrugged at me, then turned his attention back to the teacher as though nothing had happened. She was smiling nervously, though she had certainly meant it as a jab. Still, no one was supposed to get that ruffled.

Does it seem odd that I've remembered so clearly the details of this and other perfectly unremarkable days, and all the queasy little emotions I had that accompanied them, that I can pinpoint the beginning of wanting to make Lance tell me the truth to the moment I noticed he dyed his hair? At the time I was puzzled by that myself, but I've come to suspect, since the blurry string of nights listening to Lance whisper—stopping often to rest, trying to make do on the little puffs of breath his clogged lungs could provide—his recollections of childhood and relatively short adulthood, so that someone on earth would know what had meant something to him, that memory doesn't weed out what's important. Isn't it just as likely that we confer meaning on things because they were remembered? Thus the most ordinary conversations and events—an outing with our parents, an item of clothing that at the time meant nothing more to us than a way to hide our bare and embarrassing skin from the world—become laden with meaning simply because they happened to lodge in our memories. And that which is forgotten is, necessarily, consigned to insignificance.

I became more and more convinced of this as I tried to understand why Lance had remembered some occasion, say a car trip with his mother and brother where he and his brother had sung everything they wanted to say—*Ro-oll down the win-do-ow pu-lee-eze, Mo-om, can we ge-et some ay-yus cream pu-lee-eze*—until their mother had pulled over the car and sobbed behind the wheel, begging them to stop. It turned out, Lance added as an afterthought (the reason for the trip having taken a back seat in his memory to the fact they'd made their mother cry), that they were driving across country because their mother had packed them up and left their father in the middle of a hot summer night, after which Lance never saw his father again.

He remembered that he was at a restaurant called The Blue Bottle and that he was holding a glass of red wine in his hand when a plainclothes policeman approached the table, knelt down beside his chair, and told him he had to go home because his brother had shot himself in the head. He described how his hand shook, spilling wine on the white tablecloth, and said he remembered thinking that the stain would spread out forever until the purple pool engulfed him and the entire table. But he didn't remember whom he'd been eating with, nor the substance of his final conversation with his brother, or when they'd last seen each other.

Once, when I was at Lance's apartment getting him some fresh clothes and checking his mail, I picked up a photo lying on the floor with the contents of a drawer that had been turned upside down by his boyfriend when he'd ransacked the place. (Whoever had done it, besides removing everything of value, had erased any trace of himself from the apartment.) For some reason, probably fear of karmic retribution, the landlord hadn't evicted Lance, though as far as I knew the rent wasn't being paid.

The photograph was of a boy standing next to the burned-out shell of a small house, his hands stretched toward the picture taker and, on his face, a belligerent *What do you want me to do about it?* expression. If it weren't for the expression, I would have taken the boy for Lance, their features were so similar, but on the back someone had written *1960, Joey after the fire.* That night at the hospital, through a series of roundabout questions—I didn't want Lance to know his ex-boyfriend had trashed the apartment and scattered the remains of Lance's life around on the floor—I managed to elicit the information that his brother had started a chimney fire by putting too much wrapping paper in the fireplace on Christmas morning, and the house had burned to the ground. When the firemen got there, they discovered that the house, part of a development, had been built on soil that was too soft and the foundation had settled and crushed the underground pipes. The house was ashes before they could locate another water source. I'm positive Lance never would have told me this if I hadn't worked him around to it with probing questions about houses and fires, yet he'd mentioned several times that every year until they'd departed, his father had given him a rabbit for Christmas—which every year he'd named Sarah, regardless of its gender—and every year, Sarah died long before the next Christmas rolled around. And he knew exactly where every one of those dead rabbits—at least the ones whose bodies had been recovered—was buried. Not "in the yard" or "near the woodpile" but under what kind of tree, how far from the house, whether the maimed little corpse was in a coffin—usually a shoe box—and so on. It strained credulity, except I couldn't think of one reason why anyone would pretend to remember information like that if he really didn't.

It wasn't until a few nights before Lance died that I understood the implications of this randomness: the world can never become an appreciably better place. A memory that doesn't function to select significant events means one can never learn from one's mistakes. Any changes for the better are coincidental and occur with more or less the same frequency as any changes for the worse. One of Sammy's science magazines had a cover headline screaming *Can History Stop Repeating Itself?*, as if our own tiny, miserable lives weren't answer enough.

I pressed Lance's hand and said, "Don't try to talk, okay? I'll just sit here for a while." He twisted his mouth like he was going to try to say something anyway. A feeding tube that wasn't attached to any food dangled from his nose, waving slightly like an upside-down antenna when he moved his head.

I sat down and started grading papers, hoping just my presence was of some comfort. I was conscious of all those pills in my pocket, the promise of each one pressing its shape into my chest. Lance seemed to be beyond whatever comfort any pill might provide, and I was scared to put anything in his mouth he could choke on. Probably the most merciful thing would have been to grind them all up into powder, dissolve them in water, and shoot the paste down the feeding tube with a syringe.

Then I must have dozed off for a few minutes, because when I woke up, I had the vague sensation of being watched. Lance's lips had dried blood on them around the outsides and at the corners of his mouth, like he'd been sucking on a blood Popsicle. When he parted them, I could see the inside of his mouth was white and spongy-looking from thrush. I'd heard horror stories about it growing out of people's mouths uncontrollably, like cotton candy.

"Can you understand me?" I asked. "Do you want anything?"

He looked over at the corner of the room, but there was nothing there. Then he whispered "ice" in a sort of water-logged voice that sounded nothing like him.

I went down the hall to the ice machine and came back with a plastic bag full of ice chips. He knew they were letting him die, if not actually speeding things along, but I had an overwhelming urge to say it out loud. I wanted to see him express some sense of injustice over it.

I pulled my chair up to his bed and put an ice chip between his lips, where it immediately melted. He must have had some kind of fever. "You know there's things they can do for you," I said. "I mean, more than here, anyway. Some bribing would smooth your way out of this. What's your cash situation?" I knew he must have some stowed away, since there was practically nothing to buy in the whole country and he had taught a lot of extra courses.

The immobility of the skin around his eyes confirmed he'd already considered and rejected the issue. But at least by broaching the subject, I thought he might tell me what he wanted done with his money. I didn't even know if he had a will. Maybe he wanted it sent to his parents, but considering he hadn't even—as far as I knew—told them he was in the hospital, I doubted it. I didn't know how to bring it up—I would have had to acknowledge that his dying was an inevitability now, and not a distant one. We had discussed his family often, but it was always in the context of events that had happened a long time ago. His parents and brother seemed frozen for him, stuck in some year of his early adolescence when their nuclear family had gone bust. I was also afraid that once we started on that conversation, he'd tell me specifically what to do with his stuff and I would have to lie, pretend that it was all still there. Nod as he went through the whole list of who he wanted to have what—Paul had been envious of his good, heavy-duty American blender, for instance—and not have it show in my face that it was all gone.

I put another chip on his tongue. "Maybe you'll come back as a millionaire," I said, "and get your Star of Africa. I dreamed it last night." I meant it as a joke, or a good omen, or something, but then realized I had actually mentioned his death; I felt terrible. I watched his face carefully to see how he took it. He had definitely heard me. His chest was moving up and down even more laboriously, and his cheeks had a waxy, bloodless sheen like a fake piece of fruit. "Lance!" I said, a little too sharply. He was scaring me. "Do you want me to get one of those slaggy nurses? What's going on, can you breathe? You're freaking me out here." He nodded, but I could almost hear the fluid sloshing in his lungs when he exhaled. "I'm getting the nurse." My voice sounded panicky.

He shook his head, and moved his arm a little so his palm was facing up, and I held onto it.

"I didn't mean it," I said. "I'm sorry..." Then for some reason, I no longer felt bad about mentioning his death. Surely, he was welcoming it. "I'll see to it you get a sky burial, the real kind, so you'll be returned to the earth with a leg up on all these other wankers," I said, trying to smile. I knew perfectly well they would burn his body before it was cold; I'd seen them whisking off other people from the AIDS wing, straight to the furnace. But maybe Lance didn't know it—after his first few days there, he'd only left his room a couple of times. No sky burial, no being gently laid to rest on a mountaintop or a roof, with birds coming to peck your flesh off, and then when only your bones are left, having your loved ones grind them up into bone meal and roll it into little balls and put those out for the birds, too—so piece by piece you're sort of returned to the air. Just some sullen-faced orderlies with gloves and masks shoving you into a burning tunnel. No, no matter what, I wouldn't die in this hospital.

Suddenly I noticed Lance's chest wasn't going down, it was stuck in an upward, inflated position, but I didn't know how long it had been since it had moved. I had been concentrating on his face, with those blurry unfocused eyes only receiving my gaze and not returning it, trying to gauge how much he understood of what I was saying.

I dashed out as quickly as I could without my cane, and when I got a nurse in there I could see immediately she didn't want to touch Lance or do anything to him, and she ran to get a doctor. When she came back with a tiny Indonesian man I'd often seen bustling up and down the corridors, I grabbed his arm and demanded, "Is he dying, is he dying?" but of course the doctor didn't know because he hadn't looked at him yet. He gently slipped around me and placed his rubber-gloved hands on Lance's chest, and the nurse turned to me and said rudely, "Yes! He's dying. *Please leave* so we can work, you must get out now," but I knew *she* was all bluster, she had no intention of doing anything to help, and even the doctor looked at her rather angrily. Still, there was no place for me right then, so I left, bundled out the door by the harsh one who didn't look strong enough to apply as much force as she did to my arm.

I stopped outside the door, now pulled shut behind me, and I could hear banging noises and the two of them speaking Thai. The doctor's voice was smooth and cold. A woman and a child walked by without looking at me. "Lance," I said to no one, "I didn't get to finish telling you..." I kicked the door twice with my good leg, hard. It hurt like hell, but I needed a physical sensation of pain right then. "I think you'll come back as a bird," I said, "sky burial or not. One of those birds that can fly for seven years straight and never have to land on earth the whole time, not once. Wouldn't that be great?" I was shouting, but neither the mother nor child, now at the end of the hall, turned around.

The same noises were still going on in the room when I left. I went out a rear door, afraid if I saw any of the nurses, I'd let someone have it. The exit, a barely used one, gave onto a dirty little row of houses. I walked down the street, trying to stay out of the loud traffic of the main road for a few more minutes, grateful for the relative quiet in which to calm down. A jet-black dog lay in the gutter, its eye sockets hollow and its jaw unhinged. As I passed, I could have sworn it moved, made a little wriggle, but it must have been dead at least a week. I stopped and stared, and it moved again. It took my eye a few seconds to distinguish in the mass of black hair the body of a cat—exactly the same color as the dog, with a thick, healthy black coat—chewing at the corpse, sending a little wave of motion through the dog that made it seem as though its front end were twitching.

The *farang* staff had a little memorial, as though they had cared deeply all along, and several of the Thai teachers who had worked closely with Lance came. Woody, who had started out life as a man but ended up as a woman, was there in three-inch heels, impeccably dressed as all the Thai ladies always were. She cried, taking off her glasses to wipe her eyes and blow her nose, which made me feel guilty because Lance and I used to poke fun at her sometimes just because she was such an easy target, with the name Woody and all. Woody was actually her old name; as a woman she went by Susi. I think we both secretly admired her for standing up to all the departmental horseshit and forcing them to let her teach again after her operation, but we never admitted it to each other. She read rather beautifully—where could she have come across it?—a Wordsworth ode I hadn't heard since high school:

> What though the radiance which was once so bright
> Be now forever taken from my sight,
> Though nothing can bring back the hour
> Of splendor in the grass, of glory in the flower;
> We will grieve not, rather find
> Strength in what remains behind.

The other Thais were nodding, trying to pretend they understood a word of it, but it was obvious from the way they sort of snapped to attention when Susi sat back down that the content was a total wash. I wished Lance could have been there, he would have gotten a kick out of catching out those fakers, or at least a smirk.

It turned out Lance did have a will, though he had never mentioned it. The Viper told me a few days later as we waited in line next to each other to serve ourselves lunch, under a tent at the annual end-of-summer departmental picnic. The picnic was held on one of the large, patchy fields on campus, but it was so hot everyone had gathered under the shade of one big tree, like a pride of lions. There was enough food for an army, of course, and the sleek, perfectly dressed faculty were busy gorging themselves.

The will had been found when Lance's desk at school was cleaned out after he'd died. Even the Viper wasn't heartless enough to order it cleaned out beforehand. He had left all his cash—she didn't say how much, but rumor had it the amount was fairly substantial—to an organization that trained prostitutes for vocational jobs—making inlaid bracelets and earrings for tourists, gilding orchids, and so on.

I stood off to one side, watching the Viper pat her mouth carefully with a napkin. When she saw me looking, she waved me over. After digging around in her purse, she pulled out an envelope. "I forgot to give you this," she said. "I donated his teaching materials to our library here. You can have these if you like." As she passed the envelope into my hand I heard one of the few Thai men in the department, a foppishly handsome fellow with a fake British accent who spoke English even to his fellow countrymen, say to a brand new young teacher, "Yes, *sick,* you know *the* sick, terrible, isn't it?"

I took it silently and turned my back on the Viper, opening the envelope as I walked away from the picnic, still in full swing. I'd had about all I could stand. Inside were all the pictures Lance had had over his desk, most of them of people who were completely unfamiliar to me. I recognized several members of his family. I kept only one—of him and some dog or other, whose paw Lance was holding in his hand, and a very faded newspaper clipping about the Star of Africa, which it turns out is the largest cut diamond in the world, mounted in the royal scepter, held under lock and key inside the Tower of London. I dropped everything else into the garbage, hoping the Viper was watching.

At the edge of the picnic, I passed a cluster of women who had taken off their shoes and were standing barefoot, their brutally high heels abandoned nearby in the grass. I debated pointing out to the owner of a pair of expensive-looking green pumps that the toddler of one of her colleagues had just removed an enormous hunk of barbecued meat from his bulging cheek and was wringing it out over her shoe. Blissful in her ignorance, she was rubbing one perfectly pedicured foot over the other. But the boy smiled so happily, watching a trickle of gray juice run out of his closed fist and into her shoe, that I decided against it. Life is full of disappointments and rude surprises, I told myself. Let this be just one more.

ABOUT RICHARD FORD

A Profile by Don Lee

Richard Ford was in France this past spring when he got the call. He had rented an apartment in Paris for a few months to escape distractions and do some writing. He had wanted to be difficult to reach. In April, he was eating dinner with a friend at a remote little restaurant, deep in Brittany, when his friend's cellular phone unexpectedly rang. It was Ford's French publisher, who explained that a lot of people across the Atlantic were trying to contact him. They had a bit of news to convey. He had won the Pulitzer Prize for his novel *Independence Day,* his sequel to *The Sportswriter.* Two weeks later, Ford received the PEN/Faulkner Award for Fiction as well—the first time the same book had won both prizes.

For Ford, the awards were a culmination to a career that has spanned nearly thirty years, made up of hard, disciplined, and sometimes frustrating work. If anything, Ford is not a lazy man. In his final revisions of *Independence Day,* he twice read aloud the entire seven-hundred-page manuscript to detect any rough spots. Then he went through two more drafts with his editor at Knopf, Gary Fisketjon. Then, as the book was about to go to press, his British editor gently commented, really as an afterthought, that there seemed to be quite a few *-ly* adverbs in the novel. Ford looked, and agreed. "In weak moments," he says, "a writer will use an *-ly* adverb when the verb isn't strong enough." He went through the manuscript yet again over the next two weeks, striking out every *-ly* adverb he could part with, and strengthening the accompanying verbs. "It seemed there were about four thousand of them."

Born in 1944, Ford was raised in Jackson, Mississippi, until he was eight years old, when his father, Parker, a traveling starch salesman, had a heart attack. Thereafter, Ford, an only child, was shuttled between Jackson and Little Rock, Arkansas, where his mother Edna's father, a former prizefighter and dining car con-

ALAIN MERCIER

ductor, managed a hotel. When Ford was sixteen, his father had a second, fatal heart attack. Up to then, Ford recalls his childhood as a happy, mirthful one, even enjoying all the driving and traveling, establishing the itinerancy for which he has become well-known (he has lived in fourteen states, not to mention France and Mexico). "Nothing ever got stale," he says. "I remember one night in 1961, I had a date with an airline flight attendant—somewhat older than I was at age seventeen—and what we did on our date was drive from Little Rock to Jackson and back again, all in a few hours. I have a pleasant memory of that."

As a teenager, Ford's only idea for a career was to be a hotel manager, like his grandfather. He attended Michigan State University, where they had a first-rate hotel science school, and where he also signed up for the Marines, joining a ROTC program called "Platoon Leader Class." Soon after he enlisted, though, he contracted hepatitis and promptly was given a medical discharge. On an impulse, he then decided to study literature, a somewhat unlikely interest, given that he was mildly dyslexic as a boy. Ford, however, doesn't think his dyslexia was a handicap, and believes it actually helped him as a writer: "Being a slow reader admitted me to books at a very basic level—word by word. That doesn't seem like bad preparation to me, if writers are people who essentially live in sentences."

Upon graduating in 1966, he applied for a variety of jobs, including one with the Arkansas State Police, but, to his chagrin, no one would hire him. Floundering, he taught junior high school and coached the baseball team for a while in Flint, Michigan, then moved to New York and briefly worked for *American Druggist* as an assistant science editor, and then went to law school at Washington University in St. Louis. Quickly, he realized that he had made a terrible mistake. He quit after just one semester and moved back to Arkansas, where he substitute-taught at Little Rock Central High School while once again testing the job market, applying for an assignment as a sportswriter for *The Arkansas Gazette* (he was roundly rebuffed: "I wasn't any good at it, I guess"), and a position at the CIA, which, for once, he was offered, but didn't accept. Ford says about some of these vocational choices: "I think it must've been that the world seemed pretty contingent and uncontrollable—a college graduate with no job, and later having 'discontinued' my legal studies—and so what could be better than to have a job in which you told everybody what to do? Being a novelist is sort of related to that, don't you think? In a much more benign way?"

At twenty-three, without gainful employment, and married by then to his college sweetheart, Kristina Hensley, the daughter of an Air Force test pilot, Ford tried to determine what he could do reasonably well that might turn into a life. Fancifully, he thought of writing fiction, something he had larked around with at Michigan State, when he was living in a fraternity house. "I'd written a couple of insignificant stories, and my teacher read them and said they were 'good.' But 'good'? Frankly, I think deciding to try to be a writer was something I did purely on instinct and whimsy. It was a gesture against the practical life of going on with law studies. It may have been—other than loving Kristina—my first important independent act." His former teacher told him to go to graduate school, and he settled on the University of California in Irvine, simply because, he confesses, "they admitted me. I remember getting the application for Iowa, and thinking they'd never have let me in. I'm sure I was right about that, too. But, typical of me, I didn't know who was teaching at Irvine. I didn't know it was important to know such things. I wasn't the most curious of young men, even though I give myself credit for not letting that deter me."

It turned out that Oakley Hall and E. L. Doctorow were at Irvine, and Ford remains, to this day, grateful for their tutelage. Yet, after finishing the M.F.A. program in 1970, he could not, for the life of him, get anything into print. "Once I got reconciled to not being a good enough short story writer even to get published," he says, "I quit thinking about publishing and got to work on a novel." An excerpt from that novel, *A Piece of My Heart,* was eventually taken by *The Paris Review,* and the book itself, through the assistance of his friend and mentor, Donald Hall, was published by Harper & Row in 1976.

Nominated for the Ernest Hemingway Award for Best First Novel, *A Piece of My Heart* tells the story of Robard Hewes, an Arkansas drifter who leaves his wife to chase after a married cousin, along the way crossing paths with Sam Newel, a law student from Chicago, on a desolate island in the Mississippi River. Though the book generally received good reviews, Ford was irritated by some, particularly those that tried to tag him as a Southern writer who was attempting a "neo-Faulknerism." "I'm a Southerner, God knows," Ford says, "but I always wanted my books to exist outside the limits of so-called Southern writing. *A Piece of My Heart* was set in Arkansas and Mississippi, and I, of course, thought that though the setting was Southern, the book somehow *wasn't* Southern. But then the people who wrote about it all said it was another Southern novel, and I just said, Okay, that's it. No more Southern writing for me."

Ford set his next novel, *The Ultimate Good Luck* (which was published by Houghton Mifflin in 1981), not only in another region, but in another country. In the book, Harry Quinn, a Vietnam veteran, journeys to Oaxaca, Mexico. In an effort to reconcile with his ex-girlfriend, Rae, he tries to free her brother from jail, where he has been imprisoned for dealing drugs. Again, the novel was fairly well-received, but Ford wasn't satisfied. His two books had sold less than twelve thousand copies, combined. "I realized there was probably a wide gulf between what I could do and what would succeed with readers. I felt that I'd had a chance to write two novels, and neither of them had really created much stir, so maybe I should find real employment, and earn my keep. Kristina was, as always, diligently employed."

With a Ph.D. in city planning, his wife was then teaching at NYU (and she would, over the years, be hired for more and more prestigious urban planning posts—she is now the executive director of the New Orleans City Planning Commission). At the time, they were living in Princeton, New Jersey, and although Ford had put in brief stints teaching creative writing at the University of Michigan and Williams College, and had just finished a year at Princeton University, he didn't want to teach full time himself. In 1981, he quit writing fiction and became a sportswriter, covering baseball and college football for a glossy New York magazine called *Inside Sports*. Ford was as content as he could expect to be. If *Inside Sports* had not folded in 1982, and if *Sports Illustrated* had given him a job afterwards, as he had hoped, he would have gladly abandoned fiction writing forever.

As fate would have it, Ford, with nothing else to do, began another novel—about a thirty-eight-year-old man, living in the fictional New Jersey suburb of Haddam, who had left a promising career as a short story writer and novelist to become a sportswriter. The narrator, Frank Bascombe, proclaims, "I had written all I was going to write, if the truth had been known, and there is nothing wrong with that. If more writers knew that, the world would be saved a lot of bad books, and more people—men and women alike—could go on to happier, more productive lives." Kristina had much to do with Bascombe's creation, encouraging Ford to write about a character who strives, albeit fitfully in Bascombe's case, for happiness. "She's a quite happy person by nature, and it might've been that she thought I'd find a wider audience if I stopped writing about dark souls and dark fates. In retrospect, I'd say she was right. I know it's much more of a challenge—for me in particular—to find language for people essaying to be better and happier, than for people wrestling with murder and mayhem."

In *The Sportswriter*, Frank Bascombe suffers a spiritual crisis of sorts during Easter weekend of 1983. Four years before, his son

Ralph had died suddenly of Reye's syndrome, and ever since, Bascombe has retreated into a dreamy solipsism, collecting mail-order catalogues, visiting a fortune-teller, having affairs with a variety of women. Eventually his wife divorces him, and the novel opens when they meet at the cemetery to commemorate what would have been Ralph's thirteenth birthday on Good Friday. Bascombe still loves his ex-wife (left nameless in the book, referred to only as "X") and misses "the sweet specificity of marriage, its firm ballast and sail," but for the moment he is preoccupied with his girlfriend, Vicki Arcenault, a nurse originally from Texas. Bascombe takes Vicki on a trip to Detroit to interview a crippled pro football player for, ostensibly, an inspirational story, but, as Bascombe sadly admits, sportswriting is a job that teaches you "there are no transcendent themes in life." Things get worse. Returning to Haddam after midnight, Bascombe is cornered by Walter Luckett, the newest member of a social/support group called The Divorced Men's Club. Still crushed by his own wife's desertion, Luckett has just slept with a man, and is desperate for counsel. Bascombe, patient and solicitous as he is, cannot be of much help. He is tired, and he is facing a long drive tomorrow to Vicki's parents' house for Easter dinner (one that will turn out disastrously), and he knows that "for your life to be worth anything you must sooner or later face the possibility of terrible, searing regret. Though you must also manage to avoid it or your life will be ruined."

The Sportswriter was released as a paperback original by Vintage Contemporaries in 1986 and was named one of the five best books of the year by *Time* magazine. A PEN/Faulkner finalist, it sold over sixty thousand copies (total sales have tripled since then, and Knopf has recently reissued the novel in hardcover for the first time). Indeed, it was the breakthrough book Ford needed, but early on, he almost didn't finish it. A well-known, flamboyant editor at Knopf had seen the first one hundred fifty manuscript pages and said Ford should forget about the novel. "He told me I should put those pages in the drawer and go back to writing what I knew best. I guess he meant the South, or maybe he meant stories set in Montana. Anyway, he was wrong. I spent six months after our conversation fretting and brooding about his 'advice,' and not writing. But finally I just said, Well, this is the book I've chosen to write. I don't actually harbor any bad feelings about that. He had the right to be wrong, and he *thought* he was giving me good advice. You just can never tell, though, how a young writer will develop."

Gary Fisketjon eventually acquired *The Sportswriter* for Vintage, and he has been Ford's editor ever since. *Rock Springs,* a collection of stories set mostly in Montana, quickly followed in 1987 and galvanized Ford's growing reputation as one of the best writers of his generation. His fourth novel, *Wildlife,* about a Montana teenager whose parents' marriage is crumbling as a nearby forest fire rages out of control, was published in 1990.

Then Ford fished around for his next project. As early as 1989, he quipped to an interviewer that he might write a sequel to *The Sportswriter* centered around Independence Day, but he didn't consider it seriously until 1991, when, unbidden, Frank Bascombe's voice reappeared in Ford's notebooks. That is his essential process, never beginning with a grand scheme, just jotting miscellany in a notebook—"some words, ideas, character possibilities, possible settings, rough ideas of interactions." Once he knew that Frank Bascombe would still be in Haddam, New Jersey, Ford camped out in a bed-and-breakfast in Princeton for a month and drove around New England, recording his impressions on a micro-cassette. He spent a year planning *Independence Day,* doing research, making notes, meticulous as ever. The smallest details—names, for instance—are given great deliberation. In *The Sportswriter,* Bascombe's last name was originally Slocum, after Joshua Slocum, the famous mariner who circumnavigated the world alone. "That was a subtextual conceit for me in writing *The Sportswriter*—sailing alone," Ford says. "That's why there are so many nautical references in the book. I thought I was pretty clever, actually. But then Donald Hall pointed out to me that Slocum was the name of the narrator in Joseph Heller's wonderful novel *Something Happened.*" On the other hand, Bascombe's ex-wife was called "X" out of default. Ford couldn't think of the right name for her, and simply marked "X" where he would insert a name later. Finally, "X" became who she was—it seemed appropriate, Bascombe not being able to bear the intimacy of saying her name (which is revealed as Ann Dykstra in the sequel).

Ford worked on *Independence Day* steadily for three additional years. "I always write with a pencil or pen," he says, "and afterwards I type it out on a word-processor for the sake of legibility. I do all my own typing, since that's a way of staying close to the book. My biggest challenge is to stay *in* the book as long as I can, since I believe that I can make things better if I just concentrate and stay close. Young writers—and I was one—are often bothered by the worry of being able to finish a book. It's a big question mark until you do it. I'm challenged nowadays, though, by a wish to stay in without finishing. Eventually I'll finish, or else there's no book there."

He is hardly finicky about *where* he writes, however. He and Kristina, who have no children, alternately live in a townhouse on Bourbon Street in New Orleans, a house in Chinook, Montana, and a leased plantation house in Mississippi. "I do like a quiet life when I'm trying to write," Ford concedes. "I wouldn't like to try writing in New York, for instance. I'm not crazy about New Orleans, either, though over the years I've written—actually written—on transoceanic airplanes, in hotels in Milan and Paris, on overnight Greyhounds... quite a variety of places. But I never imagined that was ideal, only necessary." Kristina, to whom Ford has dedicated all of his books, is always his first reader, even though he doesn't feel she is the perfect reader for him: "She's much too smart; she's much too sympathetic to me and my various efforts; and she has a great sense of humor and loves jokes. My ideal reader is somebody I have to work hard to win over... somebody like me, for instance."

Independence Day, which is now out in paperback, was published by Knopf in 1995. Taking place in the election year of 1988, five years after *The Sportswriter*'s events, the novel finds Frank Bascombe now selling, of all things, real estate—a subject Ford already knew quite a bit about, considering how many times he and Kristina have moved. Real estate gives Bascombe ample opportunity to meditate on the American character—for instance, why the Markhams, an irksome couple from Vermont to whom Bascombe has shown forty-five houses, cannot make a decision, their hesitation originating from "the cold, unwelcome, built-in-America realization that we're just like the other schmo, wishing his wishes, lusting his stunted lusts, quaking over his idiot frights and fantasies, all of us popped out from the same unchinkable mold. And as we come nearer the moment of closing—when the deal's sealed and written down in a book in the courthouse—what we sense is that we're being tucked even deeper, more anonymously, into the weave of culture, and it's even less likely we'll make it to Kitzbühel. What we all want, of course, is all our best options left open as long as possible; we want not to have taken any obvious turns, but also not to have misread the correct turn the way some other boy-o would. As a unique strain of anxiety, it makes for a vicious three-way split that drives us all crazy as lab rats."

What Bascombe wants is to subsist without too much pain, too many expectations, and to do so, he clutches to a philosophical construct, a state of mind, that he calls "the Existence Period, the high-wire act of normalcy, the part that comes *after* the big struggle which led to the big blow-up," wherein he is able to "ignore much of what I don't like or that seems worrisome and embroiling, and then usually see it go away." Of course, things do not go away for Bascombe in the next three days, as he tries to collect rent from a sullen interracial couple, shows the Markhams yet another house, checks up on a hot dog stand he co-owns, visits his girlfriend, sees his ex-wife, and ferries his troubled fifteen-year-old son, Paul, to the basketball and baseball halls of fame for "the *ur*-father-son experience," hoping to redirect him onto "the hopeful, life-affirming, anti-nullity" tack.

The reviews for *Independence Day* were ecstatic, but Ford didn't read them. "Over the years," he says, "I always read the reviews of my work, and when they were bad—as they were sometimes—I was mad, resentful, disappointed. All the usual things. When *Wildlife* was published, there were a couple of very scornful reviews, and I seemed to let that bother me overmuch. I'm like everybody else: I want the world to like everything I do and like me for doing it. Unfortunately, that rarely happens. So, when *Independence Day* was published, Kristina suggested I not read reviews, just for my peace of mind. And lo and behold, I liked not reading them. I came away from the publication of that book in much better spirits and with a greater sense of equanimity."

Getting to this point in his career has not, obviously, been easy for Ford, but, he says, "I can't really complain about writing's difficulty. No one makes me do it. If it was too hard, I'd quit. But the fact is, that whatever's hard about it is quite nicely balanced by the realization that I'm doing what Chekhov did, and that I might make a contribution to the life of another, that I often find it pleasurable, funny, personally refreshing, intellectually stimulating."

Nonetheless, if he were starting all over again, maybe Ford himself would heed the advice he would give to any young writer: "Try to talk yourself out of it. As a life, it's much too solitary, it makes you obsessive, the rewards seem to be much too inward for most people, and too much rides on luck. Other than that, it's great."

BOOKSHELF

LARGE ANIMALS IN EVERYDAY LIFE *Stories by Wendy Brenner. Univ. of Georgia Press, $22.95 cloth. Reviewed by Fred Leebron.*

Wendy Brenner's stunning first collection of stories, which won the Flannery O'Connor Award for Short Fiction, is marked by her dark humor, deft stylistic range, and joyous use of language. Whether an ice cream salesgirl in a bear costume at a Florida supermarket, or the bitter paramour of a two-bit country singer in Nashville, Brenner's characters are indeed like large animals in everyday life—awkward, out of place, and destined for a kind of extinction. Her prose is always evocative and rhythmic, and her vision is an almost impossible skew between nihilism and purposefully naïve optimism, as if her characters are willing to turn a blind eye to what they have taken so much trouble to learn.

In the opening story, "The Round Bar," the narrator is a woman who has wandered unhappily from California to Florida, only to stumble onto "a dwarfish Kentucky native" with a "baby-smelling beard" who plays guitar and sings at a rotating bar. "His stomach is hard and creates a certain space between us," she says. "His small legs in their Wranglers seem far, far away.... His dick is small and in the morning when he's gone nothing's sore and nothing smells." Even though the singer is married, the narrator desperately trails him back to Nashville and holes up in a room at the Sheraton, where she keeps company with an odd pre-adolescent girl—she has polyps, and she and her family are in town to tend to an aunt with "a tilted uterus." Yet when the woman finally sees the singer again, she is disappointed: "He steps inside, a short fat man in a tractor cap, and sits at the table, a stranger."

"The Child" chronicles the difficult familial relationships surrounding a little girl who is "scared of everything." The child has "a blasé grandmother and a passionate grandmother," and their central disagreement concerns whether the child is actually ill. "She just has a fast metabolism," the blasé grandmother argues.

"Metabolism, my God!" thinks the passionate grandmother. "The child was digesting herself out of existence, evaporating by invisible increments every minute, even now, right here in front of them!" For Christmas the child's father furtively builds her a dollhouse, while "the mother takes the child to see a behavior specialist to get her out of the way." But, ultimately, it's not the child who will be consumed, but the passionate grandmother, who succumbs to an illness she has tried so hard to keep secret.

A wonderful, frontal, in-your-face irony runs through these stories, the effect of fearless writing that is intelligent and honest and generous. In "A Little Something," Helene "knows she is not necessarily a pretty person . . . Her parents were clever agnostics who didn't believe in sadness or the unknown." Her unsatisfying relationship with Joe, whom she meets at a cocktail lounge while waiting out a blizzard, almost inexplicably develops into a consideration of living together, even though Helene is "smart enough to know about things like taking charge, responsibility, Oprah Winfrey, about independence being the redemption of the modern woman." Perhaps she is attracted to Joe because he avoids pain of any sort, "Joe, who once stood on the roof of the Sears Tower wearing only a loincloth, and another time served paella to Natalie Wood. When you let go, life is one fabulous day at a time."

As the title of the collection indicates, animals figure prominently in these stories, and it's tempting to see them as symbolic—frozen "on the center line" of the highway, finding it "impossible . . . to go forward and impossible to go back." Katie, in "I Am the Bear," dresses up as a polar bear to dish ice cream cones at the local supermarket, until she is fired due to the complaint of a teen model seeking vengeance for kissing what she'd been duped into believing was a *male* bear. "I was a beast, yes," Katie confesses, "but I also had something like x-ray vision; I was able, as a bear, to see through beauty and ugliness to the true, desperate and disillusioned hearts of all men." While even oysters and insects sing in Brenner's fiction, her people and her language sing louder, in rich voices filled with wisdom and awe.

Fred Leebron's first novel, Out West, *will be published by Doubleday in November, and he is co-editor of the forthcoming* Postmodern American Fiction: A Norton Anthology.

ALL-AMERICAN GIRL *Poems by Robin Becker. Univ. of Pittsburgh Press, $10.95 paper. Reviewed by Joyce Peseroff.*

Gathered at the edge of each poem in Robin Becker's moving fourth collection, palpable and terrible, wait the forces of chaos. Love affairs end, families dissolve, the kingdoms of childhood are lost. *All-American Girl*, despite its insouciant title, is a sad book recounting a life fully adult and aware of human limits. Becker documents a struggle for order and sense in a universe as disordered as the one at the end of "The Star Show," whose out-of-control planetarium commentator "[throws] stars across the sky, [flings] meteors / carelessly . . . / . . . punctur[ing] the darkness with white bullets."

Two events inform and shape the book: the death of the poet's sister, and the breakup of a long-term relationship. Becker is aware of how slight individual loss weighs against the heft of landscape and history. In "Solar," she writes, "The desert is butch . . . / / . . . her rain remakes the world, / while your emotional life is run-off from a tin roof." As a lesbian and a Jew, Becker claims a history of expulsion and isolation. What is astonishing in these poems is how the author uses irony and humor—abundant in imagery as well as in tone—to define rather than distance herself from such knowledge. Becker's inherently Jewish jokes can be self-deprecating and skeptical; imagining that a bird seen during her morning jog is really her grandmother "back to remind me / to learn Yiddish, the only international language," she gets not transcendence but back-talk as the bird "flies / out of sight, shouting, *Big talker! Don't run on busy streets!*" In poems like this, we encounter the poet's soul as completely as we do Wordsworth's in his *Prelude*.

Becker is alert to the play of political, familial, and sexual forces that bind intimate relationships. "Shopping" begins, "If things don't work out / I'll buy the belt / with the fashionable silver buckle," both mocking and acknowledging the way women use clothing to control and define. The poem ends, "I'll do what my mother did / after she buried my sister: / outfitted herself in an elegant suit / for the rest of her life." In what may be the book's most powerful poem, "Haircut on Via di Mezzo" reverses the Biblical story of Samson: in place of the hero shorn by a seductive woman, a little girl weeps at the loss of her floor-length hair, fixing "her gaze on her father. / Cool and serene, he nodded to her, . . . / and she, obedient . . . leaned / toward the blades and turned her wildness inside." As Becker writes in "Santo Domingo Feast Day," "there are no remedies for great sorrow / / only dancing and chanting, listening and waiting." And, I might add, reading poems of wisdom and consolation such as those found in *All-American Girl.*

Joyce Peseroff is the author, most recently, of A Dog in the Lifeboat, *a collection of poems from Carnegie Mellon University Press.*

LIES OF THE SAINTS *Stories by Erin McGraw. Chronicle Books, $11.95 paper. Reviewed by Ann Harleman.*

"Life puts us in each other's way," one of Erin McGraw's characters tells another. That is the beauty of this first collection: the characters—so real that I hesitate, wanting to use the word "people" instead—engage each other in frequent, intense, and surprising ways. A radio talk show hostess is besieged by calls from her ex-husband, who gradually woos her audience away from her; a young man who believes he's won the lottery dumps his fiancée; the wife of a recovering alcoholic struggles to accept his sobriety, feeling as if she's "been slammed onto dry land after a long storm"; a realtor dates her friend's ex-husband while simultaneously allowing herself to be seduced by the friend's lover. None of these situations has a predictable outcome; yet each ending, when it comes, feels inevitable.

The predicaments in which McGraw's characters find themselves are ones we ourselves could easily have stumbled into, ratcheted up a notch. They elicit a horrified there-but-for-the-grace-of-God fascination. At the same time, the intensity these characters bring to their lives—"there is nothing in heaven or on earth that I don't want," declares an eighty-year-old widow—inspires envy. Despite their wry wisdom—the source of quietly stunning insights which McGraw allows her characters to arrive at for themselves—these men and women continue to entangle themselves and each other in a perpetual tango of desire.

McGraw's deceptively simple prose turns each story over to her characters. Her loosely woven narration—light but with great tensile strength—lets their voices come through unimpeded; as in Flannery O'Connor's stories, the only irony is dramatic irony,

brought about by the actions of the characters themselves. Sometimes, though, McGraw homes in for a stinging image, or impales
one of her characters with a phrase: a realtor hoping for a big sale
takes a deep breath of air "sharp as a new dollar bill"; participants
in a group for the Newly Single have "the ravenous, terrified sup-
port-group look"; a man on the make moves "with calculated
detachment, occupying his body as if he'd rented it for the night."
At other times, McGraw, briefly lyrical, captures the wonder of the
ordinary world: "the sheen his skin gave off, as if it held too much
blood"; "the soil lay like cake in dark and moist ridges"; a baby
"born so full of wants."

Lies of the Saints takes its title from three linked stories that give
us the history of a family—father, mother, five children, a grand-
daughter—over the course of thirty years. This marvelous loaves-
and-fishes achievement is repeated in microcosm on nearly every
page of the book. What is unsaid matters no less than what is
said. Erin McGraw is a writer who knows how to weave the two
together, lightly.

Ann Harleman's collection of short stories, Happiness, *won the 1993 Iowa
Prize. Her novel,* Bitter Lake, *will be published in October.*

RED SAUCE, WHISKEY AND SNOW *Poems by August Kleinzahler.
Farrar, Strauss & Giroux, $19.00 cloth. Reviewed by David Rivard.*

August Kleinzahler is a poet whose freshness provokes other
poets and critics into describing him as the offspring of unlikely
matings. In one book blurb, Thom Gunn brings together Frank
O'Hara and Basil Bunting. Helen Vendler, in a recent *New Yorker*
piece, weds Berryman and William Carlos Williams for the same
purpose. Maybe Kleinzahler is really the love-child of a *ménage à
trois* starring Popeye, Olive Oyl, and the haiku master Bashō. In
other words, he is what he is (and, Zen-wise, what he isn't, as
well).

This need to trace the family tree is a reaction to a voice so
seemingly out of tune with contemporary poetry's mannerisms
that it sounds mutant. The buzz around Kleinzahler certainly
makes him seem "the next new thing," and something of a poster
boy for Bay Area poetry. In fact, *Red Sauce, Whiskey and Snow* is
his fourth book. It is evidence not so much of a departure in style

as a deepening. Inspiration in poetry is often a matter of confidence—if you've got the skills and gifts, and you believe you can say whatever you want to, in whatever way you want to, then you will probably submit more fully to the momentum of composition. That's where Kleinzahler is now.

These poems do one of the hardest of all things. They combine an impulse toward improvisatory speech with a terrific ear for clarified structures. The voice jumps off the page, alive, with the poems often beginning in the oddest spots (two snails crawling into a discarded potato chip bag, the "bummy" smell that greets one coming out of a subway station, a headline about John Tower). They arc into equally unexpected places and feelings.

The full flavor of this arcing is hard to give in short passages, but the liveliness—a playful gravity—comes across immediately. Take this cheerful bit of bad news at the start of "A Glass of Claret on a Difficult Morning": "The snip-snap worm has made eggs / and worse / in the night / six crucial bolts spent their threads / holding fast / your cargo of antibodies." Kleinzahler uses his syntactical swerviness to constantly redirect and shift diction, flashing along segues of weird idiom. One drunk on the street is described "flogging his rotors," another is "sore as the dickens." The sly, almost collaged movement from image to image, combined with a sculptural sense of line and musical effect, makes for a great deal of surprise. But—amidst all the music and the tonal verve—Kleinzahler owns a focused, enviable equanimity of spirit. Here's his brief portrait of a troubled acquaintance: "His face furrows from the inside out. / The arduousness of it all, / intent and appearance at cross-purposes. / Poor guy, you'd think he was on the ropes / the way he covers and ducks, / / Macho Camacho digging at his kidneys."

The speaker of these poems is often invisible, off to the side, so the voice will sound somewhat impersonal to many readers. Better to say Kleinzahler is attuned to *sensibility* rather than personality. Something Zen, an immediacy of spirit, comes across here. Not the affected "I'm-down-with-Bashō" manner of most Americans influenced by Japanese and Chinese poetics, but an alertness to the ambiguity of the moment. By and large, Kleinzahler—unlike most mainstream poets—eschews the narcissistic drama of the psychological. But unlike most post-modern, LANGUAGE-influenced writers (with whom he sometimes shows a glancing affinity), he's interested in rendering the feel of living into accessible speech.

Mostly what August Kleinzahler does is give pleasure. In the current scene that's a real gift, and it makes him a subversive.

David Rivard's new book, Wise Poison, *has won the 1996 James Laughlin Award (formerly the Lamont Prize) of the Academy of American Poets, and is due from Graywolf in November. He will be teaching this fall at Tufts University and Sarah Lawrence College.*

ELIJAH VISIBLE *Stories by Thane Rosenbaum. St. Martin's Press, $21.95 cloth. Reviewed by Marcie Hershman.*

This is as vibrant and provocative a collection of short fiction as I've read in years. That it is also a debut collection makes it all the more gratifying. Thane Rosenbaum, who, in his early thirties left a prestigious New York law firm in order to write, seems already an old hand at fiction, fashioning heartbreakingly astute stories out of labyrinths usually too dark, too steeply dangerous, too voracious and empty for most writers to navigate with much hope of safe arrival.

At the center of *Elijah Visible*'s nine stories is the memory of the Holocaust. Made present here through its tenacity and weight rather than by its particulars, the Holocaust is the enormous inheritance bequeathed to the young, assimilated, American-born Jew, Adam Posner, who appears in all the stories. Adam's parents are survivors of concentration camps, and their undetailed history seems more real to him than his own. As with so many in contemporary America, his is a sense-of-self in flux, yet as a child of survivors, his identity, conversely, is rooted.

The collection's ingenious structure mimics the pull between inheritance and impermanence, as story after story slightly rearranges the reader's assumption of who Adam is. In one tale, he's an adult, in the next, a child; here, the setting is Miami, there, New York City; sometimes the character is orphaned, sometimes well-sheltered and lovingly parented. Rather than create a sense of discontinuity, the shifts become a matter of fascination: Look how different, the author seems to saying, the individual caught in a web of history can be. By the end, the feel is very much like that of a novel.

"Cattle Car Complex" opens the book with a no-holds-barred Kafkaesque transformation, as Adam Posner, a yuppie lawyer, finds himself stuck after-hours in the dark, airless cubicle of a Manhattan elevator. In the lobby, his Russian limo driver and the building's Irish security guard listen to Adam's growing hysteria through the intercom: "A brief interlude of silence was then followed by a chorus of moans and shrieks, as if a ward in a veterans' hospital had become an orchestra of human misery, tuning up for a concert. 'I don't believe there are work camps! We won't be happy. We will die there! I can feel it!' ... 'What's 'e saying?' the security guard asked."

The raw power of this story is matched by the subtleties of others. "An Act of Defiance" has Adam as a dreary stickler of a professor who comes face to face with the inexplicable joy his elderly uncle—a long-lost European relative—takes in life. In the masterful and frighteningly funny "The Rabbi Double-Faults," he is a bar mitzvah boy playing in a tennis match between two reunited brothers, one a wild, ultra-liberal Miami rabbi, the other now an Orthodox Israeli rabbi (both are survivors), as they battle to declare God's presence in the universe as either "absent" or "all powerful." In "Romancing the Yohrzeit Light," Adam, an abstract expressionist painter whose hip nihilism seems empty even of emptiness's meaning, clumsily seduces a Swedish fashion model by the glow of his mother's *yohrzeit* candle, lit to memorialize the anniversary of her death.

Elijah, Visible introduces a young writer who brings with him a long past and—as seems clear—a long, artistically rich future. Thane Rosenbaum's first story collection is a cause for our celebration and reflection, both.

Marcie Hershman is the author of the novels Safe in America *and* Tales of the Master Race, *which are now out in paperback (HarperPerennial). She teaches writing at Tufts University.*

THE DUAL TRADITION *An Essay on Poetry and Politics in Ireland, by Thomas Kinsella. Carcanet Press, $17.95 paper. Reviewed by M. L. Rosenthal.*

Irish poetry has had a long, trauma-beset journey. In his book *The Dual Tradition: An Essay on Poetry and Politics in Ireland,* Thomas Kinsella leads us through its successive periods of "most radical adjustment and change." He plunges into the matter more intimately than anyone since Yeats, and in far more precise detail than Yeats ever did. But he wears his sophistication lightly. His style is direct and vivid, with pointedly apt quotations.

Kinsella's own poetic career—his subtle yet piercing original verse, together with his translations from the Irish in *An Duanaire: Poems of the Dispossessed 1600–1900*, in his anthology *The New Oxford Book of Irish Verse*, and most notably in his version of the Cuchulain saga *Táin Bó Cuailnge*—prepared him ideally for the task his new book shoulders.

His essential theme is hinted in his early poem "Nightwalker": "A dying language echoes / Across a century's silence. / It is time, / Lost soul, I turned for home." It is spelled out explicitly in his introduction to the Oxford anthology, which stresses the central force, in Irish speech and poetry, of two dual traditions. The first was created by the overlay of Christianity on an originally "pagan" culture. The second, now dominant, comes from the subordination of a Gaelic-speaking people by the military power and the language of the English invader.

All this is in a broad sense common knowledge. But Kinsella, speaking out of close attention to the slow unfolding of Irish poetry in both languages, breaks down familiar generalizations into important, unfamiliar particulars. He offers a politically sensitized historic overview that nevertheless reflects a *poet's* primary concerns. He has pondered Yeats's complaint that Ireland is "a community bound together by imaginative possessions" hard to communicate because so very few writers, or people generally, are "born to" the Gaelic any longer. *The Dual Tradition* accepts Yeats's premise and acknowledges the problem, but goes on to describe the warring phases of poetic development as an irreversible reality Irish writers must (and do) cope with as best they can.

In so doing—especially in tandem with the Oxford anthology—the book becomes an invaluable guide. The two volumes form the basis for enlightening study, whether on one's own or in a classroom. But Kinsella's main critical purpose is to clarify, through empathy with the psychological pressures underlying individual poems, the accumulated components revealed in Ireland's poetry. He is fascinated by key points of crisis: e.g., when native Irish poets felt the encroachments of Christian priesthood on the "pagan" world they had taken for granted; when the bards lost status because of the dispossession of their aristocratic patrons; and when British repression of the old Irish culture and speech completed their impoverishment and also transformed the people into colonials.

In this last context, Kinsella's discussion of the inevitable need for publication and recognition *outside* Ireland by Yeats, Joyce, Beckett, and later poets is masterful. And he is repeatedly eloquent on the whole existential tangle: "the dual state of things: the sullen Irish, dispossessed but refusing to disappear" while their "high and dry" conquerors long to feel "really at home." *The Dual Tradition* is vitally revealing in the way it shows the real, violent way in which cultural and religious power-struggles have shaped the language and spirit of Irish poetry. It is also enormously suggestive—without saying a word on the subject—when one thinks about comparable issues in the poetic history of other countries. Cultural "unity" has been forged out of bloody conquest and repression almost everywhere, and the United States is hardly an exception.

M. L. Rosenthal's most recent book of poetry is As for Love: Poems and Translations *(Oxford Univ. Press). His most recent critical book is* Running to Paradise: Yeats's Poetic Art *(Oxford).*

Rosellen Brown recommends *Lies of the Saints,* stories by Erin McGraw: "These stories are wonderfully understated glimpses of believable lives, of men, women, and—in the title novella—children in uneasy embrace, trying for honesty and grace, and sometimes succeeding." Reviewed in "Bookshelf" on page 239. (Chronicle)

Maxine Kumin recommends *Vietnamerica,* a memoir by Thomas A. Bass: "A disturbing and totally compelling account of the lives of Amerasian children left behind in Vietnam; transported to the U.S., dumped in detention centers; used in factory jobs; fated to wander rootless from place to place. Bass, like John Balaban before him, forces us to look our past square in the face. Cleanly written, clearly told." (Soho)

Lloyd Schwartz recommends *All-American Girl,* poems by Robin Becker: "Unsparing and self-knowing, Robin Becker uses irony (as in her double- and triple-edged title) as if it were a form of directness. Painful, often devastating poems contend with crushing loss, the convolutions of sexuality and family politics, the struggle to accept the self. Yet they also rage with such imaginative energy, you can't wait to read them again and again, feeling an astonished pleasure in both their accomplishment and their humanity." Reviewed in "Bookshelf" on page 238. (Univ. of Pittsburgh)

Jane Shore recommends *Meadowlands,* poems by Louise Glück: "A brilliant, funny, and heartbreaking book, both personal and universal, by the master craftsperson and muse of her generation." (Ecco)

Maura Stanton recommends *Swamp Candles,* poems by Ralph Burns: "In his new book, Ralph Burns fuses the two major strands in American poetry. His spare images dazzle us with their precision, while his colloquial voice moves us with its vital rhythms and deep emotions." (Univ. of Iowa)

Chase Twichell recommends *Flesh and Blood,* a novel by Michael Cunningham: "A contemporary family saga with vivid, memorable characters that tells a heartbreaking story without a trace of sentimentality. The writing is fluent and poetic, unselfconscious, with passages of great beauty." (Farrar, Straus & Giroux)

EDITORS' CORNER

*New Books by
Our Advisory Editors*

Maxine Kumin: *Connecting the Dots.* In her eleventh poetry collection, Kumin wisely and unforgettably expands on her favorite themes: the ties and losses of family and friends, and the natural world. (W.W. Norton)

Jane Shore: *Music Minus One.* Shore's third collection of poetry movingly traces a woman's life from childhood to coming-of-age to parenthood, the poems striking for their jazzy melancholy and intimacy. (Picador USA)

POSTSCRIPTS

COHEN AWARDS Each volume year, we honor the best short story and poem published in *Ploughshares* with the Cohen Awards, which are wholly sponsored by our longtime patrons Denise and Mel Cohen. Finalists are nominated by staff editors, and the winners—each of whom receives a cash prize of $600—are selected by our advisory editors. The 1996 Cohen Awards for work published in *Ploughshares* Vol. 21 go to:

JANET DESAULNIERS *for her story "After Rosa Parks" in Winter 1995–96, edited by Tim O'Brien & Mark Strand.*

Janet Desaulniers was born in 1954 in Kansas City, Missouri, and received her undergraduate degree from the University of Missouri and her M.F.A. from the Iowa Writers' Workshop, where she was a teaching-writing fellow. She has taught at Northwestern University, Carthage College, the University of Missouri, and recently began work as Director of the M.F.A. in Writing program at the School of the Art Institute of Chicago. Her fiction has appeared in *The New Yorker, TriQuarterly, The North American Review,* and twice before in *Ploughshares,* among other publications. She has received literary fellowships from the National Endowment for the Arts, the James A. Michener/Copernicus Society, and the Illinois Arts Council, along with a Pushcart Prize and a *Transatlantic Review* award for fiction. She lives in Evanston, Illinois, with "a man, a boy, and a Chesapeake Bay retriever."

About "After Rosa Parks," Desaulniers writes: "One afternoon, in front of a school where I was engaged as artist-in-residence, a student who had been marked for murder by a neighborhood gang was shot. Word was he had been shot five times: once in the chest, once in the neck, once in each leg, and once in the behind—the last wound, according to my students, meant to embarrass him even after he was dead. But he wasn't dead. He was at Cook County Hospital, conscious and most likely surrounded by inquiring detectives, as a bullet that missed him had grazed a teacher and raised his story to lead on the local news.

"His fellow students wanted to talk about whether he would or could or should tell the police who shot him. All agreed he knew who did it and that he'd be killed if he told. Most thought he'd be killed even if he didn't tell, as they couldn't recall anyone in the neighborhood outliving a mark. 'He's already dead,' someone said. 'He's got no choice.' That comment enraged a young woman, who claimed the wounded student did have a choice, not a choice she'd wish on anyone, but his choice, she reminded us, the one his life had brought him. She said he'd better make up his mind fast because then, at least, when they killed him, he'd die a free man.

"That's not the story that inspired 'After Rosa Parks,' but it's a parallel story, a true one from Chicago, to stand beside it."

STAR BLACK

LOUISE GLÜCK *for her poem "Penelope's Stubbornness" in Winter 1995–96, edited by Tim O'Brien & Mark Strand.*

Louise Glück was born in New York City in 1943, raised on Long Island, and attended Sarah Lawrence College for six weeks before dropping out. About her incomplete formal education, she says wryly, "It wasn't a confident dismissal of a ritual I didn't need or had bohemian contempt for. I was, at eighteen, too advanced in neurosis to manage life outside my bedroom. My education, such as it was, was psychoanalysis, augmented by a series of miraculous workshops at Columbia's School of General Studies, first with Leonie Adams, then with Stanley Kunitz."

Glück is the author of a book of essays, *Proofs and Theories,* and eight collections of poetry, including *The Triumph of Achilles,* which won the National Book Critics Circle Award in 1985; *The Wild Iris,* which received the Pulitzer Prize in poetry in 1993; and *Meadowlands,* which was released this year from Ecco Press, her publisher since 1975. She has taught at a number of universities, including Harvard, Columbia, Iowa, and Williams College, and has made Vermont her home for many years, although, beginning this fall, she will be living in Cambridge, Massachusetts, for a trial period.

"To talk about 'Penelope's Stubbornness,'" Glück writes, "I have to talk about *Meadowlands*. The poems that became that book, having been conceived almost immediately in terms of that book, were written in about five main clusters, the first a lively and absorbing flurry in the summer of, I think, 1993 in Vermont; the last, two weeks of euphoric sleeplessness in Cambridge—in buses, in cars, and, mostly, in Tom and Vera Kreilkamp's wonderful guest room—a period that ended in bronchitis when the book ended. I was, that spring, encouraged by the enthusiasm and sharply focused criticism of Robert Pinsky and Frank Bidart; enthusiasm hadn't been, at the outset, what this work attracted (except from fiction writers, perhaps because implicit structure is what they're used to recognizing). I had begun, it seemed, to write that way; I could hear *Meadowlands* very early, but what I heard was a graph of tone, so that for several years I felt haunted, tormented, like someone who can remember a song, but not its name, and not its words. In this case, a very long song.

"'Penelope's Stubbornness' was written rather early, though not in that first summer's work, and it was written easily, being one of the pieces compelled by the overall narrative (as opposed to tonal) design: finding the various tones or attitudes, I felt like an explorer; fleshing out the drama, I felt like a craftsperson. Restful, interesting, but not overwhelming. This poem was part of a more sustained duet between women, a stand-off, a fight for dominance which is (in my head) a fight also to have the last word."

BEST AWARDS Three stories from the Fall 1995 issue, edited by Ann Beattie, have been selected for prizes: Caroline A. Langston's story, "The Dissolution of the World," will be reprinted in *The Pushcart Prize XXI: Best of the Small Presses 1996–97;* William Henry Lewis's "Shades" will be included in *The Best American Short Stories 1996,* edited by John Edgar Wideman; and David Wiegand's "Buffalo Safety" appears in *Prize Stories 1996: The O. Henry Awards,* the final volume edited by William Abrahams. Two poems from the Spring 1995 issue, edited by Gary Soto, have been chosen by Adrienne Rich for *The Best American Poetry 1996:* "Skin Trade" by Reginald Shepherd and "Rednecks" by Martín Espada.

CONTRIBUTORS' NOTES

Fall 1996

RICHARD BAUSCH's short stories have appeared in *The New Yorker, Esquire, The Atlantic Monthly, Harper's, Playboy,* and other magazines. His 1984 novel *The Last Good Time* was recently made into a movie, written and directed by Bob Balaban and released by Samuel Goldwyn. This year, The Modern Library published *The Selected Stories of Richard Bausch.* His seventh novel, *Good Evening Mr. & Mrs. America, and all the Ships at Sea,* will appear from Harper-Collins this fall.

ANN BEATTIE is the author of the short story collections *Distortions, Secrets and Surprises, The Burning House, Where You'll Find Me and Other Stories,* and *What Was Mine,* and the novels *Chilly Scenes of Winter, Falling in Place, Love Always, Picturing Will,* and, most recently, *Another You.* She and her husband, the painter Lincoln Perry, now split their time between Maine and Key West.

LESLIE MCKENZIE BIENEN, a fiction writer and poet, has begun a collaborative nonfiction project on refugees, traveling last year to Somalia and Mozambique, with the photographer Fazal Sheikh. In recent years, she has taught in Bangkok, New York, and elsewhere, and has trained and exercised horses on Vashon Island in the Puget Sound. She received an M.F.A. from the Iowa Writers' Workshop in 1991 and is currently studying to be a veterinarian.

BO CALDWELL was a Stegner Fellow and Jones Lecturer at Stanford University. Her stories have been published in *Story, Epoch, Image,* and elsewhere, and her nonfiction appears in *The Washington Post Magazine.* She lives in Northern California.

ALAN CHEUSE is the author of the novels *The Grandmothers' Club* and *The Light Possessed,* and the story collection *The Tennessee Waltz,* among other works of fiction. He is also the author of a memoir, *Fall Out of Heaven.* He serves as a book commentator for NPR's evening newsmagazine "All Things Considered" and is the producer and host of The Center for the Book/NPR short story magazine for radio "The Sound of Writing." His latest book is *Talking Horse: Bernard Malamud on Life and Work,* edited with Nicholas Delbanco.

SHANE DUBOW is an adventure-trip guide and freelance writer who lives, most of the time, in Chicago. His fiction and nonfiction have appeared in *Playboy, Men's Journal, Seventeen, The Chicago Review, Summit, Chicago Magazine, The Boston Phoenix, The Chicago Reader,* and other publications.

TESS GALLAGHER is the author of a book of short stories, a collection of essays, and eight books of poetry. A new story collection, *At the Owl Woman Saloon,* will be published in 1997 by Scribner. She wrote the introduction to *All of Us: The Collected Poems of Raymond Carver,* which will be released in Great Britain by Harvill this fall, and her translations—with Adam Sorkin and the author—of the Romanian poet Liliana Ursu, *The Sky Behind the Forest,* is forthcoming from Bloodaxe this fall. She is completing the third year of a grant from the Lynd-hurst Foundation, and will hold the Edward F. Arnold Visiting Professor of English Chair at Whitman College for the 1996–97 academic year.

ANDREW SEAN GREER recently received his M.F.A. from the University of Montana. He lives in Missoula, Montana, and has just finished a novel entitled *Blue Lusitania.*

ALYSON HAGY is the author of two collections of fiction, *Madonna on Her Back* (Stuart Wright) and *Hardware River* (Poseidon Press). Her stories have most recently appeared in *Shenandoah, The Virginia Quarterly Review,* and *Mississippi Review.* She currently teaches at the University of Wyoming.

JANE KENT, a nationally recognized artist, has exhibited her work most recently at Hirschl & Adler, **MODERN,** New York. Her work is in the collections of the National Museum of American Art, Smithsonian Institute, the Brooklyn Muse-um, the New York Public Library, and Princeton University. She currently teaches at Columbia University.

DALE RAY PHILLIPS's stories have appeared in *The Atlantic Monthly, GQ, Story,* and several literary magazines. He has work forthcoming in *Esquire,* and his sto-ries have also been anthologized in *Best American Short Stories* and *New Stories from the South.* He teaches at Clemson University, where he is completing a book of stories entitled *What It Cost Travelers.*

IRA SADOFF is the author of four collections of poetry, most recently *Emotional Traffic,* as well as the forthcoming *Delirious: New and Selected Poems* (Godine, 1997). He is also the author of a novel, *Uncoupling,* and a collection of stories, poems, and essays, *An Ira Sadoff Reader.* He has published more than two dozen stories in national literary magazines and a number of anthologies, including *The O. Henry Awards.* He teaches at Colby College and Warren Wilson College.

~

SUBSCRIBERS Feel free to contact us via E-mail with address changes (the post office usually will not forward journals) or any problems with your subscription. Our E-mail address is: pshares@emerson.edu. Also, please note that on occasion we exchange mailing lists with other literary magazines and organizations. If you would like your name excluded from these exchanges, simply send us an E-mail message or a letter stating so.

SUBMISSION POLICIES *Ploughshares* is published three times a year: usually mixed issues of poetry and fiction in the Spring and Winter and a fiction issue in the Fall, with each guest-edited by a different writer. We welcome unsolicited manuscripts from August 1 to March 31 (postmark dates). All submissions sent from April to July are returned unread. In the past, guest editors often announced specific themes for issues, but we have revised our editorial policies and no longer restrict submissions to thematic topics. Submit your work at any time during our reading period; if a manuscript is not timely for one issue, it will be considered for another. Send one prose piece and/or one to three poems at a time (mail genres separately). Poems should be individually typed either single- or double-spaced on one side of the page. Prose should be typed double-spaced on one side and be no longer than twenty-five pages. Although we look primarily for short stories, we occasionally publish personal essays/memoirs. Novel excerpts are acceptable if self-contained. Unsolicited book reviews and criticism are not considered. Please do not send multiple submissions of the same genre, and do not send another manuscript until you hear about the first. Additional submissions will be returned unread. Mail your manuscript in a page-sized manila envelope, your full name and address written on the outside, to the "Fiction Editor," "Poetry Editor," or "Nonfiction Editor." (Unsolicited work sent directly to a guest editor's home or office will be discarded.) All manuscripts and correspondence regarding submissions should be accompanied by a self-addressed, stamped envelope (S.A.S.E.) for a response. Expect three to five months for a decision. Do not query us until five months have passed, and if you do, please write to us, including an S.A.S.E. and indicating the postmark date of submission, instead of calling. Simultaneous submissions are amenable as long as they are indicated as such and we are notified immediately upon acceptance elsewhere. We cannot accommodate revisions, changes of return address, or forgotten S.A.S.E.'s after the fact. We do not reprint previously published work. Translations are welcome if permission has been granted. We cannot be responsible for delay, loss, or damage. Payment is upon publication: $25/printed page, $50 minimum per title, $250 maximum per author, with two copies of the issue and a one-year subscription.

THE NAME *Ploughshares* 1. The sharp edge of a plough that cuts a furrow in the earth. 2 a. A variation of the name of the pub, the Plough and Stars, in Cambridge, Massachusetts, where a journal was founded. 2 b. The pub's name was inspired by the Sean O'Casey play about the Easter Rising of the Irish "citizen army." The army's flag contained a plough, representing the things of the earth, hence practicality; and stars, the ideals by which the plough is steered. 3. A shared, collaborative, community effort that has endured for twenty-five years. 4. A literary journal that has been energized by a desire for harmony, peace, and reform. Once, that spirit motivated civil rights marches, war protests, and student activism. Today, it still inspirits a desire for beating swords into ploughshares, but through the power and the beauty of the written word.

BENNINGTON WRITING SEMINARS

MFA in Writing and Literature
Two-year low-residency program

FICTION
NONFICTION
POETRY

For more information contact:
Writing Seminars,
Box PL, Bennington College
Bennington, Vermont 05201
802-442-5401, ext. 160

MFA
CREATIVE WRITING
UNIVERSITY OF MARYLAND, COLLEGE PARK

FACULTY – 1996-1997

Poetry

Michael Collier   Phillis Levin
Stanley Plumly

Fiction

Merle Collins   Joyce Kornblatt
Reginald McKnight   Howard Norman

RECENT VISITING WRITERS

Russell Banks
Henri Cole
Rita Dove
Louise Glück

Marita Golden
Robert Hass
Seamus Heaney
June Jordan

Philip Levine
Peter Matthiessen
William Maxwell
C.E. Poverman

Mary Robison
Marilynne Robinson
C.D. Wright
Charles Wright

For more information:

Joyce Kornblatt, Director, Creative Writing Program
Department of English
University of Maryland, College Park, MD 20742
(301) 405-3820

What the Body Told
Rafael Campo

"Rafael Campo is one of the most gifted and accomplished younger poets writing in English. More than that, he is a writer engaged in several of the pivotal struggles/issues of our era, and what he has to say about them is 'news that stays news.'"— Marilyn Hacker

"Campo's background and concerns—he writes out of his identity and experience as a gay Cuban American physician—make for a rich field of investigations, and his best work is both passionate and formally accomplished. *What the Body Told* dives into the difficult, necessary territory of physical love, desire, contagion, illness; such poems are essential to our moment. We need them."—Mark Doty

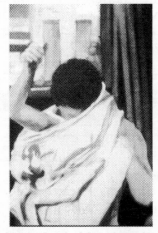

136 pages, paper $12.95,
library cloth edition $35.95

Duke University Press
Box 90660
Durham, NC 27708-0660
http://www.duke.edu/web/dupress/

Details from *Eros* by Joan R. Fugazzi. Courtesy of the artist

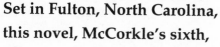